# The Secular Use of Church Buildings

# The Secular Use
# of Church Buildings

J. G. DAVIES

THE SEABURY PRESS
NEW YORK

# CONTENTS

# PREFACE

ONE OF the most, if not the most, vital debates in which theologians are engaged at the present day is that which concerns the secular nature of Christianity. So far this discussion has been mainly at the theoretical level. Attention has been paid to such questions as: What modifications in Christian theology are necessary in order to set it free from an out-dated mythology? or, How can one express the Gospel in non-religious terms? or, How can one formulate a Gospel which does not relate to a God of the gaps, i.e. to a God who exists only in the *lacunae* of our scientific knowledge, but to a God who is encountered in the midst of life in the world? One of the issues in this debate is of course that of the relationship of the sacred and the secular, and it is with this relationship that the present study is concerned. It is however not primarily theoretical but practical, in that it concentrates upon the subject of church-building.

Most books about the architecture of churches pay little attention to what went on inside them, and, in so far as they do, they confine themselves entirely to matters liturgical. But this is only one facet of the complete picture. For over a millennium and a half churches were the scene of a host of varied secular activities; to ignore them is to pass over an essential element in understanding them functionally. Moreover, the way churches were and are used implies a certain concept of the relationship of the sacred and the secular, i.e. an investigation of the activities that have taken place, do or may take place, in churches can clarify our interpretation of the unity or disunity of the two.

The first six chapters of this book are in fact a history of secular activities in churches. First the evidence from the patristic period is surveyed and then that from the Middle Ages. There follows an account of the attitudes to church buildings prevalent in some of the main Christian communions and a demonstration of how these attitudes were given architectural expression, e.g. in Baroque or in the

Gothic Revival. Taking 1430 as the approximate date of the water-shed between the Reformation and what went before, there is next a description of Paul's Walk, a veritable microcosm of the macro-cosm of Post-Reformation secular activities, and the history is then completed up to the present day. On this basis of past Christian precedents, it is then possible to examine the relationship of the sacred and the secular uses of church buildings today, to appreciate their unity and the nature of that unity and so, finally, to consider the idea of the consecration of buildings—how this is to be under-stood if sacred and secular are comprehended as twin aspects of a single totality.

In quoting from the original sources, especially from the medieval period, I have modernized the spelling to facilitate reading; the student who wants either to check the original or to pursue the sub-ject further can consult the notes printed at the end. These notes are mainly references and can be ignored by the general reader, although they are essential evidence of the accuracy of what is recorded; in the few instances where a note adds something to the text, an asterisk has been printed by the appropriate number.

The sources are themselves of the most diverse kind; indeed one can say that there is almost no genre of literature which may not and does not contain some item of information relevant to the subject. Poetry, plays, letters, journals, memoirs, account and minute books, legal enactments, records of trials, synodal decrees, wills, tracts, pamphlets, newspapers, sermons, treatises, archaeological reports—the list is inexhaustible. Because of the extent of the available material, I have had to limit myself mainly to British sources, al-though with sufficient examples from Europe and elsewhere to show that these are typical and do not constitute a regional peculiarity. I have further limited the number of examples listed of each secular use, otherwise the narrative would have become a mere catalogue and hence unreadable.

The absence of a bibliography is due to the fact that I have been unable to trace any book which deals specifically with this subject. The material is scattered throughout the sources listed in the notes and has not previously been assembled. There are two works how-ever which should be mentioned. The first of these is *Church and*

*Manor* by S. O. Addy (1913). This work has been generally neglected because its thesis is untenable. Addy sought to argue that the plan of the medieval parish church derived from that of the manor house, and in attempting to prove his point he adduced evidence to show that the same kind of activities that took place in the one were also to be found in the other. His work is therefore a mine of information about secular activities in churches in the Middle Ages, although these were not his primary concern. The second work is by W. Johnson and is entitled *Byways in British Archaeology* (1912). This includes a chapter headed: 'Secular Activities in Churches' —it is a useful miniature survey, but is inevitably restricted in scope and detail.

In conclusion I wish to record my sincere thanks to my wife for drawing most of the plans and to the SCM Press for the care taken in the publication of this book.

J. G. DAVIES

*The University*
*Birmingham*

# ACKNOWLEDGEMENTS

THE AUTHOR wishes to express his thanks to his godson Henry Sparks, for the brass rubbing which is reproduced as Plate XI; to his colleague, Professor Ellis Waterhouse, for Plates I and VII; to the Mansell Collection for Plates II, III and IV; to the German Archeological Institute in Rome for Plate V; to the Courtauld Institute of Art for Plate VI; to the Rev. G. A. Johnson for Plate VIII; to the *Illustrated London News* for Plate XII; to the *Birmingham Post and Mail* for Plate XIII; to the Rev. Canon R. S. O. Stevens for Plate XIV, and to the Religious Drama Society and Mr Houston Rogers for Plate XV.

# LIST OF PLATES

xi

# LIST OF FIGURES

# 1

## The Patristic Period

### I. THE PRE-CONSTANTINE ERA

'WE HAVE no temples and no altars.'[1] This statement, referring to Christians, comes from the pen of the apologist Minucius Felix, c. 200, and all the evidence supports its accuracy. Throughout at least the first two centuries there were no church buildings as such, and this was so remarkable that to the pagan population it was considered grounds for accusing Christians of 'atheism'. In a world notable for the number of its holy shrines and for the rivers of blood that flowed daily from the sacrificial victims, Christians were conspicuous in that they possessed neither the first nor engaged in the second. Having no church buildings, the question of their secular use does not arise and it may seem that we should proceed directly to the third century. But if we were to do this, we should miss an important clue to the understanding of the later development and a useful criterion for evaluating that development. Indeed we cannot escape the questions: why were there no church buildings? If 'atheism' is an absurd explanation, what is the correct one? And, what understanding of the relation of sacred and secular is involved in this?

At the practical level, three factors contributed to prevent the erection of specifically Christian places of worship, and these may be defined by the words poverty, paucity and persecution. In its origins and early history Christianity was predominantly a working-class movement. Although some men of property were to be found in its ranks,[2] in general it could be said that there were 'not many mighty, not many noble'.[3] For decades therefore their common funds would have been insufficient to meet the cost of any large-scale building programme. Further, these Christians met in small groups; congre-

gations numbering hundreds of people were unknown, and consequently great halls to accommodate them were not needed. Again,
although Christians did not suffer continuous persecution, it was an
ever-present possibility—in these circumstances it was scarcely
prudent for them to draw attention to themselves by erecting huge
buildings. Nevertheless these practical factors are not the only nor
the complete explanation of the absence of churches; there is an all-
important underlying theological reason that requires to be considered, and this concerns the attitude of Jesus and of the New
Testament writers to worship and to the 'place' of worship.

There is no record that Jesus ever took part in the Temple cultus.
Indeed he seems to have adopted a position of steady and determined
hostility to it.[4] On one occasion he is represented as endorsing the
statement of a scribe to the effect that to love God 'with all the heart,
and with all the understanding, and with all the strength, and to love
his neighbour as himself, is much more than all whole burnt offerings and sacrifices'.[5] In other words, man does not require any holy
sacrifice nor a mediating priesthood; his relationship to God is determined not by what he gives to him in some holy place, but by his
love of God in his neighbour. Again, Jesus rejects prayer in public
places, including the synagogue, as mere idle prattle,[6] and his exhortation to go into one's inner chamber shows that he held a man's
private room to be holier than the Temple.[7] If 'where two or three
are gathered together in my name, there am I in the midst of them',[8]
there can be no exclusive place of encounter with God; anywhere can
be the place of his presence. Nor does the so-called 'Cleansing of the
Temple' contradict this persistent rejection of the idea of a holy
place.[9] The usual title of this incident is a misnomer; Jesus pays no
attention to those parts of the Temple which were to the Jew of the
greatest and holiest significance; he is concerned only with the court
of the Gentiles, i.e. 'only indirectly with a Jewish Temple problem
and much more directly with the problem of the "Gentiles"',[10]
because he was performing an eschatological act which presaged the
access of the non-Jewish people to God.

It is also apparent that Jesus was charged with wanting to destroy
the Temple,[11] and according to the record at his death the veil of the
Temple was torn in two,[12] i.e. Jesus' end is also the end of the

Temple; the Jewish cultus has been nullified. The author of the fourth Gospel is moving in the same realm of ideas when he represents Jesus as saying: 'the hour cometh, when neither in this mountain, nor in Jerusalem, shall ye worship the Father . . . the hour cometh, and now is, when the true worshippers shall worship the Father in Spirit and truth'.[13] Here the idea of a holy place is explicitly rejected and worship is declared to be not a merely human act but the act of God in the community through the Spirit. It is entirely consistent with this that the New Testament writers use the Greek word *hieron* of the Temple, although this is employed very sparingly of it in the LXX, being reserved for the host of pagan shrines throughout the world. Just as Jewish circumcision is included by Paul in the self-mutilations of the pagan cults,[14] so the Temple belongs to the same class as pagan temples, erected on the false premiss of sacrifice and specially holy places. We have to reckon therefore with a new and different attitude to the place of worship.

The Temple, for the Jew, was the very centre of his life, in principle if not always in practice. Hence, when it was demolished by the soldiers of Titus, it could be said: 'Since the day the sanctuary was destroyed an "iron curtain" has separated Israel and Israel's Father in heaven'.[15] No Christian, apart from a small group of aggressive Judaizers, could say this—no building was the numinous locus of his worship; that locus was now the Christian community in the world. 'We are a temple (*naos*, sanctuary) of the living God', wrote Paul to the Corinthians.[16] 'Where a complete reminting of a cultic notion takes place in this fashion, it is impossible to build, say, a temple of stone as a place of worship.'[17] Poverty, paucity and persecution may have had their part to play, but the fundamental explanation of the lack of church buildings is this theological one.

The New Testament writers believed that the Church is the Body of Christ and the Temple of the Holy Spirit. There was therefore a constant relationship between the community and God—hence the cult, in the sense of a sacred action or rite to establish contact with the divine, was abolished. Alternatively, one can say that the point of confrontation between God and man was not spatially located, because that point was the person of the exalted Lord. It was then impossible to extract worship from the totality of life and enclose it in a sacred building, since the 'holy place' was as omnipresent as the ascended Christ. Indeed in New Testament times 'worship, conceived as the joyful response of Christians to God's action in Jesus Christ, was not defined first and foremost in terms of what happened in a certain *place where* and at a certain *time when* Christians assembled. What happened on those occasions was understood within the context of response to God in their total existence.'[18] So the word 'church' itself is never applied in the New Testament to a building as such but to a community. When its members assembled for corporate worship, they did not 'go to church'; they *were* the Church meeting in the private house of one of the congregation. Many early Christian writers were to emphasize this point. Hippolytus, for example, declared that 'it is not a place that is called "Church", nor a house made of stones and earth. . . . What then is the Church? It is the holy assembly of those who live in righteousness.'[19] To the same effect Clement of Alexandria asserted that 'it is not the place but the assembly of the elect that I call Church'.[20] Jesus is, of course, known in the breaking of the bread;[21] he *is* known in space, which is after all an essential aspect of the human condition, but this presence is not confined to a consecrated architectural space.

Since the focus of the divine presence is no longer a physical building but the living community in the world, any idea of the profane as the sum total of common life outside the sphere of the holy is foreign to New Testament thought, because 'profane' (*pro fanum*) means before, i.e. outside the temple, and this no longer has meaning for Christians, who in everything they think and do are now themselves the 'living stones'[22] of the temple. The division of life into a sacred area and a profane area, common to Jewish and pagan thought, is no longer valid. This does not mean that the sacred and the secular have become indistinguishable but that, through Christ, they have been united. This is apparent from the form and context of early Christian worship. The eucharist cannot be distinguished by its form from all secular acts as sacrifice can; its form is in fact constituted by the ordinary daily custom of men and its context is their daily life centred in the home. So 'it is far removed from holiness as the Jewish cult honoured it. It is characterized by the usual and the familiar, even in its prayers and actions, and it can take place wherever men satisfy their hunger with thanksgiving to God and in fellowship with the Master. The homeliness of one's own house or the beauty of the countryside take the place of the holiness of a particular building with the holy altar and sacred sacrifices.'[23]

The early Christians then did not put their church buildings to secular use, simply because they had no church buildings as such, but the physical location of their particular acts of worship witnessed to their understanding of the unity of sacred and secular in and through Christ—they assembled in private houses.[24] The New Testament tells us a little about these. At Ephesus the Church met in the home of Aquila and Prisca,[25] at Laodicea in that of Nymphas[26] and at Colossae in the house of Philemon.[27] Since the essential element in the act of worship was a meal, the dining-room would be the place of assembly. These houses, because of the relative poverty of the Christians, would have been typical cheap ones inhabited by the middle and lower classes. In the East these were one-family buildings up to four storeys high, the dining-room being the only large room and usually at the top, i.e. the upper room, *hyperoon*, mentioned in Acts.[28] The furnishing would consist of a simple table and three couches—the *triclinium*, with the members of the congregation even sitting on the window sills if no other place were available. So at Troas a young man, overcome by heat and the length of Paul's sermon, fell out through the lattice on the third floor (*tristegon*).[29] In Rome tenement houses were the norm, with apartments horizontally across them and not necessarily having a dining-room, so that the largest chamber would have to be used. Hence the eucharist was celebrated in rooms which could be used at other times for ordinary meals and often, in the houses of the poor, would serve for all purposes as a living-room.

When we move from the apostolic age to the second century we find the same situation persisting. At the trial of Justin Martyr in 163 before Rusticus, prefect of Rome, he was asked: 'Where do you assemble?' Justin replied: 'Where each one chooses and can; for do you fancy that we all meet in the very same place? No, because the God of the Christians is not circumscribed by place, but, being invisible, fills heaven and earth, and everywhere, is worshipped and glorified by the faithful.' Rusticus insisted: 'Tell me where you meet and in what place you collect your followers.' Justin said: 'I live above one Martinus, at the Timiotinian Bath; and during the whole time (and I am now living in Rome for the second time) I am unaware of any other meeting than his.'[30]

In the third century, the house-church was still the norm and there are two apocryphal works, reflecting contemporary practice, which provide evidence of this. In the *Acts of Thomas* we read of a *triclinium* in the house of Siphor which was used for teaching, baptism and the eucharist,[31] while in the *Acts of Peter* we are informed how the apostle entered the dining-room of a certain Marcellus while the Gospel was being read.[32] Nevertheless the opening decades of this century did witness a change. Previously the house would appear to have belonged to an individual who placed it at the disposal of the local congregation but continued to inhabit it and use it for his ordinary daily life at other times. With the growth of organization and of numbers, the Church now took the step of acquiring, either by purchase or gift, houses of its own, which were placed exclusively at the use of the Christian community.[33]* So one Leocadius gave his house to the Church at Bourges[34] and Tertullian is prepared to use the phrase 'house of God' of a place of assembly.[35] The main living-room continued to be used for the eucharist, and so Tertullian refers to one 'high up, open to the light',[36] i.e. the *hyperoon*.

At Dura Europos on the Euphrates we have an actual example of a house modified for use by a Christian congregation. Built shortly after 200, it underwent alteration in 231 to make it more suitable as a community house. The room opposite to the entrance across the courtyard was enlarged by knocking down a wall and merging it with the adjoining south-west room, thus providing space for some fifty people; a dais was placed, probably for the bishop's chair, against the east wall, beyond which was a small vestry. On the west side of the atrium there was another chamber, possibly used for the catechumens, and a small baptistery to the right of the entrance as one came in. The alterations did not affect the character of the building as an example of local domestic architecture,[37] nor of the eucharist as a domestic event within the family of Christians.

The new feature of the Dura Europos plan is the provision of a baptistery. In the apostolic age baptism could be administered in any place where water was to be found. It could happen in a wayside pool, as when Philip baptized the Ethiopian eunuch in the desert between Jerusalem and Gaza;[38] it could happen in a river, as when Lydia, the purple seller, was baptized at Philippi.[39] During the second century this practice did not alter, and Justin Martyr describes how candidates for baptism are 'brought where there is water'.[40] At the turn of the third century Tertullian could write: 'It makes no difference whether a man be washed in a sea or a pool, a stream or a fountain, a lake or a trough.'[41] A decade or so later the *Acts of Thomas* describe a baptism in the public baths[42] and another in a river.[43] Similarly the *Clementine Homilies* and *Recognitions*, dating in their present form from the fourth century but based upon third-century documents, tell how Peter baptized a certain Mattidia in the sea 'between some rocks, which supplied a place at once tranquil and clean',[44] and assert that for baptism is needed 'the water of a fountain or river or even sea'.[45] At Dura Europos, however, architectural provision was made within the community house,[46] so that a move was afoot to comprise all the liturgical activities of the community within one building specially adapted for those purposes. Nevertheless, the house-church at Cirta in 303 would appear to have had no baptistery, its general disposition being still that of a private house, although it belonged to the community and could be described as the place 'where the Christians customarily meet'.[47]

The house at Cirta was raided on 19th May 303 by Munatus Felix, the high priest and curator of the colony, with a body of his officials. They first cross-examined the bishop and his clergy and made an inventory of their possessions, e.g. two gold and six silver chalices. Next they went into the library and opened the cupboards, and finally penetrated into the dining-room where they discovered four casks and six large jars. The details are insufficient to give a clear picture of the house, since we are not told where the initial interrogation took place—it could have been in the atrium if there was one. The dining-room (*triclinium*) may have been the place for the eucharist or alternatively for the *agape* or love-feast, of which more will be said below,[48] or indeed for both.

Other examples of house-churches are now known, but here again, with some exceptions, the details of plan and use are by no means clear.[49] In third-century Rome, where the increase in numbers rendered one meeting place no longer sufficient, *domus ecclesiae* were established in the many-storeyed blocks that housed the urban population. 'Their resemblance to ordinary tenements would have made these *tituli*[50]* as hard to identify as the meeting-rooms of contemporary sects installed in the tenements of New York's Harlem or London's East End.'[51] By the early fourth century there were twenty-five of these *tituli* and these still exist, marked by church buildings, mostly erected from the fourth to the ninth centuries. In or beneath the foundations of these basilicas there are the remains of tenements, and it is probable that these pre-Constantinian structures included the original *domus ecclesiae*. In the case of SS. Giovanni e Paolo there can be no doubt since the ground floor, previously consisting of shops, was decorated with paintings, including such Christian subjects as the *orans*, at the beginning of the fourth century, while in the third a monumental staircase was constructed suggesting the existence of a large hall on the first floor.[52] The churches of S. Clemente,[53] S. Anastasia[54] and S. Martino[55] similarly incorporate pre-Constantinian buildings, but while their Christian use is probable it cannot be proved.

This perpetuation of domestic architecture continued well into the fourth century. At Kirk-Bizzeh in Syria, *c.* 300–30, a house was adopted for use as a community building. This consisted of a closed courtyard with porticoes out of which, on the north side, two doors led to the room for worship two storeys high. The sanctuary, at the east end, had a triumphal arch, and opposite to this was the horse-shoe-shaped ambon with cathedra, typical of many Syrian basilicas (Fig. 1).

Nevertheless, in the last decades of the third century buildings of a more monumental kind were being erected. The anti-Christian writer Porphyry refers to 'huge buildings thus imitating the structure of temples'[56] and it is probable that at Rome S. Crisogono[57] and S. Sebastiano[58] were both Christian halls of the immediately pre-Constantinian era. Nevertheless, the original Christian attitude could still be expressed as late as the Diocletian persecution when

Arnobius of Sicca demanded, expecting a negative reply: 'Do we honour God with shrines and by building temples?'[59] Yet, in spite of Arnobius, the architectural development went hand in hand with a changing concept about the nature and the place of worship.

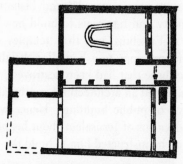

*Fig.* 1   House-church at Kirk-Bizzeh, Syria, *c.* 330

Whereas the eucharist had been initially a domestic gathering, relatively informal, with sacred and secular united, now it began to be elaborated and formalized. The Syrian *Didascalia*, *c.* 250, reveals this in the following prescription which applies to the house-church:

Appoint the places for the brethren with care and gravity. And for the presbyters let there be assigned a place in the eastern part of the house; and let the bishop's throne be set in their midst, and let the presbyters sit with him. And again, let the laymen sit in another part of the house toward the east. For so it should be, that in the eastern part of the house the presbyters sit with the bishop, and next the laymen, and then the women also. . . . But of the deacons, let one stand always by the oblations of the eucharist; and let another stand without by the door and observe them that come in.[60]

The same document shows the increasing tendency to assert a dichotomy between religion and daily life. 'The trades of the faithful are called works of superfluity, for their true work is religion. Pursue your work therefore as a work of superfluity, for your sustenance, but let your true work be religion.'[61] The contrast between this and the New Testament attitude outlined above is too obvious to require emphasis. With the accession of Constantine this tension and this division were to be increased and the church buildings erected were to be invested with the character of holy places like the Temple at Jerusalem and the pagan shrines.

## 2. THE AGE OF CONSTANTINE AND AFTER

With the triumph of Constantine and the cessation of persecution, Christianity acquired a privileged position. Houses or lands which had been confiscated were restored[62] and bishops were provided with money, property and materials to build new churches.[63] The result, according to Eusebius, was that 'temples were raised once more from their foundations to a boundless height', surpassing in their magnificence those that had been destroyed.[64] The new status of the Church demanded an architectural vocabulary corresponding to the highest class of public buildings. Hence when Constantine wrote to Bishop Macarius of Jerusalem about his plan for the site of the Holy Sepulchre, he instructed him to build the finest basilica yet seen.[65]

The emperor's use of the term 'basilica', without explication, indicates that it was well understood. It did in fact refer to a type of construction which combined religious overtones with the criteria of an official building. Within the genus basilica there was a whole variety of plans and uses. Frequently an aisleless hall, it could also have nave and aisles; it could have galleries and clerestory; it could have projecting apses. There were forum basilicas, palace basilicas, bath basilicas; they were used as covered markets, law courts, reception rooms and audience chambers. The basilica was in fact a large meeting-hall, given a religious association by the presence of the emperor's effigy, which was a feature of the cult of his divinity. Consequently the church buildings that began to be erected 'simply represented one more type of basilica created by a new demand. In Constantine's time, the Christian basilica was viewed as just another monumental public meeting-hall with religious overtones',[66] devotion to God as emperor of heaven being substituted for the imperial cult.

All this meant that at first there was no uniform plan. At Aquileia, 313–19, two halls were joined at their west end by a transverse one.[67] The cathedral at Tyre, 314,[68] was preceded by a spacious forecourt; it had three doors, with corresponding nave and aisles; an altar stood at the far end within a chancel and the episcopal throne flanked by benches for the presbyters in the apse. At Orléansville, 324, there was a nave with four aisles and an elevated apse included within the body of the building.[69] These three designs are widely different and indeed it was not until towards the end of the fourth century that anything like a uniform plan was adopted and that one can speak of *the* Christian basilica.

The general aspect of the Christian basilica was that of a single room, its horizontal perspective being emphasized by parallel colonnades which seemed to converge on the altar standing towards one end on the middle axis (Fig. 2). This was the focal point of the building and around it priesthood and laity gathered for the celebration of the liturgy, each section having its prescribed place. In the centre of

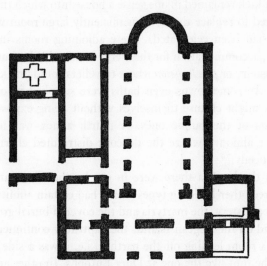

*Fig.* 2 Suvodol, Macedonia, 4th century

the semi-circular apse, roofed by a half-dome, the bishop had his throne, the *cathedra*, on either side of which were the seats of the presbyters. The superior clergy were separated from the rest of the congregation by the altar around which the deacons were grouped. It could stand on the chord of the apse or even in the body of the church well down the central nave. The rectangular hall was divided by parallel rows of columns into aisles of which there was always an odd number. The centre one, the nave, corresponded to the apse in width and was equivalent to the sum of the side aisles. It rose above the aisles, its walls pierced with windows to form a clerestory and allow the access of light. There were of course numerous differences of detail. The apse could project beyond the east wall or be contained within it. Space could be provided in front of the presbyterium by the construction of transepts. The porch might be separate or included in the building to form a narthex. Moreover, the church-building proper did not consist solely of this assembly hall. When the Church emerged from the private house, it did not make a complete break with all that had taken place there, discarding, as it were, the additional rooms and adopting instead a single hall. Indeed, the house of God, *domus Dei*, was only part of the greater house, *domus ecclesiae*, which remained in one sense a house into which the basilica was inserted to replace the now insufficiently large room where the eucharist had been celebrated. These adjoining rooms included a baptistery, accommodation for the clergy to eat and sleep and sometimes a hostelry or *pandocheion* where travellers could find shelter for the night. In some towns even baths were supplied in order that Christians might cleanse themselves without being exposed to the temptations of the public ones. A fourth annex was used as a *diaconia* or almonry where the deacons distributed charity to the poor and needy.[70]

Besides the basilica there were in use by the Christians of this period three other building types which had certain affinities: these were the baptistery, the martyria and the covered burial grounds. In Greece and on the Aegean Islands the baptistery continued to be in the main a room leading off the narthex, i.e. it was a side chamber housing the font like the one at Dura Europos. In other areas, such as Syria and Italy, the baptistery became a detached building and assumed the shape of contemporary tombs, because the sacrament was understood to effect a co-death and a co-resurrection with Christ.[71] The tomb also provided the main prototype for the martyria, which were edifices enshrining the remains of the saints. In some of the Constantinian buildings, e.g. the church of the Nativity at Bethlehem or St Peter's in Rome, an attempt was made to fuse hall and martyrium, by engaging the latter with the former at its extremity. In the East the cult of the saints became so powerful that its architectural form ultimately superseded that of the basilica for congregational gatherings,[72] whereas in the West it was associated with the regular celebration of the eucharist by connecting the altar with the tomb of the saint below, or, later, by enclosing relics within the altar itself.

The third type of building, the covered burial ground, requires a more extended consideration because sufficient examples have only recently come to light to allow this new classification to be made.[73] The buildings, all at Rome, are as follows: first, S. Lorenzo, discovered in 1950; second, S. Agnese, soundings for which were taken in 1955; third, SS. Marcellino e Pietro (Fig. 3), excavated in 1956.

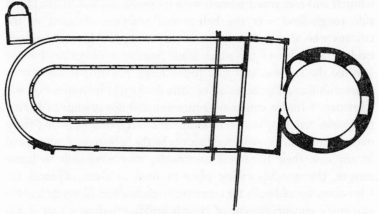

*Fig.* 3   SS. Marcellino e Pietro, 4th century

All these edifices were large structures, some 240 to 360 feet long; in all three the aisles continued as an ambulatory around the apse; the nave, as well as the aisles, was apparently roofed; tombs paved the entire floor; a martyr's grave, located in a subterranean chamber, was accessible by means of a staircase. To these three must be added a fourth building, previously known and revealing the same plan and features, viz. S. Sebastiano. All of them date from the reign of Constantine. They were undoubtedly ecclesiastical buildings and the eucharist was celebrated within them, since the Constantinian donation lists include altars and eucharistic vessels, and S. Agnese, at least, had a font. They were, however, not ordinary churches; rather they were a kind of martyrium but with the chief object of veneration, i.e. the saint's tomb, not actually included within the building.

They were in fact covered burial grounds or *coemeteria-basilicae*, which is perhaps best rendered basilican-cemeteries, since they were not cemetery basilicas.[74]* Their further function, apart from that of burial, will be considered when we turn to the secular uses of church buildings, but before so doing we must finally consider the attitude of the fourth-century Christians to these 'places' of worship.

The position of Constantine when he became sole emperor was unquestionably an ambiguous one. On the one hand he attributed his victory to the God of the Christians and on the other he was the ruler of subjects who were for the most part pagan. He favoured the Church and concerned himself with its problems, but he could not ride rough-shod over the beliefs and practices of many of the citizens who also accepted him as their master. This ambiguity is evident in the law of 321 which made Sunday an obligatory holiday —while the law was cast in a pagan form, referring to the day as *venerabilis dies solis*, there can be little doubt that its inspiration was Christian.[75] In this situation Constantine did not attempt to destroy the pagan temples, nor were Christians interested in taking them over, because they considered them to be the habitats of demons, and in any case their form was unsuitable; they were cells to house images, the worship taking place in front of them, whereas the Christians wanted halls for community gatherings. Nevertheless the emperor's encouragement of church building indicates that it was his hope that the churches would eventually replace the temples as centres of religious devotion, and part of this policy was realized by the erection of a multitude of martyria or chapels to displace the worship of the local gods by the veneration of the saints.

To foster an ambitious programme of church building of an official type as a substitute for temples was to encourage the idea that the two classes of edifice were really of the same kind, the only *differentia* being that the one provided for the cultus of false gods and the other for the cultus of the true God. Hence it was relatively easy for the terminology used of temples to be applied to church buildings. So we find *penetralia* and *adytum*, both referring to the innermost and holiest part of a temple, being used of churches.[76]* Lactantius could use *templum* of the church at Bithynia[77] and this term is frequent in the writings of Augustine.[78] *Naos* was similarly employed,[79] and also *aedes*.[80] With the vocabulary was also adopted the associated idea of specially holy places set apart for the cult. Unlike Minucius Felix, Christians of the fourth century were content to say: 'We have temples.'[81]

This changed attitude was further influenced by Constantine's plan for adorning the sites of Christ's ministry and death in Palestine. Here again the idea of specially holy places is predominant, and in his letter to Macarius the emperor explicitly declares the site of the resurrection to be sacred.[82] The church that he ordered to be built at Mamre is another illustration of his ideas. Accepting current exegesis, that the three men who appeared to Abraham at the oak were Jesus in the company of two angels, the emperor took steps to make the scene of a theophany into a sacred shrine.[83] It is not surprising therefore to learn that when he went on his Persian campaign he carried with him a tent in the form of a church;[84] he could not escape from the idea of a holy place and his example affected the Church at large.

Not all Christians were prepared immediately to capitulate. Some spoke out, as had the ante-Nicene fathers, against the identification of Church and church. Hilary of Poitiers, for example, declared that 'it is wrong to be attached to walls; it is wrong to direct your veneration for the Church towards roofs and buildings'.[85] Similarly John Chrysostom contended that 'the Church is not constituted by an enclosure of walls; it consists in the number of its members'.[86] Others, such as Gregory of Nyssa, complained bitterly of the idea of specially holy places which had become the main motive for pilgrims to visit Palestine in their hordes in the last decades of the fourth century:

What advantage accrues to him who reaches these celebrated places? He cannot imagine that our Lord is living, in the body, there at the present day, but has gone away from us foreigners; or that the Holy Spirit is in abundance at Jerusalem, but unable to travel as far as us. . . . You who fear the Lord, praise him in the places where you are now. Change of place does not effect any drawing nearer to God, but wherever you may be, God will come to you.[87]

But not all Christians were so direct and clear in their thinking. Their difficulty is to be detected in the contradictions which come from the pen of Jerome on this subject. At one time he was in agreement with Gregory:

> I do not presume to limit God's omnipotence or to restrict to a narrow strip of earth him whom the heavens cannot contain. . . . The true worshippers worship the Father neither at Jerusalem nor on mount Gerizim, for 'God is a spirit, and they that worship him must worship him in spirit and in truth'. . . . The Saviour himself, speaking to his disciples in the Temple, said: 'Arise, let us go hence', and to the Jews: 'Your house is left unto you desolate'. If heaven and earth pass away, obviously all things that are earthly must pass away also. Therefore the places that witness to the crucifixion and the resurrection profit those only who bear their several crosses, who day by day rise again with Christ, and who there show themselves worthy of an abode so holy. Those who say, 'the temple of the Lord, the temple of the Lord', should listen to the apostle's words: 'Ye are the temple of the Lord', and the Holy Spirit 'dwelleth in you'. Access to the courts of heaven is as easy from Britain, as it is from Jerusalem.[88]

Nevertheless Jerome could also say of Bethlehem: 'I know this spot is holier than the Tarpeian rock,' i.e. than the Capitol with its temple of Jupiter.[89] At one time he writes grudgingly of money spent on churches, allowing only that it is perhaps better to do this than to hoard it,[90] but at another he can compare the recently deceased Nepotian, who had adorned certain churches and martyria, with Bezalel and Hiram who worked the one on the furniture of the tabernacle and the other on that of the Jerusalem Temple.[91] We can detect him searching for reasons to support the new Christian attitude to the Palestinian sites and to church buildings. 'The Jews of old reverenced the holy of holies. . . . Does the Lord's sepulchre seem less worthy of veneration?'[92]

This comparison with the Jewish sanctuary draws attention to another factor that was promoting the changed attitude on the 'place' of worship, viz. the influence of the Old Testament. When Christians began to build their great basilicas, they turned for guidance to their bible and were soon applying all that was said about the Jerusalem Temple to their new edifices, seemingly ignorant of the fact that in so doing they were behaving contrary to the New Testament outlook. So Eusebius, in his panegyric at Tyre, called the Bishop Paulinus, who had been responsible for the cathedral, 'a new Bezalel the architect of a divine tabernacle, or Solomon the king of a new and far goodlier Jerusalem, or even a new Zerubbabel who bestowed upon the Temple of God that glory which greatly exceeded the former'.[93] He could also speak of Paulinus as 'our most peaceful Solomon who built the Temple of God'.[94] It is true that Eusebius is emphatic that the Christian community is the true temple and that it is only by transference that what is said of the Church can be applied to a church,[95] but it was easy to forget that the identification of Temple and church was figurative and then to regard it as a fact. Cyril of Jerusalem was prepared to call the baptistery 'the holy of holies',[96] a title similarly used by Ambrose[97] who also compared it with the 'second tabernacle'.[98] When the *Apostolic Constitutions* prescribed the places for the various sections of the congregation in a church, it supported its regulations by the statement that 'the same description and pattern was both in the tabernacle of the testimony and in the Temple of God'.[99]* Hence Augustine explained the rectangular shape of churches as a direct imitation of the tabernacle in the wilderness,[100] and Cyril of Alexandria similarly saw it as the model of the Christian basilica.[101]

Jerome provides a pointer to the fourth factor we have to consider. Arguing for respect for the Holy Sepulchre, he says: 'Everywhere we venerate the tombs of the martyrs . . . and yet some think that we should neglect the tomb in which the Lord himself was buried'.[102] Mention has been made above of the cult of the saints and of its steady penetration of church buildings—this penetration finally set its seal upon the outlook that the church is a holy place, towards which Christians should adopt the same attitude as Jews to the Jerusalem Temple and pagans to their shrines. Indeed, in fifth-century Egypt we hear of monks removing their sandals when they went to 'celebrate or to receive the holy mysteries'[103] in imitation of Moses at the burning bush and Joshua at Jericho, to each of whom it was said: 'Put off thy shoes from off thy feet, for the place whereon thou standest is holy ground.'[104]

It is against this architectural and theological, or ideological, background that we must now consider the secular uses of these Constantinian and post-Constantinian church buildings.

## Living and Sleeping

The use of church buildings for living and sleeping in the patristic period is related to three practices: (1) incubation; (ii) sanctuary, and (iii) shelter for travellers.

(i) Incubation, as practised by the pagan population of the Roman Empire, was a method of obtaining visions of the future through dreams fostered by worshipping a deity and then sleeping in the place most likely to be visited by him, i.e. in a temple. Its primary aspect was medical, its purpose being to obtain a cure, either immediately or by obeying the divine will revealed in the vision. The two principal healing gods in the pagan pantheon were Serapis and Aesculapius—so we read of a temple of the latter at Aegae where those 'who passed the night' were restored to health.[105] The apparent success of these two gods ensured their continued popularity, and their cults only fell into disuse when churches replaced their temples as centres of healing believed to be accomplished by Christ through his saints.[106]*

Amongst the most successful of Christian saints in curing illnesses were Cosmas and Damian, to whom a church was dedicated in Constantinople. Associated with this sanctuary are stories of a man with a fistula in his thigh who was healed in the church, of another with a haemorrhage who was told to give up meat and to eat cakes made with flour, and of a woman with a pain in her breast who was prescribed laser mixed with pennyroyal.[107] These are all examples of prescription-cures, and indeed the records tell of doctors being summoned to the church to perform what the saints had commanded. Healing, however, was by no means always immediate; hence we are informed of a man who lay seven months in the church and of another who lived there for a whole year.[108]

A second centre at Constantinople was the shrine of St Therapon and an encomium of the saint, probably written in the seventh century, records how a soldier with a misshapen body stayed there for several days and was finally directed to anoint himself with oil. A paralytic, named Theodoros, passed thirty days in the church and a woman suffering from cancer forty days.[109]

Close to Constantinople was the church of St Michael the Archangel. According to Sozomen, a lawyer named Aquiline, being severely ill, was carried there by his servant and, having passed the night, was restored to health.[110]

Another famous centre was the church of Menuthes near Alexandria; there some patients stayed over a year. The church itself was filled with mattresses and low couches on which the sick passed their days and nights, sleeping by the tomb of the saint. So great were their numbers that they overflowed into the sacristy, there being insufficient space in the worship room for them all. Some of the prescription-cures included bathing, and baths were provided in the building complex for this to take place.[111]

All over the empire churches were used in this way. At Tours, the church of St Martin housed on one occasion a certain Veranus, a sufferer from gout, who lived there for five days before obtaining relief.[112] At St Maximinus, near Trèves, Charles Martel, who had a fever, slept before the saint's tomb.[113] Bede in his *Ecclesiastical History* provides a further series of examples from England. In 616, Archbishop Laurentius of Canterbury ordered his bed to be carried to the church of SS. Peter and Paul, where he passed the night.[114] In 642, a boy with an ague was healed after watching all night by the tomb of St Oswald,[115] and in 698 a paralytic was cured after the usual vigil at the tomb of St Cuthbert.[116]

Not only those suffering from physical diseases but also the mentally deranged were to be found living in churches. According to Bede again, in 669, a mentally handicapped traveller arrived late at the church where St Chad was buried; since he could find no other accommodation, he passed the night in the church and by the following morning he was restored to health.[117] In the canons falsely attributed to the Fourth Council of Carthage, the exorcists, who were charged with the care of energumens or demoniacs, had to lay hands on them daily at home and in the church building, which was to be swept each day.[118] Indeed, 'the church seems to have been used as a sort of asylum for the insane'.[119] Here then we have abundant evidence of a secular use, with religious overtones, of church buildings to house, feed and sleep those whom one can only call residential patients.

(ii) Like incubation, the granting of sanctuary had pagan origins. For centuries before the Church received legal recognition, and therefore before its buildings could be classified as places of refuge, it had been the custom to regard temples as inviolable. The most famous example is undoubtedly that of Demosthenes, who in 322 B.C. sought sanctuary in the temple of Poseidon on the island of Calauria.[120] The basic idea was that it was sacrilege to remove by force anyone who had entered the holy precincts; he was, as it were, invested with some of the sacredness of the place and could not therefore be touched as long as he remained within it. When church buildings were included in the same class as temples, i.e. as specially holy places, it was natural that the idea of sanctuary should also be associated with them, particularly as there seemed to be some precedent in the Old Testament.[121]

In a law of 392 which indicates that churches had already been recognized as sanctuaries,[122]* public debtors are excepted from this privilege,[123]* and in another law of 397 Jews, who pretended to be Christians in order to qualify for protection, were similarly excepted[124] and slaves likewise, although later they were allowed to stay for one day.[125] The primary place of sanctuary was the altar and then the nave, and the baptistery too, was regarded in the same light,[126] and since these fugitives often stayed a considerable time, we have here further evidence of living and sleeping within churches.

Nevertheless the growing emphasis upon the sacredness of church buildings led some to regard the living-in of the sanctuary seekers as a desecration, and so to meet this situation, and still to preserve the right of sanctuary, the emperors designated a larger area than that immediately around the altar. The relevant law, issued 23rd March, 431, which sheds light on the contemporary attitude to churches, reads as follows:

The temples of the Most High God shall be open to those persons who are afraid. Not only do we sanction that the altars and the surrounding oratory of the temple, which encloses the church with a barrier of four walls on the inside, shall be set aside for the protection of those persons who take refuge, but also the space up to the outside doors of the church, which people desiring to pray enter first, we order to be an altar of safety for those who seek sanctuary. Thus if there should be any intervening space within the circumference of the walls of the temple which we have marked off and within the outer doors of the church behind the public grounds, whether it be in the cells or in the houses, gardens, baths, courtyards, or colonnades, such space shall protect the fugitives, just as the interior of the temple does. No one shall attempt to lay sacrilegious hands on them to drag them out, lest a person who dares to do this, when he seeks his own peril, may himself also take refuge and seek aid. Moreover, we grant this extent of space for this purpose, namely that it may not be permitted that any fugitive remain or eat or sleep or spend the night in the very temple of God or on the sacrosanct altars. The clergy themselves shall forbid this for the sake of reverence for religion, and those who seek sanctuary shall observe it for the sake of piety.

1. We also command that those persons who seek sanctuary shall not have within the churches any arms at all, in the form of any weapon, either of iron or of any other kind. For weapons are debarred not only from the temples and divine altars of the Most High God, but also from the cells, houses, gardens, baths, courtyards and colonnades.

2. Hereafter if any persons should flee without arms to the most holy temple of God or to its sacrosanct altar, either anywhere else in the world or in this fair city, they shall be prevented by the clergy themselves, without any injury to such persons, from sleeping or from taking any food within the temple or at the altar. The clergy shall designate spaces within the ecclesiastical enclosures which shall be sufficient for their protection and shall explain that capital punishment has been decreed if anyone should attempt to enter forcibly and seize them.[127]

Nevertheless in the Middle Ages, as will be seen below, the sanctuary seekers did continue to live for days and even years in the worship room itself.

(iii) The use of churches by travellers to sleep overnight only took place when there was no alternative accommodation. The cathedral of Brad in Syria, for example, had an adjoining *pandocheion*, consisting of a large room divided into two by a row of animal feeding troughs, which were separated by upright stones on which beams were placed to support a partition. But not all churches had such annexes, in which case it was not regarded as in any way improper to sleep in them. So Sozomen records the story of a friend of Julian the Apostate, who was on his way to join him in Persia. When night fell, he went into a church and during his sleep he had a dream foretelling the emperor's death.[128] At a later date the Quinisext Council found it necessary to forbid regular lodging in church galleries.[129]

There is a certain ambivalence in the material assembled above, in that churches were both regarded as temples and therefore holy and yet, because of this classification with pagan shrines, secular activities, such as eating and sleeping, could take place within them. Despite the emperor's attempt to regulate the extent of sanctuary, incubation and travellers alone meant that at any one time a not inconsiderable number of people were using churches as habitations.

### Eating and Drinking

The evidence adduced above of people actually living in churches is also evidence of eating and drinking, for the sick had to be fed and the law that attempted to regulate the sanctuary seekers refers to their 'taking food within the temple or at the altar'. But the practice was much wider than this and must be related to the *agape* or love feast and to the meals at the tombs of the martyrs.

There is good reason to believe that the eucharist as first celebrated in the apostolic age was a repetition of the Last Supper *in toto*.[130] This means that it began with the blessing, breaking and distribution of bread, and that there then followed a meal at the conclusion of which wine was taken, blessed and distributed. In the course of time the meal was removed, thus uniting the blessing and distribution of the bread and of the wine to establish the classical shape of the eucharist. The meal however was not discarded; it continued as a separate observance, and already by the second generation of Christians was being called the *agape* or love feast.[131] This meal was provided with its own ritual introduction in the form of the blessing, breaking and distributing of a loaf.[132]

The *agape* took place in the private homes of Christians as a form of fellowship and of charity towards the poorer members of the congregation, who were specially invited to attend, and so Hippolytus says: 'throughout the meal let him who eats remember him who invited him, for to this end he petitioned that they might come under his roof'.[133] The *agape* could of course also be held in the house-church and continued so to be in the basilicas. The Council of Gangra sought to encourage them: 'if anyone shall despise those who out of faith make love feasts and invite brethren in honour of the Lord, and is not willing to accept these invitations because he despises what is done, let him be anathema'.[134] Nevertheless the growing reverence for churches as holy places led the Council of

Laodicea to forbid the holding of *agapes* in them: 'it is not permitted to hold love feasts, as they are called, in the Lord's houses, or churches, nor to eat and spread couches in the house of God'.[135] This indicates that up to the middle of the fourth century churches could be and were fitted out as dining-rooms for a common meal.

Love feasts were held on three main occasions, of which the last two require particular attention: at marriages, funerals and on the feast days of martyrs. The first two had pagan antecedents and the third was an extension of the second.

When in the year 397 Pammachius provided a vast funeral banquet for the poor of Rome in honour of his deceased wife, the numbers were so great that they occupied the nave and aisles of St Peter's and overflowed into the atrium.[136] Pammachius was performing an act of Christian charity, but in a form that stemmed from the funeral customs of his pagan ancestors. It was the practice among the pagans to visit the tomb of a relative on the third day after burial and there to take a meal; this was repeated on the ninth day and sometimes on the thirtieth, as well as annually on the deceased's birthday.[137] Pagan tombs were often equipped with couches and tables, and even with a kitchen with water supply and drain attached. A single inscription from Sitifi near Hippo, dated 299, will suffice as an example of the general attitude:

> To the memory of Aelia Secundula
> We have already spent much on Mother Secundula's tomb
> Now we have decided to put up at the place where she rests
> A stone table, where we will together remember
> All the things that she did.
> Then when the food has been brought and the cups have been filled
> and the cushions
> Have been laid around, then in order to heal the painful wound
> Till late in the evening we shall discuss gladly and with praises
> Our honourable mother—and the old lady will sleep.
> Now she who nourished us lies here in eternal sobriety.
> She lived 72 years. Provincial year 260. Erected by Statulenia Julia.[138]

Christians were prepared to do the same. About the year 260 a dining-room was built on a site on the Via Appia, which seems to have been a provisional resting place of the relics of Peter and Paul; stone benches were disposed around the walls and the débris in the gutter—glass, chicken and fish bones—shows its use for *agapes*.[139] Another example comes from Dougga in North Africa, where three donors offered to the martyrs a *symposium* with four *cubicula*, i.e. dining-couches,[140] while at Carthage there was a *basilica tricliarum*.[141] The meal in these centres was an opportunity to distribute food to the poor and so the Christian gathering was extended beyond the pagan confines of blood relationship. The *Apostolic Constitutions* sanctioned the observance on the third and ninth days, but for the thirtieth substituted one on the fortieth in honour of Moses.[142] Augustine, however, while accepting the third day because it recalled Christ's resurrection, opposed the ninth with its connection with the *novemdialia* and *parentalia* of the pagans and proposed instead the seventh to recall the rest of the Sabbath,[143] and the day of death itself replaced the birthday as the occasion of the year's mind. This pagan custom, baptized as it were into Christianity, was to persist. In time Augustine considered that the better Christians among his flock had abandoned it, but he did not condemn it outright;[144] that was reserved for the feasts associated with the cult of the martyrs.

While particular attention was paid to the anniversaries of the martyrs, any day was acceptable for an *agape* and indeed we are informed by Augustine, in disapproving terms, that there was 'daily tippling' (*cotidianae vinulentias*) in St Peter's at Rome.[145] Similar banquets in honour of the martyrs were held in all parts of the empire, e.g. at Nola,[146] and the basilican cemeteries in Rome, described above, would seem to have been specially built for the holding of these feasts.[147] There is extant a Good Friday address from the time of Constantine which describes these gatherings. 'Then hymns, psalms and songs of praise are sung in honour of him who sees all things, and in memory of these people there is celebrated the sacrifice from which all blood and violence have been banished. Here is to be sought neither perfume nor incense nor a funeral pyre, but only pure light to illumine those who pray here; and often there is connected with this a modest meal for the benefit of the poor and unfortunate.'[148] Unfortunately this picture of decorum ceased to correspond with the facts as the years passed. The gatherings became occasions for riotousness and drunkenness.

Paulinus of Nola sought to regulate them, but Ambrose of Milan took the more severe step of prohibiting them entirely.[149] One of the first to feel the effects of this was Monica in the year 384 and Augustine recorded his mother's experience in his *Confessions*:

> It had been my mother's custom in Africa to take meal-cakes and bread and wine to the shrines of the saints on their memorial days, but the door-keeper would not allow her to do this in Milan. When she learned that the bishop had forbidden it, she accepted his ruling with such pious sub-mission that I was surprised to see how willingly she condemned her own practice rather than dispute his command. For her heart was not beset by a craving for wine nor did the love of it goad her into a hatred of the truth. . . . She used to bring her basket full of the customary offerings of food, intending to taste a little and give the rest away. For herself she never poured more than a small cupful of wine, watered to suit her sober palate, and she drank only as much of it as was needed to do honour to the dead. If there were many shrines to be honoured in this way, she carried the same cup around with her to each one and shared its contents, by now well watered and quite lukewarm, with any of her friends who were present, allowing each only to take the smallest sip. For her purpose was to perform an act of piety, not to seek pleasure for herself. But she willingly ceased this custom when she found that this great preacher, this holy bishop, had forbidden such ceremonies even to those who per-formed them with sobriety, both for fear that to some they might be occasions for drunkenness and also because they bore so close a re-semblance to the superstitious rites which the pagans held in honour of their dead. . . . Yet it seems to me that my mother would not have given up this habit so readily, if the prohibition had come from another whom she loved less dearly than Ambrose.[150]

Zeno of Verona followed suit declaring: 'God is displeased by those who run along to the gravesides, offer their lunch to stinking corpses and then in their desire to eat and drink suddenly, with pot and glass, conjure up the martyrs at the most unfitting places'.[151] Augus-tine's own respect for Ambrose was also such that he decided that his example should be followed in North Africa and in 392 he wrote to Bishop Aurelius to induce him to execute the same policy. 'Riot-ing and drunkenness', he declared, 'are so tolerated and allowed by public opinion, that even in services designed to honour the mem-ory of the blessed martyrs, and this not only on the annual festival but every day . . . they are openly practised. . . . Let this outrageous insult be kept far away from the tombs of the holy dead, from the scene of sacramental privilege, and from the houses of prayer.' Augustine objected to them on moral grounds but also because they fostered superstition. 'These drunken revels and luxurious feasts in the cemeteries are wont to be regarded by the ignorant and carnal multitude as not only an honour to the martyr but also a solace to the dead.' In his opinion 'so wide and deep is the plague caused by this wickedness that it cannot be completely cured without the interposition of a council's authority'.[152] In the following year the council met at Hippo and its twenty-ninth canon reads: 'that no bishop or clergy are to hold feasts in churches, unless perchance they are forced thereto by the necessity of hospitality as they pass by'.

Augustine supported his policy against eating and drinking in his sermons[153] but without immediate success. In 395 he determined to do all in his power to enforce the prohibition and his twenty-ninth letter describes the steps that he took. On the Wednesday before Ascension Day, he was expounding the Gospel which included the verse: 'Give not that which is holy unto the dogs, neither cast your pearls before swine.'[154] He seized the opportunity to apply this to the feasting in the churches and martyria and declared: 'they might plainly see how criminal it was to do, under the name of religion, within the walls of the church, that which, if practised by them in their own houses, would make it necessary for them to be debarred from that which is holy, and from the privileges which are the pearls of the Church'. The congregation was not large, but the word went round as to his stand and on Ascension Day itself the church was crowded. The lection included the 'Cleansing of the Temple' and Augustine proceeded to argue 'with how much greater anger and vehemence our Lord would cast forth drunken revels, which are everywhere disgraceful, from that temple from which he thus drove out merchandise lawful elsewhere, especially when the things sold were those required for the sacrifices appointed in that dispensation; and I asked them whether they regarded a place occupied by men selling what was necessary, or one used by men drinking to excess, as bearing the greater resemblance to a den of thieves.' He then contrasted with the excesses of the Christians the behaviour of the Jews who 'never held feasts, even temperate feasts, much less feasts disgraced by intemperance, in their temple'. He asserted, on the basis of I Cor. 11.20–22, that eating and drinking were 'things lawful in themselves, but not lawful in the church, inasmuch as men have their own houses in which they may be nourished'.

'Next morning,' continues Augustine, 'when the day dawned, which so many were accustomed to devote to excess in eating and drinking, I received notice that some, even of those who were present when I preached, had not yet desisted from complaint, and that so great was the power of detestable custom with them, that, using no other arguments, they asked, "Why is this now prohibited? Were they not Christians who in former times did not interfere with this practice?" ' In his morning sermon he faced these objections, explaining, 'the circumstances out of which this custom seems to have arisen in the Church—namely, that when, in the peace that came after such numerous and violent persecutions, crowds of heathen who wished to assume the Christian religion were kept back, because, having been accustomed to celebrate the feasts connected with their worship of idols in revelling and drunkenness, they could not easily refrain from pleasures so hurtful and habitual, it had seemed good to our ancestors, making a temporary concession to their infirmity, to allow them to celebrate, instead of the festivals they had renounced, other feasts in honour of the holy martyrs, which were observed, not as before with a profane design, but with similar self-indulgence.' A second discourse in the afternoon seems to have convinced the majority of his hearers of the rightness of his proposals and the practice began to disappear. It did not vanish entirely, however, in spite of later condemnation, e.g. by the Council of Auxerre, 573–603, which forbade singing and sociable feasts in churches.[155]

In the fifth century common meals were held in the Thebaid every Saturday evening,[156] and Theodoret reported yearly feasting in honour of the martyrs.[157] Gregory the Great was prepared to allow them at the dedication of churches,[158] particularly in the case of the newly converted English, although in this latter case the meals were to take place outside and around the churches.[159] We find, too, Remigius of Rheims leaving at his death, *c.* 530, a vineyard to his priests and deacons to provide *agapes* on Sundays and festivals within the cathedral itself.[160] In Armenia, in the same century, so we are informed by the Quinisext Council as it condemns it, some are 'boiling joints of meat within the sanctuary and offering portions to the priests'.[161] Some ecclesiastics were prepared to give a measure of support. According to the Capitular of Hincmar of Rheims, 858, when there was a dispute between members of guilds, they were to resolve them after mass and then receive from the priest some blessed bread and a goblet of wine.[162] The *eulogia* or blessed bread was a remnant of the practice of eating, but it was to survive in a more robust form as church ales throughout the Middle Ages.

The criticisms levelled against eating and drinking in churches, by Augustine in particular, are certainly valid in so far as they apply to excesses, but it is noticeable how the case for their entire prohibition rests upon two factors which the New Testament attitude contradicts, viz. on the parallel between the Jewish Temple and the church building and on the incident of the 'Cleansing of the Temple'.

## Dancing

Dancing in churches has a long history, although its documentation is not extensive. This activity, as so many others, was first associated with the festivals of the martyrs. So an anonymous homily, belonging to the first third of the fourth century, and delivered on the anniversary of St Polyeuctus, contains the exhortation: 'If you will, let us celebrate in his honour our accustomed dances.'[163] On St Cyprian's day in the year 360, the memorial church on the Area Macrobii at Carthage was the scene of dancing to the music of zithers.[164] Augustine, preaching some decades later in the same church, was most scathing as he recalled the incident. 'Is it proper that here, where psalms are sung, there should be dancing? And yet, not so very long ago, the forwardness of the dancers had penetrated even into this very place.'[165] Basil of Caesarea, too, reproved those women who dared to dance at the Paschal celebrations,[166] but Evagrius (*c.* 536–600), recording another instance in Syria, does so without condemning it; he describes how he saw some rustics performing a dance around the balustrade enclosing the pillar of

Simeon Stylites, within the great architectural complex reared at Qalat-Siman.[167]

Dancing in churches continued throughout the Middle Ages despite regular condemnations by councils and bishops. A whole series of such statements are extant from the sixth to the ninth centuries, indicating its persistence during this period. A brief resumé will illustrate their extent. Dancing in churches was attacked by a council at Auxerre (573–603), by one at Chalon-sur-Saône (639–654), by one at Estinnes (743), by a Roman synod in 826 and by Leo IV (847–855). These were not ritual dances but the popular expression of high spirits associated with the Church's festivals in general and no longer merely with saints' days, so, e.g. a constitution attributed to Childebert I, who died in 596, refers to dancing 'in the sacred buildings, at Easter, Christmas and other festivals'.[168]

## The Sale of Goods

More sparse are the references to the selling of goods. A canon ascribed to a synod of Tours in 461 declares that 'it has been related to the holy synod that certain priests in the churches committed to them (an abuse hardly to be mentioned) have established taverns, and so through tavern-keepers (*caupones*) sell wine or allow it to be sold'.[169] A canon to similar effect was promulgated by the Quinisextan Council: 'It is not right that those who are responsible for reverence to churches should place within the sacred precincts an eating place, nor offer food there, nor make other sales. For God our Saviour, teaching us when he was tabernacling in the flesh, commanded not to make his Father's house a house of merchandise.'[170]

How extensive this practice was it is impossible to determine. It could well have been a frequent accompaniment of the martyrs' feasts and certainly in the Middle Ages the common use of churches for fairs and the sale of all kinds of goods indicates a connection with the festivals of the saints. This appears to be borne out by a passage from the monastic rules of Basil of Caesarea:

Scripture shows us that buying and selling conducted at martyrs' tombs is not fitting for us. For it is incumbent on Christians to be seen at the martyrs' tombs or in their neighbourhood for no other reason than that of prayer and in order that, remembering how the saints contended even unto death on behalf of godliness, we may be initiated to a like zeal. We must remember the fearful wrath of the Lord, who though he was always and everywhere meek and lowly of heart, as it is written, yet on one class —those that bought and sold in the Temple precincts—inflicted a castigation, since their trafficking turned the house of prayer into a den of thieves. Others may have corrupted the accustomed order of the saints, and in place of praying for one another . . . may have used the time and place as a market and fair and common emporium. But it ill befits us now to follow their example.[171]

## Meetings

The term 'basilica', as previously noted, referred initially to a large meeting-hall. Although its primary function, when adopted by the Christians, was to provide for the liturgical assembly, its general connotation remained valid. Churches were used for a variety of meetings of a non-liturgical character.

(i) *Councils.* A large number of synods and councils were held in churches. The opening sessions of the first ecumenical council at Nicaea in 325 were held 'in a simple house of prayer'.[172] The second ecumenical council at Constantinople in 381 also met in a church which was later called the *Homonoia*, and Evagrius explains that it had received this appellation, meaning the church of concord, because of the consensus achieved by the bishops at that assembly.[173] The third ecumenical council at Ephesus was 'in the church called Mary'[174] where the Gospels were placed upon the throne in token of the presence of Christ.[175] Chalcedon in 451 assembled in the martyrium of Euphemia, a description of which has been left by Evagrius. It consisted of three structures: a basilica with aisles, an atrium and a round domed building enshrining the relics of the saint. The general sessions of the council took place in the basilica, but for the formulation of the Definition of Faith the bishops retired to the round building where they drew up the statement and then came back into the basilica to present it to the whole council.[176]

Other smaller synods met in churches, and while an exhaustive list is unnecessary a few illustrations may be given. In 359 the council of Seleucia gathered in the church.[177] In 394 a meeting at Constantinople, under its Bishop Nectarius and Theophilus of Alexandria, held its sessions 'in the baptistery of the most holy church'.[178]

Moving to later centuries, the council of Constantinople in 754, which was concerned with the iconoclastic controversy, assembled in 'the temple of the holy and inviolate Mother of God and Virgin Mary, surnamed in Blachernae',[179] while the second Nicene Council of 787 was held in 'the holy church of God which is named Sophia'.[180]

It may be objected to this evidence that it scarcely falls within the category of secular uses. It is however doubtful if a distinction can be maintained in this clear-cut fashion. The council of Nicaea of 325 may serve as an example of this ambiguity. It is true that the primary concern of this assembly was to achieve a settlement of the doctrinal controversy which had been initiated by Arius, but the emperor, who was present at several of the sessions, certainly did not regard this as a simple religious and internal Church question. The unity of the Church was to him a matter of political concern; a disrupted Church would not play the part that he envisaged in his policy for preserving the cohesion of the empire—sacred, or religious, and secular therefore are in this instance but two aspects of the same thing.

(ii) *Elections.* From early days the laity had an important part in the appointment of bishops. Cyprian, describing how Cornelius was made Bishop of Rome, says that it was 'by the testimony of almost all the clergy, by the suffrage of the people who were then present, and by the assembly of ancient priests and good men'.[181] He was emphatic that the 'ordination of priests ought not to be solemnized except with the knowledge and in the presence of the people'.[182] The evidence of the fourth century is similar. Of Athanasius, we read that the people shouted that he should be bishop and that he was then elected by the other bishops present 'in the sight of and with the acclamations of all the people'.[183]

These elections took place in church buildings. So, for example, Ambrose, when presiding over such an election as the governor of the province, was acclaimed by the people of Milan despite his protests.[184] On occasion there were elections and counter-elections. At Jerusalem in 451 the people assembled in the Anastasis to elect Theodosius in opposition to the orthodox Bishop Juvenal,[185] while in Alexandria Timothy was elected in the great church of the Caesareum in opposition to Proterius.[186] Probably the worst example of all was the election in Rome disputed between Damasus and Ursinus in 366; the adherents of the former met in the basilica of Lucina and of the latter in the Julian basilica, and much blood was shed before Damasus emerged supreme.[187]

(iii) *Discussions.* A church building was obviously an admirable hall for debates and was so used from pre-Nicene times. At Ancyra in Galatia at the end of the second century upholders of the orthodox party 'discoursed for many days in the church' against the Montanists.[188] Later we hear of the emperor Valens entering the church at Caesarea in Cappadocia in 371 in a vain attempt to convince Basil of the rightness of Arianism. Amongst those contributing to the debate was a cook named Demosthenes who was guilty of a solecism and this called forth a remark from Basil: 'We have, it seems, a Demosthenes who cannot speak Greek; he had better attend to his sauces than meddle with divinity.'[189] The zealous emperor also went to Tomi and held a meeting in the church at which he tried to win over the bishop to his Arian viewpoint.[190]

Augustine used this method of public debate both against the Manichees and the Donatists. His first discussion with the Manichee Fortunatus was in the Baths of Sossius,[191] but twelve years later, in 404, he met Felix in the church.[192] The first Donatist debate also took place in the public baths, in the hall of the Baths of Gargilius,[193] but in 419 in Caesarea of Mauretainia Augustine debated in the church.[194] The African bishop saw nothing wrong in this particular non-liturgical use of the church building.

## Legal Proceedings

On the basis of Paul's injunction that the faithful should not go to law before unbelievers,[195] the bishop had come to exercise a certain measure of jurisdiction. This received state recognition in 318 when Constantine authorized the transference of cases to the episcopal courts.[196] The venue of these hearings is seldom stated; they could take place in the *secretarium* or sacristy[197] or even in baptisteries[198] and it is reasonable to assume that on occasion the liturgical room itself was put to this secular use.

It is this state recognition of the magisterial office of the bishop that explains the purely secular activity of manumission which took place in churches. Since the result of manumission was legally to confer Roman citizenship upon a slave, each act required formal state cognizance, and so it had to be performed, in theory, in the presence of a magistrate.[199] With the assimilation of one of the functions of a bishop to this office, the way was open to give them authority to supervise manumission, hence the law of 18th April, 321:

If any person with pious intention should grant deserved freedom to his favourite slaves in the bosom of the Church, he shall appear to give it with the same legal force as that with which the Roman citizenship formerly was customarily bestowed under observance of the usual formalities. But it is our pleasure that such right to manumission in the churches shall be allowed only to those persons who give freedom under the eyes of the bishops.[200]

We find this endorsed on the Church's part not only in practice but also by canon, viz., canon 8 of the synod of Carthage, 15th or 16th June, 401.

The procedure, i.e. the 'usual formalities', is described in one of Augustine's sermons. The slave was led into the church by his master. After a period of silence, the document attesting his freedom was read out and the master declared: 'I give this man out of my hands. He has faithfully served me in all things.' The contract of sale was then torn in two.[201] In the sixth century we find a slight elaboration of detail. The slave, holding a taper, was led three times round the altar by the priest and was then presented with a certificate of his free status upon a tablet; hence one could speak of those freed 'by taper and tablet'.[202]

Churches were also used for the drawing up of documents, of deeds, of wills[203] and legal enactments, e.g. the law relating to tithes agreed and signed by Ethelwulf in 855 'at Winchester in the Church of St Peter before the great altar'.[204] The altar was the place for the taking of oaths, either in relation to a contract, e.g. about the items in a marriage settlement,[205] or to prove one's innocence of a criminal charge, e.g. the case of the lady shop-lifter at Albi who raised her hands to swear before the tomb of St Eugenius.[206]

## Publishing of Notices

As a centre of legal activities and also of general concourse, a church was an ideal place for the communication of official notices such as imperial edicts. Two examples will suffice to illustrate this use. An edict of Theodosius was read out by one Deomphilus before the people assembled in church at Constantinople,[207] and in 482 Pergamius, the newly appointed procurator of Egypt, published Zeno's *Henoticon* in church at Alexandria.[208]

## Storing

The supposed sanctity of church buildings and the fact that they were often more strongly built than the private house made them central depositories for all kinds of goods. When in 532 Theuderic invaded Auvergne, his soldiers broke into the church of St Julian at Brioude to pillage the possessions of the poor that had been stored there,[209] while in 585 the church of St Vincent in Agen was being similarly employed to house the inhabitants' treasures.[210] But storage was not confined to valuables. Theodulf of Orleans was prepared to allow corn to be deposited in churches[211] and animals too sometimes found shelter there. This latter usage, in certain circumstances, was even sanctioned by ecclesiastical canon:

No one may drive any beast into a church except perchance a traveller urged thereto by the greatest necessity, in default of a shed or resting-place, may have turned aside into the said church. For unless the beast had been taken within, it would have perished, and he, by loss of his beast of burden, and so without means of continuing his journey, would be in peril of death. And we are taught that the sabbath was made for man: wherefore also the safety and comfort of man are by all means to be placed first. But should any one be detected without any necessity such as we have just mentioned, leading his beast into a church, if he be a cleric let him be deposed, and if a layman let him be cut off.[212]

## Teaching and Library Facilities

Many churches were used for instruction, although in this period this was religious rather than general education. So Cyril of Jerusalem, *c.* 350, according to the *Catechetical Lectures* ascribed to him, delivered many of them in the Martyrium,[213] while at Milan

Ambrose made use of the baptistery.[214] This latter annex was also employed by Hilary of Rome who is said in 461 to have made two libraries in the Lateran baptistery,[215] while Paulinus provided books at Nola in one of the side apses.[216]

In his *Antiquities of the Christian Church*, issued in ten volumes from 1708 to 1722, Joseph Bingham had this to say about how the early Christians used their buildings:

They employed them only as the houses of God, for acts of devotion and religion, and did not allow of anything to be done there, that had not some tendency towards piety, or immediate relation to it. They might be used for religious assemblies, for the election of bishops or clergy, for the sitting of councils, for catechetical schools, for conferences and collations about religion; but not be put to the use of common houses, to eat, or drink, or lodge in.[217]

The evidence surveyed in this chapter shows that Bingham was not correct—churches were employed for numerous secular activities. The ante-Nicene concept of the unity of sacred and secular in terms of church buildings was not entirely given up.

# 2

# The Middle Ages

## I. FORMER SECULAR USES CONTINUED AND ELABORATED

WHEN WE move onwards through the centuries from the patristic period to the Middle Ages we find, first of all, a continuation of the same classes of secular activities in churches as formerly, but with an increased variety within those classes, and we also encounter evidence of a host of new non-liturgical uses of the nave, of both cathedrals and parish churches. Reaction to these facts may be initially one of surprise, for the conception of the church as a sacred place, which we have previously seen to have arisen in the fourth century, was more and more emphasized and it might have been supposed therefore that this 'apartness' of the building would necessarily limit its use to religious activities.

The identification of church and temple was now complete. Whenever a medieval writer discourses on the subject, he invariably employs terminology taken from the Old Testament cultus. According to Walafrid Strabo (c. 808–49): 'The tabernacle of Moses and the Temple of Solomon, with their various utensils and ornaments, have served as designs and models for the construction and building of all that is now done in the church.'[1] Honorius of Autun (d. 1136) writes, to similar effect: 'It is because the tabernacle of Moses and the Temple of Jerusalem prefigured the Church of Christ that Christian people build their churches according to the form of both.' He goes on to assert that the sanctuary corresponds to the holy of holies, and the nave to the holy place.[2] Abbot Suger of St Denis (d. 1161) considered that the Solomonic Temple and his church were built for an identical purpose and had both the same divine author.[3] William Durandus, Bishop of Mende from 1285–96, is equally dogmatic. 'From both of these, namely, from the tabernacle and the Temple, our material church takes its form.'[4] So he can compare the piscina with the laver of Exodus 38.8[5] and even derive the cloisters from 'the watchings of the Levites around the tabernacles, or from the chambers of the priests, or from the porch of Solomon's Temple'.[6] It was therefore entirely in keeping with this range of ideas that, in 1095, Abbot Baldwin planned a new church at Beadricesworth, i.e. Bury St Edmund's, 'after the fashion of Solomon's Temple'.[7] We also find several passages from the Vulgate translation of the Old Testament being applied to cathedral fabric departments: so Solomon's chief officers supervising the work of building the Temple—*praepositi qui praeerant singulis operibus*[8]—were regarded as the prototype of the monk *qui caementariis praefuit* at Canterbury.[9]

The rites of consecration, which were devised in the eighth and ninth centuries, also rest upon this equation of church and Jerusalem Temple. Just as Moses anointed the tabernacle, the ark and the vessels of the sanctuary, together with the altar,[10] so Christians did likewise to their churches and altars. According to the *Missale Francorum*, wine mixed with water is to be put on the horns of the altar, sprinkling seven times, and poured upon its base, and this ceremony is prescribed in words taken from Exodus 29.12 and Leviticus 8.11, where Moses is said to have put the blood of a bullock upon the horns and around the base and to have sprinkled oil seven times—the only difference between the two is that the wine and water have replaced the blood and oil.[11] Just as Solomon had dedicated his shrine,[12] so Christians in direct imitation consecrated their buildings.[13] Hence in the order preserved in the forty-first of the *Ordines Romani*, the Bishop knocks upon the church door and an antiphon is sung taken from Ps. 24: 'Lift up your heads, O ye gates; and be ye lift up, ye everlasting doors; and the King of glory shall come in'.[14] Another antiphon, sung later while he approaches the sanctuary, is 'Then will I go unto the altar of God' from Ps. 43.4.[15] So Old Testament texts, originally applying to the Jerusalem Temple, are referred, quite literally, to Christian church buildings and their furnishing.

The consecration rites also give a further indication of the medieval understanding of a sacred space. The period was one dominated by a fear of hell and a dread of the devil and his minions. There was indeed a 'medieval habit of looking for the devil everywhere in nature'.[16] So the sacred space was conceived as one in which men were safe from these terrible enemies. Hence, in the consecration service, use was made of water, previously exorcised, to sprinkle the building, its walls, its altars and its floor. The effect of this, as a prayer for blessing the water in *Ordo* 42 makes clear, was to drive away all demons.[17] Durandus' exposition is quite accurate when he says that the purpose of consecration is 'that the devil and his power may be entirely expelled' from the church, which thereby 'ceases to be the resort of demons . . . for holy water, from its proper virtue, avails to drive them away'.[18] In the dedication ritual of the sacramentary of Dodo, Bishop of Metz (826–55), the expulsion of the evil spirit is given dramatic form. Prior to the entrance of the bishop into the new church, one of the clerics is directed to hide himself within it; when the doors are finally opened, after the perambulation of the church and three blows upon them, then 'he who was at first inside is to make his exit, as if fleeing',[19] i.e. he plays the part of the devil driven out in the course of the rite.

This disinfective property of the consecration rite was reinforced by the architectural embellishments. The imposing scene of Christ in judgment, which appears upon so many tympana, reminds the devils that their doom is certain, while the fearful shapes of gargoyles are to strike them with terror and ensure that they are kept at bay. In a world that was subject to Satan, churches were so many havens of security, little portions of territory recovered from his grasp and assigned to God's sovereign ownership in perpetuity.

The medieval understanding of the world as the domain of evil, reinforced by the popularity of the monastic movement with its affirmation that renunciation of the world is the highest form of Christian life, together with the identification of church and temple, explains why so many leading ecclesiastics fulminated constantly against the secular use of churches, seeking to suppress any worldly activity that might take place within them. What is less easy to explain is the continued and developed use of them in this way.

The first factor that contributed to the ignoring of the censures of the authorities was undoubtedly the Christianization of Europe. Christians were no longer a minority in a pagan society; however nominal their faith may have been, the centre of their life and so of the whole local community was the church. Moreover, in towns and villages the church was the one really strong building and the sole one large enough for community gatherings for either business or play. For centuries local councils had no meeting place of their own nor had the trade guilds their own halls, i.e. there were no other public buildings to be used as alternatives to churches. Moreover, the churches were, after all, theirs. Frequently they had helped to build them with their own hands; they had added to them; they had kept them in repair; they embellished them during their lifetime and left gifts to them in their wills. With no other public building to rival them, where else should they or could they meet? Further, the rigid division of nave and sanctuary, which characterized the churches of that era, gave an apparent justification to the idea that the former could be the scene of non-liturgical activities as long as the latter was preserved inviolate.

The architecture of these churches has been aptly described as consisting of two rooms—the one, the smaller, was the choir with the altar and was the place for the priest; the other room, the larger, was the nave where the laity could gather (Fig. 4). Bishop Sicared of Cremona (d. 1215) explained this two-fold division as a reproduction of the same arrangement in the Mosaic tabernacle and in the

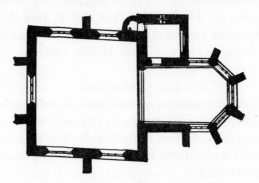

*Fig.* 4   Holy Cross, Zittau, 1260–80

Jerusalem Temple.[20] The distinction was emphasized by the custom relating to the repair of the two rooms. The rector or vicar was responsible for the sanctuary and the parishioners for the nave. So, for example, in 1250 Archbishop Walter Gray decreed that the rector or vicar should keep the chancel wall and roof, the glazed windows, the desks, stools and benches in repair, while the laity were to look after the nave.[21] In 1296 at Reculver, in the diocese of Canterbury, a box was kept in the church in which the parishioners were to place their offerings for the upkeep of the fabric; it could only be opened by two of the laity, elected by their fellows, in the presence of the vicar.[22] Or again, Bishop Brantingham of Exeter (1370–94) laid it down that 'the work of constructing and repairing the chancels of all mother churches belongs to the rectors of the parishes, but that of the nave pertains to the parishioners without regard to any contrary custom'.[23]

The contrary custom occasionally arose when the rector failed to fulfil his duty, e.g. at Hennock, in the archdeanery of Totnes, in 1342, rain was falling through the centre of the main window on to the high altar and even into the chalice at mass.[24] In such circumstances the laity sometimes undertook the repair themselves, if only to preserve their church from ruin. So the worshippers in St Perran in Zabulo, Cornwall, in 1331 undertook the upkeep of the chancel.[25] In general, however, the distinction was observed and one can understand the reluctance of the inferior clergy to dictate to their flock how exactly they used that room of the two for which they were so directly responsible, as long as the sanctuary itself was preserved from 'desecration'. The laity were not slow to avail themselves of this liberty to have community activities in the nave, as will be seen as we survey the secular uses in the Middle Ages.

### Living and Sleeping

In the patristic period, as we have seen, churches were used for living and sleeping in connection with three matters: (i) incubation, (ii) sanctuary, (iii) travellers. In the Middle Ages these three activities continued with (i) and (iii) decreased in importance and (ii) very much increased.

(i) *Incubation*

The shrines of the saints continued to be great centres of healing, so that, for example, during the two centuries from 1000–1200 thousands flocked for this purpose to the Benedictine Abbey of Fleury.[26] But because of the greater facilities for accommodating travellers, which will be considered below, the practice of sleeping all night in church was not so widespread in Western Europe as in previous centuries. Nevertheless there are many examples. So *c.* 1012 Bernard of Angers visited St Fides at Conques in Rouergue and there saw the sick inhabiting the church,[27] while in 1248 invalids passed their nights awaiting their cure in a chapel of Notre Dame at Paris 'near the second door'.[28] In England the shrine of Edmund, King and Martyr, at Beadricesworth, later known as Bury St Edmund's, was a famous centre for incubation. The chronicles tell how, under Edward the Confessor, there was a woman with withered legs who used to beg before the church and sleep just inside the west door; one night she was visited by the saint and cured.[29] In 1088 Edmund, son of Yvo, one of the knights of William Rufus, was afflicted about the eyes with red warty substances covered with hair and was unable to see. He went to the shrine on the eve of the martyr's feast and, having slept there until daybreak, awoke completely healed. The cure of another blind person, a girl named Lyeveva, after a night's rest is recorded for the year 1095, while in the reign of Henry I another girl, born without use of arms or legs, after a night asleep in the church, is said to have been restored.[30] Even at St Thomas's Hospital it was the church rather than the ward that was the place of the cure, as may be seen by a reference to it in 1400, viz., 'the old aisle where the sick poor lie within the church of the hospital of St Thomas the Martyr in Southwark'.[31]

(ii) *Sanctuary*

If the records relating to incubation are not always extensive, those that provide information about sanctuary are by contrast superabundant. The number of sanctuary seekers was very large indeed. The Staffordshire Assize Rolls of 1271–2 reveal that in that single year there were twenty people in sanctuary in the county, while the Assize Rolls of Cornwall for 1283–4 list seventy-eight cases, of which twenty had committed murder and fifty-eight had confessed to various forms of robbery.[32] If we pass to a later date, we find that the sanctuary seekers in the great priory church at Durham from 1464–1524 numbered three hundred and two.[33] Indeed at any one time there was a strong likelihood that a church would be housing one or more persons, and so familiar a custom was this that Abbot Suger of St Denis made specific mention of it in the verses that he had inscribed on the tombs of the patron saints in the upper choir:

> This place exists as an outstanding asylum for those who come;
> Here is safe refuge for the accused, where the avenger is powerless
>    against them.[34]

The length of stay of those inhabiting churches varied of course according to circumstances. In 1232, Richard, a deaf mute, who had killed one John Baldwin, is recorded to have been living in the church of Abbots Kerswell, Devonshire, for the past eight and a half years;[35] whereas in 1369 William de Wallan, who had stolen a horse, fled to the church of Cromwell, Nottinghamshire, on the Saturday before St Valentine's Day and only remained there until the following Thursday.[36] While in 1416, John Russell, who had slandered an alderman, took refuge in St Peter's, Westminster, and was there for nine months.[37]

The time an individual fugitive spent living and sleeping in a church depended not only upon his own individual case but also upon legal enactments and upon the difference between a limited number of important sanctuaries and the ordinary parish churches. In 1285, in order to regulate the practice, Edward I ordered a watch to be kept on churches to which felons had fled so that they might not escape before an investigation had taken place;[38]* if, after the enquiry, the person concerned was judged guilty, he was given up to forty days at the end of which he was to abjure the realm.[39] Abjuration of the realm meant leaving the country and going into exile. In passing sentence, the coroner designated both the port from which the condemned man was to set sail and the route to be taken to it. So in 1362 John de Bokenham, a horse-stealer in the church at Mildenhall, was required to proceed to Yarmouth, being allowed three days for the journey, with a stop at Thetford on the first night and one at Norwich on the second.[40] To some this could be a real convenience and the object of the law was unfulfilled. Scots raiders in the north of England regularly retreated into churches when there was any fear of their being caught; all they had to do then was to abjure the realm and make their way home unmolested across the border.[41]

Occasionally we hear of men slipping from one sanctuary to another. On 13th January 1345 a man who had waylaid a traveller in a wood and robbed him of ten shillings, reached St Mary Magdalene, Ecton, Northants. On 14th February he escaped to St Peter's, Cogenhoe, only finally to abjure the realm eight days later.[42] On other occasions criminals used this means to escape altogether. In 1231 one George Russel, who had stabbed Ralph Wayvefuntaines, gained the safety of St Peter's, Westminster, and from thence was able to disappear; an enquiry was duly held about the failure of the sheriffs to prevent his absconding.[43] On 25th November 1343 two men serving sentence in the gaol of Oxford Castle broke out and entered the church of the Friars Minors; there they remained until 13th December when they stole away and vanished without trace.[44]

When a person refused to abjure the realm, pressure was put on him to force him out of the church, e.g. in 1464, Thomas White, who was in St Mary Incombusta, Norwich, would not leave after the forty-day period; proclamation was therefore made that no person should 'give, send or throw food' to him.[45] At any time of day or night a man might burst into a church and there settle down to live and sleep. By way of illustration we may cite the case of Roger de Ludyngton, arrested for felony, who was being taken in custody to the court, when he broke away and reached St Peter's, Bullbridge, Wiltshire, there he took up his abode in the chapel of St Thomas the Martyr until the following day when he decided to abjure the realm.[46]

The forty-day period was only exceeded, after Edward I's enactment, either in those cases where the fugitive stubbornly refused to move or in those sanctuaries with chartered rights, such as Westminster Abbey and Durham Cathedral, which were greater than those that appertained to all consecrated buildings. Here a man might remain for the whole of his life. Nevertheless the area of sanctuary recognized at these centres was much greater than the actual church building. At Westminster Abbey it included the church, the churchyard and the close, while at Beverley Minster it extended for some one and a half miles in every direction, the boundaries being marked by crosses. The limits of the abbey of Colchester ran from Hollane to the east of the church; thence to the corner of the wall enclosing the abbey on its south side, to the corner of the wall on the west, then through Courtstyle to the end of Loderslane and finally through the northern extremity of St John's Green.[47] This meant that in the great sanctuaries, where people lived for years, they did not necessarily stay and sleep in the actual churches; they were safe as long as they were within the prescribed limits. Nevertheless, in any one year as many as a thousand people could be found accommodated in the sanctuaries of England up and down the land,[48]* and a large proportion of these lived in the worship area.

(iii) *Travellers*

We have seen previously that in the patristic period churches could be used by travellers in case of necessity. In the Middle Ages the number of travellers had increased enormously but the necessity had been largely removed. Pilgrimage-itis had begun in the fourth century with the adornment of the Palestinian sites by Constantine, and so great did it become that thousands were prepared to visit the supposed location of Job's dunghill in Arabia. In the Middle Ages the developed cult of the saints, the traffic in their relics, the erection of great shrines and the opening up of the way to the East through the crusades, led to a renewal of interest in sight-seeing, especially when this was linked with indulgences and with a belief in the benefits to be derived from these visits. 'The fundamental idea of the Christian pilgrimage was that the Deity exercised a benevolent influence operating through the sacred *media* in some definite building or locality'.[49] The concept of the specially 'holy' place was thus very much at the basis of the mass movements of Christians during this period. Provision was, however, made for their accommodation so that churches were no longer so necessary as night shelters.

The monasteries, of which each European country had a considerable number, possessed their guest houses in which it was their duty to welcome all comers. This accommodation was supplemented by the foundation of 'hospitals'; so Archbishop Hubert Walter (1193–1205) established the Hospital of St Thomas the Martyr at Canterbury for the reception of poor pilgrims, and in 1202 Archbishop Boniface created the Hospital of Newark for those passing through Maidstone on their way to Becket's shrine.[50] Further accommodation was provided by inns, such as the Pilgrims' Inn at Glastonbury, erected *c.* 1475, for those visiting the holy place of St Joseph of Arimathea and the relics of St Dunstan.[51]

Nevertheless some did use churches for shelter. This would appear to be the reason for one of the parish clerk's duties at St Nicholas, Bristol, in 1481. He was ordered to fasten the doors 'with a sure search in the said Church for fear of Sleepers'.[52] A similar situation obtained at Lincoln Cathedral in which there was a chamber for the 'searchers'. These men were required to shut the doors, toll the large bell forty times, after which they were allowed to consume some bread and beer before walking round and searching the whole building.[53]

To shelter for travellers must be added shelter for those without any homes. In 1516–17 we learn from a petition to the Star Chamber that a certain Margery Clerke had been expelled, together with her late husband and their five children, from their house by the abbot of St Werburgh and 'were compelled of necessity to go to their parish church, and there continued by the space of three weeks'.[54]

(iv) *Miscellaneous*

Living and sleeping in churches also took place in connection with several miscellaneous activities. Many buildings had people to sleep in them as guardians. At Southwell the sacristan was ordered to sleep always in the church,[55] while at Colyton in Devon the deacon was the one who had to pass his nights there.[56] This, however, need not necessarily have been in the worship area itself. Whereas at Hythe, Kent, 1480–1, Thomas the Bedesman was paid sixteen shillings for watching the organs and 'for lying in the church',[57] at St Margaret's, Westminster, there was a bed in the vestry for the clerk provided in 1500 by the sister of the Bishop of St Asaph.[58] At St Mary-at-Hill, 1501–2, fourteen pence was paid for 'a Bedstead for the priest's chamber that keepeth the first mass'; by 1526–7 this had been worn out and a new one was purchased.[59] Sometimes the persons concerned slept in the steeple, like the sexton at Faversham in 1506;[60] sometimes a special chamber was built. So at Cransfield, Bedfordshire, on the north side of the chancel there is a two-storeyed addition, the upper floor being reached by a circular staircase and containing a fireplace.

Hermits and anchorites also lived in close proximity to, if not actually in, churches. They could occupy a cell in the churchyard; this was the kind of habitation adopted by the Lady Julian of Norwich in the parish of Conisford; she died shortly after 1413 and had various successors occupying her retreat. Dame Agnes was a recluse there in 1472, Dame Elizabeth Scott in 1481, the Lady Elizabeth in 1510 and in 1524 Dame Agnes Edrygge.[61] Sometimes the recluse would lie in the church itself, like Thomas the Chaplain, described in 1415 as long continuing in St Nicholas, Gloucester, although possibly he lived in the chamber over the porch.[62] Sometimes the cell was built on to the church, and a window, through which the sacrament could be received, was opened into it.[63]

## Eating and Drinking

The ecclesiastical authorities, who were jealous of the privilege of sanctuary, were anxious to see that the fugitives in their churches were provided with sustenance. Accordingly, in 1268, the papal legate to England, Othobon, forbad both the dragging of people out of church and the prevention of their being supplied with food.[64] Hence in 1291 we hear of a complaint to the civil authorities in Ireland because they would not permit victuals being given to the sanctuary seekers and even kept them in chains in the churches themselves, e.g. at Loughrea in the diocese of Cloufert.[65]

State sanction was given to the supplying of food by the first statute of 9 Edward II, section 10, i.e. 1315–16: 'so long as they be in the Church, they shall not be compelled to flee away, but they shall have Necessaries for their Living, and may go forth to empty their Belly'.[66] This law was reinforced in 1377 by William of Wykeham,

Bishop of Winchester, who proceeded to excommunicate certain folk because they had not observed it.[67] The type of menu sanctioned may be illustrated from the experience of Elizabeth Woodville, the queen of Edward IV, who sought sanctuary in Westminster in 1470, in the company of her daughter, her mother and another lady, and was allowed by the abbot half a loaf and two 'muttons' *per diem*.[68] The consumption of food was a necessary corollary of sanctuary.

The main occasion, however, for eating and drinking in churches in the patristic period was the holding of *agapes* and we have to consider if there are any traces of this practice in the Middle Ages. There were indeed four survivals of this: at funerals, at weddings, at baptisms and in the form of the holy loaf. In the fifteenth century the historian Fabyan directed in his will that bread, ale, pieces of beef and mutton and roast ribs of beef were to be provided in church for those who attended his funeral.[69] According to the *de Subventiae Pauperum* of Juan Luis Vive, written between 1524 and 1527, there should be a public distribution of bread and meat at all funerals.[70]

A natural extension of this practice was to provide food and drink for the yearly *obit* or anniversary of a person's death; many testators in fact gave such directions in their wills. In the twelfth century Savani, Bishop of Bath and Glastonbury, granted the benefice of Pilton to the canons of Wells on condition that they fed a hundred people in the church on the day of his year's mind.[71] Four centuries later, one William Plesyngton directed in his will that yearly a barrel of beer and some bread were to be dispensed in the church to the poor of the parish.[72] Extracts could be given from a whole host of wills to this effect—a few examples will suffice. The annual increment from a certain field was to be spent on bread and ale 'amongst poor people in the church of Hadlow'. Some lands were entailed to provide yearly in Bromley church three shillings and four pence in bread and beer. One Jane Smith bequeathed sufficient to provide two bushels of wheat for bread, peas, a hundred white herrings and malt for ale 'to be dealt in St Margaret's church to poor people who will come to take it'. Edward Pratt made provision for 'nine bushels of wheat in bread and ten bushels of malt in drink, on Midlent Sunday, in the church of Hoo'.[73] Some of this may have been taken home for consumption, but the records indicate that most, if not all, was eaten and drunk in the church itself. These bequests fulfilled exactly the same intention as the funeral *agapes* of the patristic period, viz. to commemorate the deceased and to provide charity for the needy.

A possible relic of the marriage *agape* may be found in the practice, enjoined by the Sarum use, of blessing a maser or bowl of wine in which were soaked small cakes or wafers, known as sops, and these were then given to the newly married bride and groom at the end of the nuptial mass. In a number of French churches the guests also shared in the consumption, references to this practice being contained in copies of the *Rituale* of Autun of 1503 and 1523 and in that of Rheims of 1504.[74]

*Agapes* at baptism are not attested in the first Christian centuries, but as an occasion for community rejoicing they cannot be deemed inappropriate. The medieval evidence is not extensive, but Henry VII in his prescriptions for the baptism of a prince or princess ordered 'the sergeant of the spicery and two butlers to be ready with spice and wine, then when the prince is christened, the gossips (i.e. godparents) and other estates may take spice and wine'.[75]

But these were not regular occasions; one undoubted survival of the *agape*, however, which was to be found in all parts of Christendom every week was the blessed bread, distributed and consumed in the church after mass. This was known as the *antidoron*[76]* in the Eastern Orthodox Churches, as *pain bénit* in France and as the holy loaf in England. Distribution in England was normally a duty of the parish clerk, and so at Trinity Church, Coventry, 1462, one was instructed to give the portions to the parishioners in the south aisle and the other to those in the north.[77]

The great opportunities for eating and drinking were the regular scot-ales. Coulton believed that these were to be derived from the Anglo-Saxon drinking bouts baptized into Christianity[78] and this may be so; if correct, then a reminiscence of the *agape* could have given it some support and encouragement. A scot-ale may be defined as a parish feast held with the object of making money. Frequently the prefix 'scot' is omitted and a word is inserted to denote the special purpose of the gathering. A leet ale was one to which all the residents in a manorial district contributed; a bid ale, or a help ale, was to assist a parishioner in financial difficulties; a bride ale was to defray the expenses of a wedding; a clerk ale to raise a clerk's wages, a church ale for the upkeep of the building[79]* and a give ale, also called a soul ale and a dirge ale, was one financed by bequests from individuals to have a feast in their memory.[80]* Information about the last is of course contained in wills, such as that of John Devell who ordered that, after his wife's death, an acre known as Pilchland should be used as a source of income for a give ale in All Hallows, Hoo.[81]

Numerous references to these ales, which are held, in addition to the anniversary days of testators, on dedication festivals, at Easter for the clerk and at Whitsun for the poor, are to be found in the Churchwardens' accounts, e.g. those of St Peter Chepe, London, 1447, which record: 'Recd. the 27th day of May for a drinking in the Church, 18s. 4d.',[82] and those of Walberswick, Suffolk, which contain among the entries for 1453: *Item de uno Cherche Ale in Festo omnium Sanctorum . . . 16s.*[83] Those of St Laurence, Reading, 1506, record the payment of fourpence to a man named Macrell for cleaning out the church 'for the drinking'—the menu on that occasion comprised flesh, spice, baked pasties and ale.[84]

These jollifications were held in the nave; witness Archbishop Reynolds, 1325, who bitterly condemned 'certain sons of gluttony and drunkenness, whose god is their belly, hastily swallow the Lord's body at Easter, and then sit down in the Church itself to eat and drink as if they were in a tavern'.[85] As there were no pews to inhibit them, trestle tables were erected for the convenience of the company.[86]

It seems highly probable that several carvings in English churches refer to these ales and illustrate some of the things that went on. On the porch of Chalk Church, Kent, there is an acrobat and a jester with a drinking pot—probably actual performers at a church ale.[87] On the bench ends at Stevington, Bedfordshire, there are two men drinking from a bowl—again probably a scene from a church ale,[88] while some of the gargoyles on the nave parapet of Cirencester Church, Gloucester, may depict medieval revellers at a Whitsun ale—some are playing musical instruments, including the tabor, pipe, rebec and double recorder.[89] Sometimes the players would be amateurs from amongst those present; sometimes instrumentalists were hired, as was the case at Barnstaple.[90]

Although each parish was usually responsible for arranging its own ales, there is evidence of the custom of two or more joining together to make a big event of the occasion. In the Dodsworth Manuscript an indenture of pre-Reformation date reads as follows:

The parishioners of Elvaston and those of Okebrook in Derbyshire agree jointly to brew four ales, and every ale of one quarter of malt between this and the feast of St John the Baptist next coming, and every inhabitant of the said town of Okebrook shall be at the several ales, and every husband and his wife shall pay two pence, and every cottager one penny. And the inhabitants of Elvaston shall have and receive all the profits coming of the said ales, to the use and behoof of the church of Elvaston; and the inhabitants of Elvaston shall brew eight ales between this and the feast of St John, at which ales the inhabitants of Okebrook shall come and pay as before rehearsed; and if any be away at one ale, he is to pay at the other ale for both.[91]

These occasions of eating and drinking were not favoured by the episcopacy. From the thirteenth century onwards a regular series of condemnations was issued, e.g. in 1223 by Richard Poore of Sarum; in 1229 by William de Bleys, and in 1237 by Alexander of Stavenby.[92] In 1311 Durandus of Mende wrote contemptuously of the ales 'at which both clergy and layfolk swill'.[93] Although this persistent attack did not result in their discontinuance for many centuries, it did have one effect. As the centuries passed many churches were able to afford to build a church-house, e.g. at Croscombe, Somerset, in 1481, £12 2s. 11d. was laid out for such an addition.[94] Where such existed, from the end of the fifteenth century, the church ale was often transferred to it, but, as we shall see, plenty of examples remain of an enduring and sturdy indifference to episcopal censure.

There can be no doubt that medieval Christians enjoyed their social gatherings and were ready to arrange them as often as they could. Few activities took place in connection with a church without their being accompanied by eating and drinking. When the bells were hung at Yatton, Somerset, in 1446, fish, flesh, cheese, bread and ale were to hand,[95] and similarly in St Mary-at-Hill, London, in 1510–11.[96] When a crucifix was brought to Walberswick, Suffolk, in 1496, one shilling and five pence was spent on meat and drink, and a further shilling for the same items when it was put in place.[97] When a weathercock was placed on top of the 360-feet high steeple of Louth Church, on the First Sunday after Trinity in 1518, ale and bread were dispensed to all in attendance.[98] The parish accounts repeatedly list similar items, e.g. in St Margaret's, Westminster, 1478–80, bread, wine and ale were consumed in the roodloft on the day of their patron saint.[99] At St Mary Woolnoth in 1539 bread, ale and wine were given 'to the priests and clerks on reading of the Passion on Palm Sunday'[100] i.e., the performers received refreshment during the singing of the passion from the roodloft; this explains the briefer entry in the records of St Laurence, Reading, 1524, which reads: 'for drink in the rood loft on Palm Sunday'.[101] Those who watched the Easter Sepulchre also expected provisions, and so at St Mary Devizes a note is made of the bread and drink they received in 1533,[102] and when the feast of Easter was over and the sepulchre itself had to be dismantled further consumption took place, e.g. in St Mary-at-Hill in 1519–20.[103] The same accounts record payments 'for bread, wine and ale for priests and clerks in the church upon dedications and other festival days' (1479–81), and 'for bread and ale set at high feasts in the church' (1518–19), and in 1519–20, on St Barnabas' Eve, ale and wine for the clerks and children at mass and drink for the clerk at evensong.[104] At Magdalen College, Oxford, two shillings were spent in 1514–15 on the consumption of meats in the chapel on the three nights before Easter and at the time of the Nativity.[105]

The annual auditing of the accounts in the church was another opportunity for eating and drinking. For St Edmund's, Sarum, in 1461, twenty-four gallons of ale were purchased for a halfpenny a gallon and twelve cups of ashwood for seven pence;[106] while in St Martin-in-the-Fields in 1531 the bread, ale and cheese consumed 'in the Church' by the parishioners at the passing of the accounts cost eighteen pence.[107] Sometimes, however, the venue was not the church, so at St Margaret's, Westminster, 1508, the 'perusing and overlooking of the last wardens' accounts' and the partaking of bread and drink took place 'in the curate's house'.[108]

The annual audit involved the entire parish, more restricted feasting was enjoyed by the guilds. These also had their meetings in churches, until such time as they were rich enough to build their own guild halls, and at the annual general meeting a meal was customary. So a sixteenth-century preacher complained of

many country folk who keep certain guild commemorations and come together on certain days of the year and hold their feasts within the churches, perhaps because they have no houses large enough to hold so great a company, and thus with surfeiting and drunkeness and other filthiness they do profane the sanctuary of God.[109]

Two specific examples may be given by way of illustration. The Guild of St George, founded some time before 1446, held its assemblies in Chichester Cathedral. The members were fortunate enough to have a bequest from Bishop Sherborne, which was to be used for the purchase of wine to be distributed after their chief mass of the year on St George's Day. They drank this and were then dismissed by the bedel, with the words: 'All is over, pray for Lord Robert's soul.'[110] The Guild of the Holy Name of Jesus, which was founded in 1459, used to meet in the crypt of St Paul's, London, for worship, especially on the feasts of the Transfiguration and of the Holy Name. After mass, bread and ale, to the sum of ten shillings, were distributed among the members in the chapel.[111]

The hospitality provided in churches was by no means solely due to the initiation of the laity. At St Paul's, in the twelfth century, newly installed residentiary canons were required to have bread and ale taken nightly to the church for the juniors in the choir[112] and the forbidding of public banquets and drinking in Exeter Cathedral, especially in the choir, in 1358, may well have been aimed in the first instance against members of the chapter.[113]

Although at times the eating and drinking were clearly to excess and therefore not to be condoned, the vast majority of the laity and a by no means small number of the clergy in the Middle Ages clearly saw nothing wrong in their use of churches for social gatherings.

### Dancing

We have seen that music was often a feature of church ales and in all probability dancing took place. Dancing at other times may be divided into two categories: first, that more or less sanctioned by the Church authorities at set seasons of the year, and second, that which was probably of popular origin in certain localities.

According to Belethus, writing in the twelfth century, dancing in cathedrals and collegiate churches took place on Christmas Day, St Stephen's Day, St John's Day and either on the Feast of the Circumcision or at Epiphany. The deacons were the principal performers on the first day, the priests on the second, the choir boys on the third and the subdeacons on the fourth.[114] Durandus provides identical information[115] and there is an almost contemporary reference to their being performed in the cathedral of Notre Dame in Paris.[116] The title often given to these revels, and more particularly to those on the final day, was the Feast of Fools, which seems to have been observed mainly in France, sporadically in Germany and Bohemia, and in some parts of England, especially at Lincoln and Beverley. The ruling idea of the feast was the inversion of status and the burlesque performance by the inferior clergy of functions proper to the higher grades. It therefore involved much more than dancing, and included activities which are best considered later in relation to games. It was continually under attack, so that, for example, in 1212 a national council at Paris forbade its continuance, but in vain.[117] At Villarceaux in Normandy, *c.* 1250, there was dancing in the church on the feasts of the Holy Innocents and of St Mary Magdalen. At the same period there was dancing in the church at Gournay on St Nicholas' Day, while at Sens there was one called the *cazzole* on Easter Day.[118] A vivid portrayal of what was involved is contained, over two centuries later, in a letter of 12th March, 1445, addressed by the Faculty of Theology at Paris to the bishops and to the deans of the chapters of France:

> Priests and clerks may be seen wearing masks and monstrous visages at the hours of the offices. They dance in the choir dressed as women, panders or minstrels. They sing wanton songs. They eat black pudding at the horns of the altar while the celebrant is saying mass. They play at dice there. . . . They run and leap through the church.[119]

In Bohemia the revellers also wore masks and the clergy turned their garments inside out and danced with vigour.[120] At Châlons-sur-Marne singing and dancing were essential features of the feast.[121]

For local dances, not connected with the Feast of Fools, we have the evidence of Giraldus Cambrensis (1147–*c*.1223) who witnessed a dance of peasants in and around the church of St Elined, near Brecknock; the various occupations of village life, such as ploughing and sowing, were represented in mime.[122] At Limoges, on the feast of St Martial, the people danced in the choir to the singing of psalms, but instead of the concluding *Gloria*, they substituted: *Saint Marceau pregas per nous, et nous epingarem per vous*, i.e. 'St Martial, pray for us and we will dance for you'.[123] There was a similar dance at Aix and at Chalon-sur-Saône on Whitsunday; this latter was obviously a lengthy affair since it is stated that all the clergy should be allowed the opportunity to sing each a song.[124] At Echternach in Luxembourg, an annual dance was led by the clergy; it began on the banks of the Sûre, thence to the church and so along the north aisle, around the altar and back down the south aisle; this is said to have begun in the eighth century,[125] and was held on the Tuesday after Whitsunday. On the same day there was dancing in St Lambert at Liège and this continued to be observed until the cathedral was destroyed in 1794.[126]

Sometimes the dances were a feature of partisan displays. At Oxford there was a division of the students into 'nations', the Boreals and the Australs, i.e. north and south countrymen. These two groups made different churches their centres and sported themselves there, until *c*. 1250 an edict was issued forbidding 'dances with masks or any noise in churches or streets'.[127]

Sometimes the dance was of a mournful nature; such appears to have been the *danse macabre*, or dance of death. The origins of this lugubrious festivity are uncertain,[128] although Emile Mâle has argued that it began with mime[129] and L. Gougaud has drawn attention to a mid-fifteenth century Spanish manuscript describing a sermon on death which served as an introduction to a dance.[130] Whatever the origin, the dance of death was performed in churches, e.g. at Caudebec in 1393 and in the church of St John at Besançon in 1453 by the Franciscans at the end of their provincial chapter.[131]

Attempts to expel dancing of all kinds from churches were many and persistent. It was condemned by councils at Avignon (1209), Rome (1231) and Cognac (1260). At Puy in 1327 the clergy were forbidden to dance on the Feast of the Circumcision. In 1435 a council at Basel pronounced against it.[132] Antonino, Bishop of Florence, also in the fifteenth century, was unhappy to learn that 'in the churches themselves they sometimes dance and lead carols with the women'.[133] But although a Provincial council of Rheims, held at Soissons in 1546, forbade masquerades, plays, dances and buying and selling in churches, this was but another attack without effect.[134] Indeed in England, at St Edmund's, Sarum, we find in 1490 payment to William Belrynger for cleaning the church 'at ye Dawnse of Powles', i.e, for a maypole dance in the nave.[135]

The attitude of the clergy to all this was somewhat ambiguous. In general the bishops desired to stamp out what they regarded as desecration, advancing, among other arguments, the thesis that it was because of dancing that John the Baptist lost his head.[136] The cathedral canons and village priests, on the other hand, were prepared to tolerate it, either in order to control it or to engage in it wholeheartedly regardless of episcopal opinion; indeed after the celebration of his first mass a newly ordained priest often danced in the church with his mother.[137]

## The Sale of Goods

The sale of goods in churches in the patristic era arose in connection with the martyrs' festivals; the same factor was operative in the Middle Ages, and many a fair owed its establishment to the observance of saints' days. Pedlars and other vendors saw in the crowds that assembled for the celebrations an admirable business opportunity and they brought their wares and set up booths. In many places the church nave itself became the scene of the fair; there, protected from possible bad weather, stallholders could be sure of a steady supply of shoppers and the would-be purchasers could circulate at their ease, unhurriedly deciding what to have.

A regular series of condemnations provides evidence of how widespread this practice was. In the year 1230 English archdeacons were seeking to discover, in order to regulate, this use of churches.[138]* Six years later, Henry III forbad the holding of Northampton Fair in the church or churchyard of All Saints, and Robert Grosseteste, Bishop of Lincoln, followed this by prohibiting fairs in all churches, asserting that he was acting in imitation of the king who had made 'the like reformation at Northampton'.[139] In 1287 a synod at Exeter condemned the conduct of secular affairs in churches.[140] In 1367 Archbishop Thoresby prohibited markets on Sundays in churches and churchyards.[141]

The matter was then taken up by the pamphleteers, the anonymous author of *The Lantern of Light*, *c.* 1400, declaring: 'Against this (the fourth) commandment the fiend and his members give leave to chapmen to buy and sell, yes, within the sanctuary, on the holy Sunday, and victuallers of the country hold common markets',[142] and in the fifteenth-century *Dives and Pauper* the markets set up in churches and churchyards by 'victuallers and other chapmen' are roundly condemned.[143] Yet in 1444 Archbishop Stafford decreed that 'fairs and markets should no more be kept in churches or churchyards on the Lord's day and other holy days, except in time of harvest',[144] and so by allowing them at harvest time he did sanction this secular use of church buildings, despite the fact that previously, in 1427, the king had ordered that no fair or market should take place in sanctuaries in the city of London.[145]

From other statements we learn that at Salisbury a horse-fair was held not only in the precincts but in the cathedral itself,[146] that in the fifteenth century Exeter Cathedral was the scene of the sale of goods,[147] and that at St Audrey's Fair booths were erected in Ely Cathedral for sale of laces made of silk.[148] Bishop Braybrooke of London (1382–1404) felt the need to denounce the profanation of St Paul's by the marketing and trading that went on there in his day. 'In our cathedral, not only men, but women also, expose their wares, as it were, in a public market, buy and sell without reverence for the holy place.'[149] In the cathedral of Chartres food was retailed, and in the nave wine merchants sold their products; nor was this considered to be improper as long as it was carried on in an orderly fashion.[150]

Not only did the laity see little amiss in this buying and selling, they also found it a source of income for their churches. A number of entries show that pedlars, etc., were charged for the right to sell their goods on church ground. At St Edmund's, Sarum, in 1490, money was received for 'diverse cheese-sellers who stood at the church wall', and the wardens of St Laurence, Reading, were paid 'at the Fair for a standing in the Church Porch'.[151] These people either refused to interpret the 'Cleansing of the Temple' in the way contemporary preachers were wont to do or did not acknowledge its applicability to their situation.

## Meetings

As the most spacious and therefore commodious buildings in any locality, cathedrals and parish churches were used, as in the patristic period, for meetings of all kinds. The different types of gathering may be classified as: (i) councils, (ii) elections, (iii) discussions, (iv) audits and (v) degree congregations.

### (i) *Councils*

These assemblies may be divided into three: ecclesiastical councils, parliaments and city councils.

It would be a mistake to assume that ecclesiastical councils were solely religious in their concerns. The close unity of Church and State in the Middle Ages and the fact that many of the prelates were officers of the realm meant that at every meeting there was an inextricable mixture of the secular and the religious. In 1215 Stephen Langton, Archbishop of Canterbury, summoned to St Paul's all the bishops and leading barons of England: the main item on the agenda was an agreement to compel King John to sign a charter that would ensure the liberties, both religious and civil, of the land, and the following year another assembly publicly endorsed Magna Carta.[152] In 1224 Langton again presided at a council, the purpose of which was to assess and grant a subsidy to the king.[153] But when in 1232 the papal legate Otho and in 1268, his successor, Othobon, sat in St Paul's, it was in order to issue their constitutions, the contents of which were essentially ecclesiastical.[154]

St Paul's, too, was the home of the convocation, so for example Archbishop Arundel (1396–1414) and his successor Chichele (1414–1443) held almost annual meetings there, and this was the constant practice until Wolsey had it transferred to Westminster[155] —but the venue would appear to have been usually the Chapter House rather than the choir and nave of the cathedral itself.

The church of the Black Friars in London was often used for parliamentary sessions. In 1450, under Henry IV, parliament began its sitting at Westminster, was adjourned to Black Friars and finally moved to Leicester. In 1524 it opened its discussions of the royal demand for an £800,000 subsidy in Black Friars and then transferred to Westminster. Five years later parliament was in Black Friars again to condemn Cardinal Wolsey.[156]

The use of churches for the meetings of town councils has a history which endured for many centuries and, in certain towns, until long after the Reformation. At Northampton, there is documentary evidence concerning the period 1381–1467 which shows the town council in session in St Giles. The everyday business of the town was discussed, decisions were reached and by-laws promulgated. So in 1381 an ordinance was passed relating to the horse-bread used by innkeepers and in 1547 it was decreed that pigs were not to be allowed to run about the streets.[157] At Sandwich the mayor sat in St Peter's every Thursday, and on other days too, if the pressure of business demanded it, to consider matters of dispute brought before him.[158] In 1407 the vicar of New Romney paid the jurats (i.e. the mayor and corporation) three shillings and four pence not to hold their meetings in the church during service time.[159] That the city council should have done this at all may seem strange but for two facts. The laity at the medieval mass were essentially passive and non-communicating spectators; only at the elevation was their attention really required; hence the jurats could well have occupied themselves with secular affairs as long as they allowed a few moments of recollection and devotion at the appropriate point in the service. Further the church itself consisted of three oblong halls, each with its separate entrance and divided by low walls; it was therefore quite possible to hold a meeting in one, while mass was being said in another, although the practice, as we have just seen, did not fully commend itself to the incumbent.

At Southampton the council met at first in the church of St Cross or Holy Rood, and at Dover the barons of the Cinque Ports assembled in St James.[160] At Fordwick, near Canterbury, there was a regular meeting in the church to consider the estates of orphans in the custody of the corporation and to determine other matters of real estate.[161] At Newcastle-on-Tyne, the nave of St Nicholas was the place for the transaction of public business,[162] while from 1361–82 the commonalty of Hedon, near Hull, met in the chapel of St James[163] and the nave of St Giles, Edinburgh, was used by the town council and the Lords of Session.[164] There is no need to continue the list of examples; sufficient has been said to illustrate the extent to which medieval churches were regarded and used as the equivalents of the modern town halls and council chambers.

### (ii) *Elections*

By the turn of the first millennium the quasi-democratic character of the Church had been lost. The development of the feudal system, with the bishops as great landowners and lords spiritual, the spread of the practice of patronage and the rigidly hieratic nature of the ecclesiastical institutions all combined to deny the laity as a whole any real say in appointments. If the election of bishops was ratified in cathedrals, this was now no more than a formality. But other elections did take place in churches, viz. those of churchwardens, of mayors and of guild officers.

The election of churchwardens was an annual event performed at the same time as the auditing of the parish accounts. Since a full description of this last activity is given below, we may pass on to the election of mayors. The use of churches for sessions of the town council has already been noted and their further use for the appointment of mayors is a natural corollary of this—ten examples may be cited.

At Sandwich, in 1301, and probably before, on the first Monday in December at 1 p.m., the town serjeant sounded his horn and gave out the notice: 'Every man of twelve years or more go to St Clements church; there our commonalty hath need. Haste, haste!' The mayor was then duly nominated and voting took place.[165] At Dover, 8th December was election day in St Peter's; this was the venue before and after 1357. At Folkestone the same date obtained, the mayor being elected in the chancel; at Lydd the electors of the bailiff collected around a tomb in the parish church on 22nd July.[166] At Southampton the mayor took his oath of office in St Michael's, probably in the north chancel aisle which was called 'Corporation

Chapel'.[167] The bailiff and mayor of Yarmouth were both elected in the church *c.* 1310,[168] and similarly at Fordwick, near Canterbury,[169] at Boston and at Grantham.[170] At Salisbury, up to the year 1579, the mayor's election was held in St Edmund's church.[171]

Previous notice has been taken of the guilds and the way in which their members were accustomed to have refreshments in church at their annual meetings. This was the occasion of the election of their officers, of master, skevins, proctors, dean, clerk, summoner and others. The ordinances of the Guild of St George, Norwich, founded in 1385, require all its members to be present at a yearly requiem on the morrow of St George's Day, and to make choice of the officers for the year following immediately afterwards in church.[172] Similarly the Guild of St Katherine, Stamford, was to meet on St Leonard's Day, or the Sunday after, at 1 p.m. in the chapel of St Katherine, 'and there have their yearly speech, and provide and ordain for the worship, profit, and all things necessary at that time for the welfare of the same Guild'. This assembly therefore was held in church, despite the fact that they had their own Guild hall to which they repaired after the elections for their annual dinner.[173]

### (iii) *Discussions*

A church building can obviously be an admirable debating hall and was so used throughout the Middle Ages. In 1149 on the Sunday after Pentecost an arrangement was made for Abelard and Bernard to enter into a discussion in the cathedral of St Stephen at Sens.[174] In 1136 in St Sophia and St Eirene, Constantinople, a debate was staged between Archbishop Nicetas and the historian-philosopher Anselm of Havelberg, a German imperial bishop and envoy.[175] In the thirteenth century there were debates between Christians and Jews[176] and these public disputations eventually became a feature of university life in the form of the *disputatio legitima*.[177] But churches could also be the scene of discussions of an entirely secular character, as when the countryfolk of Alvingham, Lincolnshire, went to St Leonard's, Cockerington, to reach agreement upon a day for mowing the grass of their common pasture.[178] Or again, when the journeymen saddlers met in St Mary-le-Bow in 1380 to discuss grievances.[179]

(iv) *Financial Transactions*

Reference to audits has already been made in connection with eating and drinking, with which they invariably concluded, and with the election of churchwardens and of guild officials, which formed part of the business. It now remains to describe these occasions in more detail.

At Croscombe, Somerset, the audit was held in the parish church. The form of the churchwardens' accounts is really a description of the proceedings. The contributors are represented as coming into the church and there presenting their offerings. So we read under 1474: 'Comes John Joyce and William Brand, and brings in of the King's revel', i.e. the proceeds of the Epiphany merrymaking.[180] Next come the Webers, i.e. the weavers, followed by the Tuckers or Fullers; then Robin Hood, who in 1482–3 was impersonated by one Richard Willes.[181] There are also the young men, the maidens and the Hogglers, i.e. the guild of the lowest class of handworkers. As each sum was accepted and recorded, a small amount, referred to as the stock, was returned for use by the contributors during the next year, when once again they could come bringing the 'stock and the crece'. i.e. the increase. The annual audit was also the day when individuals brought in their rents for houses or property owned by the parish. It was the day too when gifts were made in person, e.g. on 14th January, 1520–1 Anys Yng presented a book, a chalice, some vestments, an apparel for the altar and a gold ring.[182] Announcements were made of other recent gifts and bequests, such as sheep, bulls, hives of bees, cows, pigs, etc. Items of business were next settled, e.g. in 1524–5 six four-year-old ewes had been presented by John Felyppes and his wife; at the audit terms were agreed for the leasing of these to one Hew Morganne; he was to have them for seven years on payment of two shillings annually; if they were to die, he was responsible at the rate of sixteen pence for each animal.[183] The outgoing wardens then produced their bill of expenses, and the new wardens, having been duly elected, were assigned the church goods in hand.

The Croscombe meetings are clearly stated to have been held in the church,[184] but often the wardens do not specify the location, presumably because it was known to all. Yet even in default of definite statements, it is frequently possible to deduce that the meetings were in church from other entries in the records. The documents relating to St Mary-at-Hill, London, refer to the amount of money being placed in the church box at the meeting[185] or to the amount in the box being counted and declared[186]—since these boxes were fixed in the church, the venue of the meeting is obvious. Further, the numbers present were often too large for anywhere else but the church to have been used, e.g. at the meeting on 23rd January, 1522-3, there were in attendance fifteen named persons and an unspecified number of other parishioners—too great an assembly to be held in the vestry and it must therefore have been in church.[187]

The guilds, besides contributing to the parish funds, had their own accounts to keep and approve. So the Guild of St Benedict, Lincoln, included in its constitution directions that there was to be a meeting in church to receive money and to arrange its financial affairs.[188] This was the occasion 'when the year's accounts were squared, the guild chattels were laid on the checker, points were promulgated, defaulters announced, new members enrolled'.[189]

In addition to the accounts of the parish church and of the guilds, there were also those of the city councils which were presented and received in churches. At Romney, the townsfolk paid to have seats placed in St Laurence's on the day of the Annunciation when the audit was held.[190] The Rye accounts were similarly made up in the church, but at the end of the calendar year.[191] The inhabitants of Lydd were under agreement to pay a certain sum of money to those of Romney, and their officers annually appeared before the jurats in St Nicholas with their accounts and with the cash to render their dues,[192] while at Lydd itself in 1471 there was an expenditure entered up for a meeting in the church to enquire 'what livelihood men have in Lydd'.[193]

Finally the church was the place where executors were accustomed to meet to audit their accounts, e.g. in St Mary's, Bury St Edmunds, in 1504.[194]

## (v) *Degree Congregations*

Descriptions are extant of degree congregations held in Oxford

University in the late Middle Ages. The degrees were conferred after mass in St Mary's—although during the rebuilding of that church from 1478–1519 this was transferred to the church of the Austin and Grey Friars. Matthew Stokes, writing *c.* 1530, records how a scaffold was erected at the east end of the nave for this purpose.[195] The ordinary meetings of the Regents and non-Regents, later called Convocation, also occupied the chancel, and as they grew in number they were distributed around the building; the non-Regents in the chancel, Theologians in the Congregation House; the Decretists in St Anne's Chapel; the Physicians in St Catherine's; the Jurats in St Thomas's and the Proctors with the Regents in the Chapel of St Mary. The court of the Vice-Chancellor, too, was held on Fridays in the chapel of Adam de Brome.[196]

## Legal Proceedings

State recognition of episcopal legal powers in the fourth century and the institutional development of the Church, which of necessity involved the formulation of rules and regulations, resulted in a great body of canon law. Collections were made, one of the earliest and most important being that of Dionysius Exiguus, a Scythian monk living in Rome at the beginning of the sixth century, and codifications were undertaken, of which the most outstanding was the *Decretum* of Gratian, *c.* 1140. The existence of such a corpus of law required a corresponding system of courts to administer and apply it. So there appeared courts of the archbishops, courts of the bishops and of the archdeacons. These usually conducted their business in cathedrals or churches, appropriately administering justice in buildings that were often decorated on their exterior with carvings of the Last Judgment and on the interior with frescoes of the same subject on the walls of the nave or across the west end. Indeed, so close was this association of court and church building that the Court of Canterbury, which dealt with the provincial appeal business of the archbishop, derived its name from the church in which it held its sessions. The Court of the Arches used to meet in St Mary-le-Bow, London, a church which according to Stow, was built 'on arches of stone' and so the court 'taketh the name of the place'.[197]

All over Britain these courts assembled regularly in churches, e.g. in the collegiate church at Ripon.[198]

In the diocese of Canterbury the Consistory Court sat inside the cathedral, probably under the north-west tower of the nave. In 1373 it met at intervals of three weeks for three days at a time, but by 1397 its business had so increased that four-or five-day sessions were common. On some days the court assembled elsewhere than in the cathedral, and on Saturdays, in particular, it often occupied the chapel of St Thomas's Hospital on the East Bridge. Right up to the Reformation, however, the cathedral was its main centre, except from 7th April to 6th October 1505, when it moved to the church of Adisham. The Consistory Court also went on circuit in the southern parts of the diocese, so in 1464 it sat at Dover in St Martin's, at Hythe in St Leonard's and at Romney in St Nicholas's. The archdeacon's court of the same diocese also transacted its business in church, but it had no permanent home like the Consistory, e.g. from 11th January 1499 to 12th November 1524, it sat in the churches of St George, of Holy Cross, Westgate, of All Saints and in the Hospital of the Poor Priests.[199] It too went on circuit and when visiting the deanery of Sandwich met in St Mary's, St Clement's or St Peter's.

On occasions these courts dealt with matters relating to sanctuary seekers. In 1279 Godfrey Giffard, Bishop of Worcester, presided in his cathedral at an enquiry into the execution of William de Lay, previously a fugitive in the Church of SS. Philip and James, Bristol. He had apparently been removed by force by Peter de la Mare, Constable of Bristol Castle.[200] Or again in 1458–9, one Henry Mullyng had been dragged from Ely Cathedral, and so the bishop, William Gray, appointed a commission to hear the case in the cathedral and Mullyng was allowed to choose to return either to sanctuary or to gaol.[201]

On other occasions the courts heard cases of heresy. So on 17th August 1415, John Cleydone, a Lollard, was tried in St Paul's before the Archbishop of Canterbury and others.[202] But the matters with which these courts dealt were not exclusively ecclesiastical; they were concerned with perjury, theft, defamation of character, debt, affiliation, etc. This intertwining of the secular and the religious, exemplified by the dispute between Henry II and Becket concerning criminous clerks, meant that medieval Christians saw nothing untoward in using churches not only for ecclesiastical courts but also for civil ones, nor anything strange in the latter hearing ecclesiastical matters as when, in 1333, the mayor and sheriffs of Chester, sitting in St Mary-on-the-Hill, gave judgment in a case of sacrilege.[203] However, before surveying the evidence there are certain survivals from the patristic period that have to be mentioned.

The practice of slavery was to continue throughout the Middle Ages, and Thomas Aquinas was quite prepared to recognize it both as morally justifiable and economically necessary.[204] Hence the liberation of slaves remained a charitable possibility. In the Cathedral at Orleans there was extant in the eighteenth century a medieval inscription recording the manumission of a certain Letbertus and another, dating from *c*. 1497, which gives information about the emancipation of a young woman.[205] We may note further the Gospel Book of Bodmin, Cornwall, of the tenth or eleventh century, which preserves the texts of certain manumissions 'on the altar of saint Petroc'.[206] But this secular legal proceeding was only one of a large number of which churches were the scene.

As in the patristic era, so in the Middle Ages, churches were the customary places for reaching agreements, drawing up contracts and ratifying them. White Kennett records the death of Robert de Oily in 1090 and notes that he had previously conveyed to the monks of Abingdon 'before the high altar' some land of £10 annual rent.[207] In 1238 a title to land was surrendered by the owner in the church before the parishioners of Hooton.[208] In 1273 the monks of Melrose, before many persons both clerical and lay, in the church of Boulden, agreed to pay the monks of Kelso a yearly sum in lieu of the meals they had been accustomed to provide.[209] These particular monks seem to have been of a litigious nature and usually resorted to St James, Roxburgh, for the hearing and settlement of their disputes—cases involving them being listed in 1263, 1291, 1295 and 1309.[210] Frequently these agreements related to land conveyance; thus in 1287 land was granted by William de Fedreth and Christine his wife to Sir Reginall le Chene in the cathedral of Elgin; in 1318 a deed relating to property was executed in Felkirk church, near Barnsley, before all the parishioners, and in 1361 a lady made a grant of land to her kinsman Colin Campbell in St Martin's in Ardscodinis.[211] Solemn agreements were entered into upon Teliau's tomb at Llandaff, e.g. in 1234, and upon the tomb of Prior Senhouse at Carlisle.[212]

The basis of this custom was the idea that as the church was a specially holy place, oaths of ratification there were themselves especially binding; hence it was customary to take them before the high altar and over the relics enshrined in it. A detailed illustration of this is provided by an incident in Macclesfield Chapel, on 24th April 1412. The proceedings began with a reading by Sir Robert Grosvenor's counsel of the deeds relating to a settlement of various manors and lands by the Pulford family. Claim to these was then laid by Sir Thomas Leigh and his wife, and it was agreed that Sir Thomas should take a solemn oath on the body of Christ. Mass was next said by Sir Robert's chaplain who, in due course, held aloft the consecrated host, before which Sir Thomas knelt and, after the deed had been read out, swore that he believed it to be true. The affair was concluded when the sheriff and fifty-seven knights and gentlemen of Cheshire had declared themselves witnesses of the oath.[213] Not infrequently, when the contract related to some material object, a symbol of it was placed upon the altar to declare its trans-ference, e.g. a clod of earth, knotted blades of grass, church keys, a candlestick, some coins, a book or the actual charter of the con-tract.[214]

To be associated with contract oaths are also oaths of fealty and of compurgation. In 1452, in St Paul's, London, Richard, Duke of York, took his oath of fealty to King Henry on the sacrament before the assembled peers, while in 1461 in the same building homage was rendered by the lords of England to Edward IV.[215] Compurgation could be practised by lords and commoners alike; this was the swearing of an oath to establish one's innocence when charged with some misdemeanour or crime. So in 1458, in Gnosall Church, Lichfield, one William Godthank, who had been accused of theft, stood before the altar and swore that he was not guilty; eight of his neighbours then swore likewise that they believed him and he was declared innocent.[216]

The ordeal comes within the same range of ideas and since it involved the invocation of the judgment of God this too had its place in churches. The sequence of events was as follows: the irons were placed before the altar and then removed by the priest with a pair of tongs to the fire which had been kindled in the nave. Two witnesses were then admitted whose task it was to certify that the iron had reached the required heat. Meanwhile mass was celebrated and the accused communicated. He then took up the irons and carried them a measured distance of nine feet. His hand was next enclosed in a wrapping which was sealed. Three days later, the bandage was removed and the wound examined; if any festering blood was found he was deemed guilty, but if the wound was clean he was declared innocent of the crime imputed to him. This barbarous practice was in use down to the year 1219.[217]

Amongst the Frisians in the Middle Ages there was an ordeal by lot, also conducted in churches. If a man were slain, his relatives summoned seven parishioners who were then put to the oath. Two pieces of wood were placed on the altar, one having a cross on its under side. The priest then prayed that God would indicate if the seven had sworn truly and picked up one of the sticks; if he selected the one with the cross, they were declared innocent. A parallel custom in Ireland consisted in placing the names of suspected persons in a chalice on the altar and the one extracted was regarded as guilty.[218]

Even trial by combat had its connection with the church building, although the fighting was kept outside. In the reign of Henry II a charter of liberties was granted to York Minster and this ordained that before any trial by combat the parties were to take an oath upon the relics in the church and that, after the duel, the victor was to offer the arms of the vanquished within the sacred precincts.[219]

We pass next to the secular courts and, in the first instance, to the different types. Churches provided accommodation for folk-moots, e.g. St Paul's in 973,[220] and for manorial courts, since although many of these assembled in the house of the lord of the manor there are records of their meeting in churches, e.g. on 8th January 1181 in the church of Kirkby-le-Soken, Essex,[221] at Ruthin on Sundays

in 1295 and 1296, in the church of Yoxall from the reign of Edward
II onwards,[222] and at Ashburton, Devon, in the chapel of St
Laurence.[223] Churches also housed court-leets, as at Bolton. They
provided space for assize courts, as did York Minster in 1238,[224]
and for courts for the view of frankpledge, as Cherry Hinton, near
Cambridge, in 1278, and Chingford, Essex, the following year.[225]
They were used by the royal judges, as were St Nicholas and St
Andrew, Norwich, in 1280,[226] or as in 1462 the Grey Friars Church
at Bridgewater where they examined prisoners accused of theft and
assault.[227] The burgomasters of Strassbourg regularly heard law
suits in their official pew in the Cathedral during daily mass.[228] The
court of the Lord Warden of the Cinque Ports met in a consecrated
building,[229] while at Sandwich the bailiff summoned the Hundred
Court every three weeks to meet in St Clement's for a view of
frankpledge, for pleas of land, questions of trespass, covenants, debts,
battery, bloodshed, etc.[230] Prior to the building of the Guildhall in
1411, the court of Aldermen met in St Mary Aldermanbury—hence
the name—near Sion College in London.[231]* Finally, there were
inquests taking place at all times of the day and year in churches up
and down the country.

Some indication of the range of cases dealt with by these courts
has already been given in connection with the Hundred Court at
Sandwich, but further illustrations are needed to show the full
extent of secular concerns investigated. We may begin with the last
item listed above, viz. inquests. A ruling of the city of London of
1243 reads: 'If a person is slain within the City, a Sheriff ought to
come and hold Inquisition of the venue (i.e. the neighbourhood) as
to who slew him.'[232] According to this ordinance, inquests are to be
held at the place where the crime was committed or discovered in
the hope of obtaining sufficient information from those in the vicin-
ity to allow an arrest to be made and a verdict to be reached. This
explains why some inquests were held in churches, as in the following example dating from 1276–7. A certain William le Clerke had
been discovered dead in St Stephen Walbrook; an inquest accordingly took place in the church and it was found that the victim had
died after a fall from a beam while seeking pigeon's eggs.[233] In 1285
a clerk was drowned in the river Cherwell at Oxford and his body

was conveyed to St Cross; it was in that church therefore that the coroner's inquest had to be held.[234]

Sanctuary seekers provided another reason for the holding of coroner's courts on consecrated ground. When an officer of the law learned that someone had sought sanctuary, he had to go to the church and enquire into the case. Hence, according to the legal treatise written by Britton under Edward I:

> When any man has fled to church, we will that the coroner, as soon as he has notice of it, command the bailiffs of the place that he cause the neighbours and the four nearest townships (to form a jury) to appear before him at a certain day at the church where the fugitive shall be; and in their presence he shall receive the confession of the felony; and if the fugitive pray to abjure our realm, let the coroner immediately do what is incumbent upon him.[235]

From the records we can gather details of the proceedings, e.g. the case of one Colson of Walsingham, Co. Durham, who had fled to the cathedral on 13th May 1467. The register entry reads:

> On the arrival of John Raket, coroner of the ward of Chester-le-Street, Colson made confession of his felony, and standing there took his corporal oath of abjuring the realm of England with as much dispatch as possible and of never returning. This oath he took at the shrine of St Cuthbert before George Cornforth, sacrist of the cathedral shrine of Durham, Ralph Bows, knight and sheriff of Co. Durham, John Raket, Robert Thrylkeyy, under sheriff, Hugh Holand, Nicholas Dixson, and many others. By means of which renunciation and oath all Colson's accoutrements were forfeited by right to the aforesaid sacristan as pertaining to his office. Therefore Colson was ordered to take off his clothes to his shirt and to deliver them to the sacristan for his disposal.[236]

So it was customary in the Durham register to enter the names of several witnesses; often one or more would be officials of the cathedral, as the sacristan in the case of Colson; often they were just called in off the street to hear the confession, and some times masons, engaged on repair work, made their appearance. Records of these hearings abound from all over Britain. First, two examples from London—in 1275–6 William de Lindseye, who had sought sanctuary in the chapel of St Mary Berkingcherche, was charged with the murder of Gervase le Noreys. He eventually acknowledged his guilt before 'the Chamberlain and Sheriffs, and other good and trusty men'.[237] In 1289 Walter Bacum was cross-examined in St Paul's by the coroner and the warden of the city of London on the charge of stealing silver from a merchant of Lucca.[238] In Cornwall, in St Petroc's we hear of a John de Trenton as coroner in 1283-4, hearing the case of Richard de Penteryn[239] and in 1377 of John Philpot's confession, before two coroners in the chapel of St Mary in the monastery of St Andrew, Northampton, that he was a thief and a murderer.[240]

In addition to inquests and enquiries relating to sanctuary seekers, courts in churches dealt with many other matters. In 1258 certain Oxford scholars came to St Alban's and complained before the king in St Oswin's chapel that the Bishop of Lincoln had restricted their liberties in violation of the statutes.[241] In the fourteenth century, the Chancery court of the Cinque Ports, in St James', Dover, considered the unlawful arrest of ships, trespass, tolls and customs, using the chancel in the south aisle.[242] In 1308 divorce proceedings were heard in Winster Church, Derbyshire. In 1425 John Cokayn and James Strangeways received letters patent from Henry VI to hold an assize of novel disseisin for the aldermen and brethren of St Mary's Guild in Chesterfield church.[243]

Whatever part of the country we turn to, whatever century we investigate, the story is the same—courts everywhere, on all days of the week, even on Sundays, in churches. Ecclesiastical condemnation had no effect. Individual churchmen such as Jonas of Orleans,[244] William Durandus[245] and Archbishop Thoresby[246] might object to secular pleas in churches; the Provincial Council of Tours in 1253 might forbid law suits,[247] and similarly synods at Exeter and Winchester in 1287,[248] but it all fell on deaf ears. When, in the mid-fifteenth century, the Bishop of Exeter himself, in dispute with the mayor, could allow the matter to be argued within the cathedral itself,[249] it was unlikely that the ordinary parish priest would raise any serious objection.

Three other legal transactions remain to be surveyed: these are payments, penalties and tithes. Churches were normal centres for the settling of debts and for the paying of fines. At St Paul's, London, there is an unbroken history of over a hundred years of these dues being handed in to creditors. From 1362 there is a note of one such payment[250] and in 1415 there was a demise of lands in Henbury, Yorkshire, the yearly rent of which was to be paid in St Paul's. From 1487 there is a receipt for forty marcs paid in the cathedral, and in 1530 there was an agreement between the Earl of Shrewsbury and Sir George Darcy which involved the payment of £200 'on the day of St Nicholas next at the Font in St Paul's Cathedral'.[251] This practice was neither confined to London nor to cathedrals. In the thirteenth century the manor of Beighton, near Sheffield, was conveyed by Sir Walter de Furneaus to William his brother for fourscore marcs and a yearly rent of a penny due at St Radegund's church. In the fourteenth century, one farthing in silver was to be paid each year in the chapel of Birchover on Michaelmas Day for land at Stanton in Derbyshire, and in 1424 an agreement was concluded involving the payment of the sum of £10 at the altar of St Mary in the parish church of Stamfordham. In 1494 the purchaser of the Sun Inn at Strood, Kent, agreed to pay in £5 instalments in the parish church of Ryarsh, near Maidstone.[252]

Church buildings were often the scene of rent payments. In 1429 James I of Scotland granted land to John Lech at a yearly rent of two pennies or a pair of gloves to be paid or rendered in the parish church of Bute.[253] The Chapter of Norwich received its rents on the tomb of Chancellor Spencer and the stone was worn by the frequent ringing of money.[254] As an example of the payment of a fine we may cite a case from 1366 when all the tenants of the manor of Heworth, Durham, who had trespassed on the corn or grass of Richard del Kytchin had to go to Jarrow church on the following Sunday and make satisfaction for the damage done.[255]

Penalties, however, could be in a different form. It was not unusual for justices to require slanderers, etc., to make public satisfaction for their faults and the church was the normal place for so doing. In 1382 a man named Robert had spread malicious rumours of theft about Johanne Wolsy; he had to go to St Mildred Poultry at the hour of mass and there admit his false witness.[256] In 1463 a burgess, who had offended an alderman, was required to be present in St Nicholas, Aberdeen, there to ask forgiveness both of the individual and of the whole city council. Similarly in 1523 one who had disobeyed the bailies had to go to high mass and ask for pardon.[257] In

1502 Geoffrey Bocher of Horton, one of the butchers who had been found selling meat illegally on Sundays, was ordered to walk before the cross in his parish church in the Sunday procession with a candle in one hand and a shoulder of lamb in the other.[258]

A not insignificant part of the parish income was derived from tithes, and both the determination of these and their collection took place in churches. So a court in Holy Trinity, Berwick, in 1279, sat to give sentence upon the payment of tithes.[259] Once each householder knew the amount he owed, he had to bring it to the church. According to the Gambara inquisition of 1195, tithes were delivered in the church of the village of Paono and there divided into four— one part for the abbot, two for the local nobility and one for the church.[260] This was not always done with a good will, and so we find Bishop Quivil of Exeter complaining in 1287 of those who maliciously had not brought their tithe of milk to church in the usual form of cheese but 'in its natural state and finding none there to receive it, pour it out before the altar'.[261] Payment of tithes in money instead of in kind is, for example, recorded of the abbot and convent of Selby who gave four shillings per annum at the altar in Holme church.[262]

## Publishing of Notices

Since medieval churches, as will now be obvious, were such centres of social life, they were admirably suited for the publishing of notices of community concern. With the announcements of entirely liturgical activities, such as the time and day of the next celebration of mass, there were proclamations of completely secular affairs, which it was important that the parishioners should know. So in 1491, in Ashton Chapel, Lancashire, the priest included among his notices the declaration that a local landowner intended to make a ditch through his moss or bog.[263]* In Cumberland stray sheep were announced in church on Sundays, and in Rotherham church the penalties decreed in the manor court were made public by the bailiff.[264] In 1469 at Chesterfield notice was given of the administration of the goods of an intestate.[265] Or again, on 15th July 1519, the Venetian ambassador reported that the election of Charles V as emperor had been proclaimed in the cathedral of St Paul's.[266]

Sometimes the form of public notices was nothing if not bizarre. Bernard Gilpin (1517–83), at one time Archdeacon of Durham, records how, when visiting a certain church, he saw a glove hanging in a prominent position and, upon asking what it meant, he was informed by the sexton that 'it was a glove which one of the parish hung up there as a challenge to his enemy, signifying thereby that he was ready to enter combat hand to hand with him or any one else who should dare to take the glove down'.[267]

## Storing

Because churches, compared with most other medieval buildings, were larger, stronger and more durable and because there were often people in them throughout the day and night, they formed excellent repositories for goods. Individuals were accustomed to deposit their valuables there for safe keeping. Thus when William of Scotland ravaged the country around Carlisle in the twelfth century, the inhabitants of Plumbland, near Cockermouth, flocked to the church and lodged their goods inside it.[268] Or again, after the battle known as the 'Fair of Lincoln' in 1221, when the Earl of Pembroke routed the French army under Prince Louis, the victors proceeded to pillage the churches and, breaking open chests, made off with silver, gold, clothes, ornaments, rings, goblets and jewels.[269] Or, a final example, we are informed that in 1327 there were delivered into the keeping of Roger de Waltham the goods and chattels of Robert de Baldoke, previously deposited in St Paul's.[270]

Deeds were another item preserved in churches, e.g. in 1275 a collection of these are said to be kept in a chest behind the high altar in St Paul's.[271] Sanctuary seekers too, if they had the time, were apt to bear their possessions with them into churches, e.g. in 1483 Elizabeth Woodville sought refuge again in Westminster and took with her 'chests, coffers, packs and fardels'.[272] Not only private individuals but guilds as well housed their money and documents in churches. The Guild of the Kalendars had their valuables in the roodloft of All Saints, Bristol, only to have them destroyed by fire in 1318,[273] and the Guild of St Peter, founded in 1406, kept their goods in St Peter's-on-Cornhill, London.[274]

Not only were items of considerable worth thus provided with safe keeping, but all sorts of goods were stored in church. According to the *Capitulary* of Theodulph of Orleans (d. 821), which was translated into Old English in the tenth or eleventh century, 'we have seen also often in the churches corn and hay and all kinds of secular things kept'.[275] Specific instances of this have been chronicled. In parts of Germany husbandmen had the right to store their corn-bins anywhere in the church, and the men of Kent also had their chests full of corn in the nave. At Parma, *c.* 1240, corn was habitually stacked in the nave of the cathedral.[276]* In 1242 we hear of a Roger Meylok who went to the church of Llanblethian, Glamorgan, 'siezed the corn, threshed it and carried it away'.[277] Similarly at Codyntone in 1397 the rector was reported to keep hay in the tower and even to quarter his cattle there.[278] Wool was stored in a church in Southampton,[279] wine in the church cistern at Avry,[280] according to the visitation returns of the diocese of Lausanne, in 1416, wine and corn in one of the churches in the district of Worms,[281] and, according to a visitation by Bishop Stapledon of Exeter in 1301, in St Mary Church, Devon, ale was actually brewed in the nave.[282]

The visitation returns of the archdeanery of Josas, in the diocese of Paris, for 1458–70, contain a whole series of further examples. The parson of Magny-les-Hameaux is said to have taken his corn into church and there winnowed it; the church of Ver-le-Petit had been similarly used. In 1459 one Nicholas le Roux threshed his tithe sheaves in church. In 1460, at Asnières, Jeanne la Mulote stored her barrels and household chattels. In 1461 at St Yom the visitor discovered Jean Mansel threshing his barley in the nave.[283]

In addition to inanimate objects, animals too, were brought into the sacred precincts. Sometimes this was to prevent their being seized, debtors affording themselves of this means to defeat the ends of justice, and hence the Constitutions of Clarendon declared that cattle forfeited to the king could not be kept in churches or churchyards.[284] Often, however, it was simply a question of shelter in immoderate weather, as was frequently the case in the larger Irish parish churches. Medieval Christians saw nothing unusual in this, since they were accustomed to attend church with their pets, and the

*Stultifera Navis* by Sebastian Brant, translated into English by A. Barclay in 1508, describes folk going to services with their hawks and their hounds.[285] Indeed the *Ménagier de Paris*, written 1392-4, and containing instructions on wifely duties, directs how, in the training of hawks, they are to be taken regularly to church to accustom them to gatherings of human beings.[286] Indeed, on St Paul's Day in the cathedral at London a buck was brought up to the high altar—the body being later sent for baking and the severed head, fixed on a pole, was borne before the cross in procession. According to Stow this practice began in 1274 and was the annual rent in kind for some land.[287]

The instances given above of the storing of goods were, apart from the guilds, mainly the concern of individuals, but churches were also used to house all sorts of implements and other items which were related to the community as a whole. The standard village weights and measures were frequently kept in the church. At Axmouth, Devon, and Petton, Salop, there survive stone receptacles said to be old 'Lord's Measures'.[288]* In some Somerset villages the length of a chain was determined by a multiplication of the length of the nave.[289] In old St Paul's, from the twelfth century, there was, carved on the base of one of the pillars, the foot of Algar, first Prebendary of Islington, and this was used as the standard measure for legal contracts of land.[290] The church was even used for such a simple everyday matter as obtaining a light for the fire—in St Mary Ottery a lamp was kept burning continually, not solely for reverence but for anyone who wanted the means to kindle a fire at home.[291] Protection against fire was also needed and so the church stored the parish fire-fighting equipment, such as buckets, long hooks to pull down burning houses, etc. The parish store of arms and weapons was also guarded in the church and when an Act was passed in 1466 requiring butts to be set up and all men to practise on Sundays and holidays, their bows and arrows were added to the list of armaments already in store.

To these categories of objects and livestock deposited and sheltered in churches must also be added the large number of votive offerings—crutches from those who had been healed, wax anchors from sailors who had been saved from a storm, etc. But, further, we must also take note of the curios in medieval churches which were used as the equivalents of the modern museum. In the church of Sugolia, on the borders of Hungary, and also in Enisheim Chapel, Alsace-Lorraine, meteors were on show. At Pennant Melangel, in Montgomeryshire, a giant's rib was on show—in fact it was a mammoth's rib. At Chesterfield there was the supposed rib of the Dun Cow of Warwick—in origin the jaw of a whale—and also in St Mary's, Redcliffe, another whale bone was believed to have come from the cow which once, according to the legend, had supplied the whole town of Bristol with milk. Canute's knee-bone could be seen at Canewdon near Rockford, Essex, and the cathedral of St Bertrand-de-Comminges, Haute Garonne, was the proud possessor of a stuffed crocodile.[292] But then, where else, if a remarkable object were obtained, could it be more publicly or better displayed than in a church?

## Teaching

The educational record of the Middle Ages is by no means negligible. These centuries witnessed the foundation of many schools that remain famous down to the present day, and a large number of these owed their origin to individuals, such as archbishops and prelates, and members of the clergy in general. But most of these benefactors sought to provide buildings of their own for these schools so that their history largely falls outside the scope of this study. Schools in churches, which is our particular concern, may be divided into two categories: those which provided a general education, although with the accent necessarily upon instruction in the Christian faith, and those whose limited aim was to train boys for the choir. It is frequently impossible to be certain from surviving references to which type a particular school belonged.

According to the decretals of Gregory IX (c. 1148–1241), all parishioners are to send their children to be taught by the parish clerk in the church;[293] this suggests a general, as distinct from a choir-oriented, education. Examples of schools in churches of this type are the one at Canterbury, 1310–11, in St Elphege or Alphage,[294] and the grammar school in the chapel of Our Lady at Chelmsford, 1375.[295] There is the doubtful case of St Andrew in Oldborne, 'in the which church', according to Stow, 'or near thereunto was some-time kept a Grammar school'.[296] At Threlkeld, near Keswick in Cumberland, there was a school in the parish church in 1461.[297] Twenty years later the directions for the parish clerk at St Nicholas, Bristol, contain the injunction that books are not to be removed from the choir 'for children to learn in', while the clerk at Faversham in 1506 had to instruct the children to read.[298] An account of the life at Eton School in 1530 records how there were two preposi-tors in the body of the church and two in the choir 'for speaking of Latin in the third form'.[299] The school in the conventual nave of Kirkham Priory in the East Riding of Yorkshire (1496) was, how-ever, to teach local boys for the choir, and this was the normal aim of monastic educational facilities.[300]

Whereas many of these schools occupied the nave or choir, in some churches other rooms were used, e.g. in St Michael's loft above the Lady Chapel of Christchurch Priory in Hampshire there still survives the sixteenth-century desk and chair where the master sat; at Howarth the raised chamber over the west end of the south aisle was employed and at Walpole St Peter's the room above the south porch.[301]

Even when schools had their separate buildings, it was not unusual for the pupils to gather in churches for what would now be called 'speech days'. William Fitzstephen, who died in 1911, has left an account of these relating to three London schools in the reign of Stephen and Henry:

Upon Festival Days the Masters made solemn meetings in the Churches, where their Scholars disputed Logically and demonstratively; some bringing Enthimens, other perfect Syllogisms: some disputed for shew, others to trace out the truth; cunning Sophisters were thought brave Scholars, when they flowed with words. Others used fallacies: Rhetoricians spake aptly to persuade, dressing the precepts of Art, and omitting nothing that might serve their purpose. The boys of diverse Schools did cap or pot verses, and contended of the principles of Gram-mar. There were some which on the other side with Epigrams and rhymes, nipping and quipping their fellows, and the faults of others, though suppressing their names, moved thereby much laughter among their auditors.[302]

*Library Facilities*

Schools required a number of text books and these too were kept in churches, but the contents of parochial libraries were more extensive than this. So St Margaret's, New Fish Street, London, had, in 1476, fifty-seven service books and twelve others. Boston church had bequeathed to it in 1457 copies of the *Polychronicon* and *Dieta Salutis* and in 1469 a common law book.[303] Sometimes located in vestries and church towers, these libraries could have a home in the worship area itself, e.g. in All Saints, Derby, *c.* 1325, nine books are listed as being chained in the Lady Chapel, and at Aylesbury, Buckinghamshire, there were books in a wainscote press in the north transept.[304]

Cathedrals, with their resident chapters and often their schools attached, had extensive libraries. Up to the fifteenth century, these were usually kept either in an aumbry cupboard by the altar or in a chest in the treasury; it was only from *c.* 1450 that separate library buildings began to be erected.[305] The Inns of Court naturally required works of reference and we are informed that in 1381 the rebels of Essex attacked the Temple and 'took out of the Church the books and records that were in Hutches'.[306]

Sometimes, regrettably, churches were the scene of the reverse process, i.e. not of the storing but of the destruction of books. In 1527, before Cardinal Wolsey, seated on a specially constructed scaffold in St Paul's, copies of Tyndale's translation of the New Testament into English were burned in the nave.[307]

In the Middle Ages, the nave of the church, according to G. M. Trevelyan, was 'the "village hall" for most communal purposes'.[308] The correctness of this description has been amply demonstrated by this survey of non-liturgical activities within churches which have a continuous history from the patristic period, although some of them have been elaborated and extended as the centuries passed. The size of many medieval parish churches now becomes understandable. They were frequently far too spacious to accommodate the normal worshipping congregation from the immediate locality, but their dimensions are to be understood, not simply in terms of devotional display, but as the necessary means of providing for the multitude of activities which took place within them. Nor has the list of activities been exhausted. We must now proceed to consider those secular uses which had no precedents in the days of the Early Church and only came into being in the course of the Middle Ages.

# 3

# The Middle Ages Continued

## 2. NEW SECULAR USES

THE PRESENT chapter will be concerned with those secular activities within the medieval cathedrals and churches for which there was no direct precedent in the patristic era. Nevertheless, these new uses were in most instances no more than a natural extension of those that had gone before. If churches could be employed for eating and drinking, in particular for funeral *agapes* which were a means of giving charity to the needy, they could equally be centres for organized poor relief. If music and dancing could take place within them, there was obviously no reason why games and plays should not also be accommodated there. If they were suitable for the storage of goods, they had only to be adapted a little to make them strongholds for community defence. We have to concentrate then mainly upon poor relief, games, drama and military architecture.

### *Distribution of Poor Relief*

Poor relief in the Middle Ages was more often in kind than in cash, and the raising and distribution of the latter belongs rather to the period after the Reformation. But in the 'Ordinance for a Common Chest', drawn up in 1523 by Luther in conjunction with the citizens of Leisneck, Saxony, we find a combination of the two. The directions for poor relief in kind are as follows:

There shall be ordered for God's house and kept in place for all time, two casks or council chests in which bread, cheese, eggs, meat and other food and provisions shall be placed; and there shall also be a box or two wherein money shall be put for the upkeep of the common chest.[1]

As regards the common chest, it was directed that this 'Receptacle shall be kept in a safe place in God's house and shall be closed with four different and particular keys and locks'.[2] The sources of money for this are then detailed. They include rents, altar offerings, income from fraternities, fines, compensation money, free-will offerings from days of healing and from bequests, etc. All this was to be most carefully administered by ten guardians or overseers, democratically elected. We shall see a considerable development of this charitable work in the centuries succeeding the Reformation.

### Playing of Games

Games in churches fall into two distinct categories: there were those that had a liturgical or quasi-liturgical setting, and these formed the great majority, and there were those that were entirely and unashamedly secular.

Those games associated with the liturgy are to be noted mainly in connection with the Feast of Fools. This observance, which seems to have arisen in the twelfth century, was variously known as *festum stultorum*, *fatuorum* or *follorum*; as *festum subdiaconorum*, since the subdeacons were usually in charge of it, and as *festum baculi* since the rod (*baculus*) of the master of ceremonies was received and wielded by a representative of the subdeacons. Its main characteristic, as previously stated,[3] was the inversion of status, the inferior clergy fulfilling the offices of the superior in a mood of almost unlicensed revelry. As the feast has been very fully investigated and described by E. K. Chambers,[4] there is no need to go into great detail, but his summary, which gives a clear indication of its range, is worth quoting to show what actually went on:

The fools jangle the bells (Paris, Amiens, Auxerre), they take the higher stalls (Paris), sing dissonantly (Sens), repeat meaningless words (Châlons, Antibes), say the *messe liesse* (Laon) or the *missa fatuorum* (Autun), preach the *sermones fatui* (Auxerre), cense *praepostere* (St Omer) with pudding and sausage (Beauvais) or with old shoes (Paris theologians). They have their chapter and their proctors (Auxerre, Dijon). They install their *dominus festi* with a ceremony of *sacre* (Troyes), or shaving (Sens, Dijon). He is vested in full pontificals, goes in procession, as at the *Rabardiaux* of Laon, gives the benedictions, issues indulgences (Viviers), has his seal (Lille), perhaps his right of coming (Laon).[5]

It was also observed in Bohemia, Germany and Spain and in England at Beverley, Salisbury and in St Paul's.

At Sens in the thirteenth century this feast was known as the *asinaria festa* and this arose from the fact that an ass was actually brought into the church at the singing of the Prose of the Ass.[6] At Beauvais an extension of this buffoonery to recall the flight into Egypt took place on 14th January, when the ass was stationed on the Gospel side, mass was celebrated, and the *introit*, *Gloria* and *credo* all ended with a braying, while instead of the usual dismissal the priest was directed to bray three times and the people to respond in similar manner.[7] Needless to say, repeated efforts were made by the ecclesiastical authorities to reform, if not to abolish, this combination of games with the saying of the hours and the celebration of the eucharist.[8]

The Feast of Fools originally referred to the jollifications on 1st January, under the direction of the subdeacon; on 27th December, the vigil of Holy Innocents' Day, the choirboys took the lead, their Boy Bishop corresponding to the holder of the *baculus* on the Feast of the Circumcision. He sat on the bishop's throne, delivered a sermon, gave the blessing and presided at the eating and further merry-making that followed.[9]

For the next game associated with the Church's calendar we move on towards Lent and to the preparatory cycle represented by Septuagesima and the two following Sundays. One of the features of the mass was the chanting of the Alleluia, as an expression of joyful praise. It was, however, not considered fitting to sing it during penitential seasons, and so Gregory the Great had ordered its discontinuance from Septuagesima to Easter. In the Middle Ages, cessation of the Alleluia was marked on the eve of Septuagesima in ways that can only be described as belonging to the category of games. In churches in Paris it was the custom for a choirboy to whip a top, bearing the word Alleluia in gold letters, from one end of the choir to the other.[10] Another way of signifying the temporary decease of the Alleluia was specified in a fifteenth-century statute of the cathedral of Toul. This directs that on the Saturday evening before Septuagesima, between noon and vespers, the boys of the choir are to carry a bier, representing the dead Alleluia, accompanied by cross, torches, holy water and incense. They are to weep aloud and go in procession to the cloisters where an open grave has been prepared—the bier is then placed inside it.[11] In England, at Lincoln Cathedral, a piece of turf replaced the bier.[12]

Ball games would seem to be necessarily secular, but even these could be given a religious association. Belethus in the twelfth century[13] and Durandus in the thirteenth[14] both record games played with a *pilota* in the cathedrals of Amiens and Rheims, especially at Christmas and Easter. A chapter minute from Auxerre of 18th April 1396 reveals its continuation there in the fourteenth century. Indeed, on 19th April 1412, the same chapter passed a decree to the effect that the ball should be made smaller and yet of such a size that it could not be held in one hand alone. Not all clerics were easy about this activity and so we find on 14th April 1471, i.e. Easter Day, one Gérard Royer being made a canon of Auxerre and refusing to provide a ball for the customary game. He asserted that he would not do so because the Bishop of Mende, i.e. Durandus, had expressed disapproval of the practice. The dean, however, insisted that all should be as usual and so the ball provided the previous year by Etienne Gerbault was brought and the game proceeded.[15]

A description of this *pilota* game has been preserved. At one or two in the afternoon the newly elected canon had to be ready in the nave of St Stephen's, holding the ball against his chest. He then passed it to the dean or to the most senior dignitary present. The dean, pressing the ball against his own chest with his left arm, clasped another canon with his right hand and began a dance in which the whole chapter joined. The prose *Victimae Paschali* was sung to the accompaniment of the organ, while the ball was thrown backwards and forwards from one dancer to another. The climax was a meal in the chapter house at the expense of the newly installed canon.[16] This game was not confined to France, for in 1385 Robert Braybrooke, Bishop of London, denounced it in England: *necnon ad pilam infra et extra ecclesiam ludunt.*[17]

Apart from the singing of the prose, this game was primarily secular, as were also games of forfeits and skittles. Forfeits were played at Nantes, according to the minutes of a council meeting in 1431. The laity, at their Spring festivities, were accustomed to capturing people and then exacting a payment before setting them free. At Nantes apparently the clergy had been hurried from their beds on Easter Monday, dragged into church and sprinkled with water at the altar.[18]

At Evreux, in the thirteenth century, there was a religious festival from 28th April to 1st May. The participants went to gather branches in the bishop's woods and, wearing masks, returned to the church to the violent ringing of bells. The choir-clerks took the high stalls and the choirboys recited the offices—a reversal corresponding to the Feast of Fools. In the intervals, the canons played at skittles over the vaults and there was dancing and singing 'as at the time of the Nativity'.[19]

The Evreux proceedings obviously had close affinities with village folk customs and the same may be said of the 'summer games' with their accompanying election of Lords of Misrule and Summer Lords and Ladies, which were another object of ecclesiastical censure. Robert Grosseteste, Bishop of Lincoln from 1235–53, condemned the ceremony known as *Inductio Maii sive Autumni*.[20] Walter Cantilupe, Bishop of Worcester, prohibited in 1240 what he called *ludos de Rege et Regina*.[21] Nearly a hundred years later, Bishop Baldock of London censured 'games, dances, wrestlings and other sports meetings' at Barking in the parish church and in the church of the nunnery.[22] In 1287 a synod of Exeter prohibited the 'pollution' of churches with *ludos*.[23] The thirteenth-century *Manuel de Péché* also attacked carols and games in 'the holy church', and a free adaptation of this into English, *c.* 1303, the *Handlyng Synne* repeated this censure of summer games in churches and churchyards.[24] It is not always clear what the games comprised—for example, we do not know what the clergy were playing when reprimanded by the Bishop of Exeter in 1306[25]—but dancing was certainly a feature and notice of a maypole in church has been previously made,[26] while Bishop Braybrooke of London (1382–1404) attacked the clergy of St Paul's for playing 'at ball and other unseemly games, both within and without the church',[27] and among the early statutes from King's, Cambridge, is one forbidding 'incautious and inordinate games', including dancing and wrestling, in the chapel and hall.[28]

The Lady Fast Wheel was perhaps hardly a game, but it is not far from being one with a serious intent. There were six festivals in honour of the Virgin Mary and any one of them could be the beginning of a fast. An individual would decide which one to choose by means of a Lady Fast Wheel, two of which survive in the churches of Long Stratton, Norfolk, and Yaxley, Suffolk. The sexton made the wheel revolve and the enquirer caught at one of the six strings which hung from it; whichever he managed to seize determined the day on which his fast began.[29]

All in all, medieval Christians, even if at times they were prone to excess, saw their faith as embracing matters both grave and gay and sported themselves happily within the shelter of both church and cathedral. Perhaps the clearest illustration of this is provided by the account of the eighth-century saint John of Beverley, written at the end of the thirteenth century. This tells how a play was being performed in the churchyard of St John's. There was so great a crowd that those at the rear were unable to see and so they went into the church 'either to pray or to look at the pictures or to beguile the weariness of the day by some kind of recreation and solace'.[30]

### Acting

To investigate the production of plays in churches is to assist at the birth or rebirth of European drama. The Fathers of the Early Church had been bitterly opposed to the theatre, partly because under the Empire comedy and tragedy had been replaced by farce and pantomime of a licentious character, and partly because theatrical presentations had a close association with devotion to the gods of the Roman pantheon. These bawdy productions were condemned as much by pagan moralists as by Church spokesmen.[31] The great classical plays were hardly ever performed and 'with the fall of the Roman Empire the greater part of the dramatic achievement of the ancient world passed into obscurity'.[32] This did not mean that interest in drama vanished; instead it found a new focus in the celebration of mass.

The pioneer in the interpretation of the eucharist as an elaborate drama was Amalarius of Metz (*c.* 780–850), whose *Liber officialis* was to have a continuous stream of imitations right up to the

Reformation. Accepting the normal twofold division of the rite into the ministry of the Word and the mass of the faithful, Amalarius sought to demonstrate that the first part, up to and including the Gospel, corresponds to the preparation for the coming of Christ, to his birth and his ministry, and the second part to the final week of Jesus' life culminating in his death and resurrection. A few details of his exegesis will indicate how he worked out this correspondence. He referred the introit to the Old Testament prophets foretelling the coming of the Messiah, the *Gloria* to his nativity, the collect to his presence in the Temple at the age of twelve, the first lection to the preaching of John the Baptist and the Gospel to the ministry of Jesus. The opening prayers of the canon he understood as parallel to Jesus' prayer in Gethsemane and to his death and entombment. The commixture, i.e. the placing of a particle of the consecrated host in the wine in the chalice, he saw as declaring the reunion of Christ's soul and body and so the resurrection. The fraction or breaking of the bread made him known as at Emmaus and the kiss of peace is his greeting of the disciples on the first Easter Day. Within this history of redemption, each of the participants at mass had several roles to play. The priest took the part of Christ; the congregation was at one time the Chosen People longing for the fulfilment of prophecy and at another the shepherds adoring the new-born Saviour.[33] The whole was then a ritual drama covering the entire history of redemption.

A single passage from the pen of one of Amalarius's successors will be sufficient to demonstrate the continuity and elaboration of his understanding of the mass. In his *Gemma animae, c.* 1100, Honorius of Autun wrote:

It is known that those who recited tragedies in theatres represented the actions of the protagonists by gestures in front of the people. In the same way our tragic author (i.e. the priest) represents by his gestures in the theatre of the church before the Christian people the struggle of Christ and teaches them the victory of his redemption. So when the celebrant says the *Orate fratres* he represents Christ agonizing for us, when he commanded his disciples to pray. By the silence of the *secreta* he represents Christ as a lamb without voice being led to the sacrifice. By the extension of his hands he represents Christ being extended upon the cross. When he chants the preface he represents Christ's cry from the cross. . . . By the *pax* and its exchange, he represents the peace given after the Resurrection and the sharing of joy.[34]

So far we have been concerned with what is known as the ordinary of the mass, i.e. with those major portions of it that are invariable and remain the same from celebration to celebration. We must next take account of the proper, i.e. of those smaller sections of the mass which change according to the day or season of the Church's year.

The Christian calendar is in fact—saints' days apart—a cycle which commemorates events in the life of Christ by means of a series of special festivals and seasons. Advent foretells his coming and Christmas Day his birth; eight days later there is his circumcision, followed by the visit of the magi on Epiphany. The climax is reached in Holy Week when there is a day-by-day correspondence with Christ's last week in Jerusalem, and indeed, on Maundy Thursday and Good Friday almost an hour by hour correspondence. The cycle of the Church's year, integrated in the mass by means of the proper, sets out at length the same drama of redemption as the ordinary of the mass itself, as expounded by Amalarius and his successors. It was from these variable portions, within the context of the ritual drama, that the medieval plays were to develop. An anticipation of this is to be found as early as the fourth century in Jerusalem with its Palm Sunday procession and its Veneration of the Cross.[35] The bridge in this transition from ritual to representational drama is provided by the *Quem Quaeritis*.

The *Quem Quaeritis* is a dialogue with actions which seems to have originated in the tenth century. Its early history is by no means clear, but it is likely that it was at first part of the preparations for the vigil mass of Easter and was later detached.[36] In the *Regularis Concordia*, approved by a Synod of Winchester, *c.* 970, it formed part of the Nocturn on Easter morning and was a combination of dialogical chant and mimetic action. The main 'property' was the sepulchre, a model of the tomb of Christ in which a cross had been placed on Good Friday to represent his burial.

While the third lesson is being read, four of the brethren shall vest, one of whom, wearing an alb as though for some different purpose, shall enter and go stealthily to the place of the sepulchre and sit there quietly, holding a palm in his hand. Then, while the third respond is being sung, the other three brethren, vested in vests and holding thuribles in their hands, shall enter in their turn and go to the place of the sepulchre, step by step, as though searching for something. Now these things are done in imitation of the angel seated on the tomb and of the women coming with perfumes to anoint the body of Jesus. When, therefore, he that is seated shall see these three draw nigh, wandering about as it were and seeking something, he shall begin to sing softly and sweetly, *Quem quaeritis*. As soon as this has been sung right through, the three shall answer together, *Ihesum Nazarenum*. Then he that is seated shall say, *Non est hic, Surrexit sicut praedixerat. Ite nuntiate quia surrexit a mortuis*. At this command the three shall turn to the choir saying: *Alleluia, Resurrexit Dominus*. When this has been sung, he that is seated, as though calling them back, shall say the antiphon *Venite et videte locum*, and then, rising and lifting up the veil, he shall show them the place void of the Cross and with only the linen in which the Cross had been wrapped. Seeing this, the three shall lay down their thuribles in that same sepulchre and, taking the linen, shall hold it up before the clergy; and as though showing that the Lord was risen and was no longer wrapped in it, they shall sing this antiphon: *Surrexit Dominus de sepulchre*. They shall then lay the linen on the altar. When the antiphon is finished, the prior, rejoicing in the triumph of our King in that he has conquered death and was risen, shall give out the hymn *Te Deum Laudamus*, and thereupon all the bells shall peal.[37]

In the eleventh century, liturgical drama took a further step forward with the production of Christmas plays, all modelled on the *Quem Quaeritis*, their subjects being either the visit of the shepherds or the adoration of the magi, the former attached to the introit of the Christmas mass and the latter most frequently to matins at Epiphany.[38] In the course of time a whole series of episodes, including complex resurrection plays, were developed, but these were not regarded as separate entities, rather they were parts of a single cycle based on the propers, which found their unity against the background of the Church's year. The dramatization of the propers enabled them to correspond with the dramatic character of the ordinary, and the whole was integrated so that the proper was not seen as an alien intrusion. But at the same time a movement was taking place from ceremony to representation and this allowed the introduction of more historical elements, with a consequent elaboration of the scene or scenes, and a simultaneous pruning of the ceremonial associations, which ultimately issued in their being detached from direct connection with the liturgy.

At some point before the middle of the twelfth century, this liturgical drama divided into two branches. The first advanced in the direction of complex Latin plays, preserving ceremonial features and a ritual dramatic structure. The second developed into vernacular plays, such as the two twelfth-century Anglo-Norman texts, the *Mystère d'adam* and the *Resurrecion*, which are fully representational and independent of the liturgy with certain non-dramatic sources.[39]

The existence of tenth- and eleventh-century manuscripts reveals play acting in churches; notices of the actual performances are somewhat later. In 1180 William Fitzstephen referred to the popularity of religious drama in the London churches of his day.[40] Many of his contemporaries viewed this with disfavour, presumably having in mind the vernacular rather than the liturgical plays. Herrad von Landsberg, abbess from 1167–95 of Hohenburg, near Strasbourg, deplored the general lowering of standards:

The old Fathers of the Church, in order to strengthen the belief of the faithful and to attract the unbeliever by this manner of religious service, rightly instituted at the Feast of Epiphany or the Octave religious performances of such a kind as the star guiding the Magi to the new-born Christ, the cruelty of Herod, the dispatch of the soldiers, the lying-in of the Blessed Virgin, the angel warning the Magi not to return to Herod, and other events of the birth of Christ. But what nowadays happens in many churches? Not a customary ritual, not an act of reverence, but one of irreligion and extravagance conducted with all the licence of youth. The priests, having changed their clothes, go forth as a troop of warriors; there is no distinction between priest and warrior to be marked. At an unfitting gathering of priests and laymen the church is desecrated by feasting and drinking, buffoonery, unbecoming jokes, plays, the clang of weapons, the presence of shameless wenches, the vanities of the world, and all sorts of disorder. Rarely does such a gathering break up without quarrelling.[41]

While Herrad had no objection to the old liturgical plays, even these were frowned upon by Gerhoh of Reichersberg who, in 1161, attacked the clergy who turned their churches into theatres, and his condemnation embraced the Nativity cycle.[42] In sympathy with this was Archbishop John Thoresby of York, the second of whose constitutions, issued in 1363, reads:

Whereas some, being turned to a reprobate sense, meet in churches on the vigils of saints, and offend very grievously against God and his saints, whom they pretend to venerate, by minding hurtful plays and vanities, and sometime what is worse; and in the exsequies of the dead turn the house of mourning and prayer into the house of laughter and excess, to the great peril of their own souls—we strictly forbid any that come to such vigils and exsequies, especially in churches, to exercise in any such way plays and uncleannesses.—And we strictly enjoin all rectors, etc. that they forbid and restrain all such insolencies and excesses from being committed in their churches and churchyards by the sentence of suspension and excommunication according to the canon.[43]

Nevertheless, from the fifteenth and early sixteenth centuries there are many notices of plays in churches, although frequently it is impossible to determine whether they were exclusively liturgical or not. Some of these notices simply state that the plays were in church, others are more explicit as to the actual part of the building used.

At St Mary's, Stamford, in the year 1427, the wardens paid six-pence to the 'players' and this was probably for a Corpus Christi play in the north chancel.[44] From 1444 onwards the accounts of St Margaret's, Southwark—a building that was eventually pulled down when the parish was amalgamated with that of St Mary Overy—record annual performances on the day of the patron saint and sometimes an additional one on St Lucy's Day.[45] In 1469, according to the archdeacon of Josas, the play of St Sebastian was rehearsed in the chapel of St Vrain (Seine-et-Oise)[46] and in the same year the cathedral chapter of Lincoln paid for a play of the Assumption on St Anne's Day in the nave.[47] In 1474, according to the corporation manuscript of Rye, the actors of Romney performed in the church, and in 1476, on the day of the Purification, the Winchelsea players were there.[48] In 1479 there was a Christmas play at Yarmouth[49] and in St John's, Peterborough.[50] On Whit Monday, 1483, a performance was given in one of the churches of Colchester[51] and in the same year there was a repeat of the Assumption play in the nave of Lincoln cathedral.[52] The choir of St Edmund's, Sarum, was used for 'plays in the summertime' in 1490,[53] while of St Mary's, Leicester, in 1491, it is simply recorded that there was a performance on New Year's Day 'at Even in the Church'[54] and there is an identical entry for 1492 in the accounts of St Martin's, Leicester.[55] In 1499 St Mary's had moved its play to the Sunday in the octave of the Epiphany.[56] In 1518 the *Quem Quaeritis* was presented in

Magdalen College Chapel.[57] On Christmas Day, 1522, a play of the Nativity was acted in the chapel of the Earl of Northumberland at Leconfield, Yorkshire.[58] A play of St Swithun is noted in St Michael's, Braintree, Essex, 'acted in the Church on a Wednesday' in 1523 and two years later a play of St Andrew in the same building,[59] and another performance is recorded in Halstead Church, Essex.[60] In All Hallows, London Wall, a play was staged in 1528 to raise money for a new aisle.[61]

This evidence shows that plays were staged in chancels, choirs, side chapels and naves. Their setting could, of course, be quite simple; it could also be elaborate. For the Easter play a sepulchre was required; if in some churches this was no more than a chaste niche, in St Mary's, Redcliffe, Bristol, it was most ornate. On 4th July 1470, the wardens received

a new Sepulchre, well gilt with fine gold; an image of God Almighty rising out of the same Sepulchre, with all the ordinance that longeth thereto; that is to say, a lath made of timber and iron work thereto. Item, hereto longeth Heaven, made of timber and stained cloths. Item, Hell made of timber and iron work thereto, with Devils the number of thirteen. Item, for knights armed, keeping the Sepulchre, with their weapons in their hands; that is to say, two spears, two axes, with two shields. Item, four pair of Angel's wings, for four Angels, made of timber, and well painted. Item, the Father, the crown and visage, the ball with a cross upon it, well gilt with fine gold. Item, the Holy Ghost coming out of Heaven into the Sepulchre. Item, longeth to the four Angels, four Perukes.[62]

Examples of the elaborate structures, stage properties and mechanisms required for these plays have been collected by K. Young:

The representation of the *castellum* with its supper-table in some versions of the Peregrinus; the contrivance for raising the *imago Christi* in the dramatic ceremony of the Ascension; the tree for Zacchaeus, the tomb for Lazarus, the room for the Last Supper, the *sedes* for Mount Olivet, and the cross for the Crucifixion, in the Passion plays from Benediktbeuren; the furnace of Nebuchadnezzar, and the ass of Balaam, in the *Ordo Prophetorum* of Rouen; the device for lowering Saul from the walls of Damascus, in the *Conversio Sancti Pauli*; the carefully erected stages for the ceremony of the Presentation of the Blessed Virgin Mary; the kitchens and other *sedes* in the play of Isaac and Rebecca; the *lacus* for lions, and the arrangements for *regalia*, battles and pageantry in the plays of

Daniel; the church, and the contrivance for transporting Adeodatus, in the miracle play *Filius Getronis*; and the impressive deploying of platforms in the Antichrist. With the increase in the number, size and elaborateness of the *sedes*, probably the playing-space was extended from the choir of the church into the nave; and some plays, such as the *Ludus de Antichristo*, if played within the building must have taxed its entire resources.[63]

Even when plays were presented in the open air, their arrangements were often a reproduction of that which had been customary within the church building. There survives a plan of a sixteenth-century stage from Donaueschingen; this is divided into three distinct sectors corresponding to the sanctuary, choir and nave; heaven is at the far end occupying the place of the altar; the cross is where it would stand in the church and the sepulchre is in its normal position.[64]

As the Middle Ages came to an end, there were some straws in the wind to suggest what might be the possible future of drama in churches. A council of Seville in 1512 considered these plays and, while not condemning them as wrong in themselves, insisted that they were to take place only with special permission;[65] this was to become the official policy for the post-Tridentine Catholic Church. The Protestant attitude was adumbrated in the Wycliffite *Tretise of miraclis pleyinge* of the late fourteenth century, which affirmed that plays violated God's law and prevent Christian belief and that they are worldly[66]—the Puritan attitude thus had its clear forerunner.

## Defence and Guidance

While using their churches for recreation, Christians of the Middle Ages were well aware of the dangers that beset them and of their need for vigilance and protection. In particular, those who lived on sea coasts or near frontiers, such as the borders between Scotland and England or England and Wales, were conscious of the possibility of attack from marauders, ready to plunder and to kill. Whereas many a lord had his fortified manor or castle, the homes of the common people were quite insufficient for defence. Consequently it was natural for the community to see in their church, with its stone walls and great tower or steeple, a possible stronghold within which they would be safe if any physical danger threatened. But more than this can be said: both the locations and the architecture of many churches are only explicable on the grounds that from the outset they were planned deliberately as strongholds to withstand brief onslaughts and even sustained siege.

As regards location, it is to be noted that many churches have been built on elevated sites, at some distance from the houses of the worshippers and in places often difficult of access. While some of these positions may be accounted for on the grounds of a vision of a saint instructing his devotees to build a shrine in his honour, it has to be recognized that the choice has often been determined by a concern for defence. The more isolated, elevated and hard to approach the building was, the greater was the chance of beating off attackers. So at Bishopstone, Sussex, the village lies in a chalk coomb but the church is on a hillock dominating the dwelling houses.[67]

The general disposition of numerous churches and their structure provide proof of their builders' intention to use them as the equivalents of castles. The churches at Pixley and at Aylton, Herefordshire, are both surrounded by moats—these can only have been for military protection. It was, however, the towers to which particular attention was given. Frequently they had no exterior entrance, e.g the church at Piddinghoe, Sussex, the tower of which was erected *c.* 1120 on rising ground above the river Ouse. It was evidently a watch-tower for pirates and was also capable of withstanding attack. When there were exterior doorways, they were protected by a portcullis, and in the tower of Bedake Church, near Richmond, Yorkshire, the groove is still to be seen. Alternatively, the doors could be strengthened and that at Great Salkeld, Cumberland, is not only massive but is plated with iron and has iron bars fitted on the inside. At Oystermouth, Glamorgan, the tower batters from the base, i.e. it slopes inwards and upwards; it is surmounted by battlements and most of the windows are simply slits. The tower of Newton Nottage, in the same area, has a row of massive corbels projecting two feet from its east face; these originally supported a covered wooden balcony from which missiles could be discharged. Square holes in the tower walls of Cheriton, also in Glamorgan, suggest that it too had once a similar fighting gallery. The round towers of Ireland, of which some seventy-six have survived, must have served a similar purpose.

There are also examples of the entire building being fortified. The church of Newton Arlosh in Cumberland, built by the Abbot of Holme Cultram in 1303, has a battlemented tower with slits just wide enough to allow the passage of arrows from within. The tower door is only two feet nine inches wide, and no window in any of the church walls is less than seven feet from the ground or more than one foot wide. Albi Cathedral, in southern France (Plate 4), was begun in 1277. It is an imposing mass of red brick, with a huge square west tower rising to two hundred and fifty-six feet having loophole windows and corner turrets—even the gateway has a brick tower to protect it. At Cuernavaca, in Mexico, work on the cathedral started in 1523, immediately after the conquest. Strong castellated walls reveal the intention of its Spanish builders to make it a haven of defence against the unpacified native population.

The evidence available is not confined to the location and architectural detail of certain churches and cathedrals; there are records of their actual use for defence. In 1127 the assassin of Charles the Good, Count of Flanders, sustained a siege in St Donatien, Bruges. In 1304 the men of Flanders blockaded the church of La Bassée (Pas-de-Calais) and in 1428 the defenders of the church of Rouvray-Saint-Denis (Eure-et-Loire) surrendered to the Earl of Shrewsbury. The following year the pope granted indulgences for the rebuilding of the fortified church by the inhabitants of Saint-Etienne, near Boulogne.[68]*

Two of the features that made towers suitable for defence, i.e. their height and their occupation of elevated positions, also rendered them serviceable as landmarks. On dark and stormy nights beacons were lit on their summits, e.g. the chapel of St Adhelm on St Alban's Head, Dorset.[69] The Merchant Adventurers of Bristol actually built the tower of Dundry, Somerset, to fulfil this purpose.[70] The subsidiary tower on the north side of the chancel at Blakeney, Norfolk, was also formerly employed for a beacon, while the tower of St Nicholas, Newcastle-upon-Tyne, served to guide travellers across the moor.

There can be no question that in the Middle Ages the church was an all-purpose building. It is difficult to think of any secular activity that had no connection with it. If people wanted to go from one place to another, they were quite prepared to make a thoroughfare of the church. So in 1378 there was a complaint regarding an illegal restriction of the right of way through St Michael le Quern, London, it being stated that 'the old door should stand open for the common passage of the people through the said Church during the day'.[71] If a king had to make arrangements for his army, the church was liable to serve as a centre for the operation. So in 1166 Henry II issued a royal mandate requiring chests to be placed in all churches for deposits for a crusade.[72] In 1418 there was a proclamation concerning men and supplies for the war in Normandy. Men were to appear before certain named persons in St Dunstan's-in-the-East, London, to declare how much food they could provide, and those who were to serve in the army had to attend for instructions where they were to board ship.[73]

In all, there was no conscious irreverence. The church was a home from home, where people could sleep, live, eat, drink, play, act and meet. It was part and parcel of everyday life; it was there to be used and used it was. Its decorations reflected the pursuits and home life of the parishioners, as when carvings represented a quarrel between husband and wife, or the ugly spectacle of a bear-baiting. The style might change from Romanesque to Gothic and churches might grow larger as aisles and chapels were added to them, but their use was constant and increasing. There was ample space for every activity, since it was only towards the end of the period under review that fixed pews on any large scale were introduced. Sacred and secular were united and while excesses were perpetrated, what made them condemnable was not the place but the excesses themselves. We are bound to conclude therefore that a knowledge of the liturgy alone is insufficient to describe the use of medieval churches —this was one important facet, but only one of many activities in these multi-purpose buildings. Except when they were isolated for reasons of defence, they nestled in the centres of towns and villages, closely related to the surrounding houses and shops and proclaiming in this way the integration of the whole of life in Christ.

# 4

# Attitudes and Buildings

ALTHOUGH THE history of the use of churches in the patristic and medieval periods involves a mass of complex detail, there was throughout these centuries one important unifying aspect—all these buildings belonged to one Church and were regarded in the same light. Because of the relative homogeneity of western social and cultural life, because of the existence of Western Christendom, it has been reasonable to assume that what took place in Cornwall or Yorkshire would have its parallels in Provence or Saxony—and indeed such was the case. With the Reformation, however, the situation changed drastically. There was no longer one Church but several divided Churches. There was no longer one single type of church building. The attitude to churches ceased to be uniform. The contrast, for example, between the Roman Catholic understanding and the Quaker is immense and this difference in outlook led to differences in plans and uses. Consequently, before we can proceed with this history of secular activities, we must first familiarize ourselves with the post-Reformation attitudes towards church buildings and with their plans  which were in part the result of these contrasting approaches.

## I. ATTITUDES

The Roman Catholic understanding of the sacred space was unaffected by the intellectual turmoil of the sixteenth century. The ideas that a church is a holy shrine and that Solomon's Temple was its prototype, consistently held and taught throughout the Middle Ages, remained dominant. Thus Cardinal Bellarmine in his *Disputations*, published between 1586 and 1593, maintained that the

plan of church buildings was a deliberate and proper imitation of
that of the Jerusalem Temple. Taking his point of departure from
the description in I Kings 6 and 7, which tells how the temple was
divided into the *debir*, or holy of holies, and the *hekal*, or holy place,
the Cardinal declared: 'in the likeness of Solomon's Temple, in
which there were atrium, holy place (*sancta*) and holy of holies
(*sancta sanctorum*), almost all churches have three parts'.[1] The
canonist Emmanuel Gonzalez equally asserted that 'the form of the
ancient church was like that of Solomon's Temple'.[2] The church
historian Cesare Baronius, in his *Annales Ecclesiastici* (1588–1607)
made the same identification,[3] and similarly Cardinal Bona.[4] So in
post-Tridentine thought the church was understood to be a holy
place, a space set apart for no other purpose than worship and
adoration.

The hold upon Roman Catholic thought of this concept, and the
extent to which it could be elaborated cannot be better illustrated
than from the pages of a book by J. B. Thiers published at the end
of the seventeenth century. In 1679 Thiers issued his study of
church porches. He was led to do this because of what he regarded
as a scandalous situation, viz., the use of them for the sale of goods.
To him this was a blasphemous profanation and he set out to
demonstrate that such had been the view of the leading ecclesiastical authorities throughout the ages. To historical precedent and the
quotation of synodal decrees, he added doctrinal comments. In this
connection his most important statement is the following:

I hold that it is necessary to distinguish different degrees of holiness
between the various parts of a church; and I have no doubt that the altar,
for example, is more holy than the rest of the sanctuary; that the sanctuary
is holier than the choir; that the choir is holier than the nave; and that the
nave is holier than the porch.[5]

It is a remarkable fact that these words can be exactly paralleled
in Jewish thought, as expressed in the *Tractate Kelim* of the *Mishnah*.
This states:

There are ten degrees of holiness. The Land of Israel is holier than any
other land. . . . The walled cities are still more holy. . . . Within the wall
of Jerusalem is still more holy. . . . The Court of Women is still more
holy. . . . The Court of the Israelites is still more holy. . . . The Court

of the Priests is still more holy. . . . Between the Porch and the Altar is still more holy, for none that has a blemish or whose hair is unloosed may enter there. The Sanctuary is still more holy, for none may enter therein with hands and feet unwashed. The Holy of Holies is still more holy, for none may enter therein save only the High Priest on the Day of Atonement.[6]

Whether Thiers knew of this passage, it is impossible now to ascertain; nor is it important. What is important is to recognize the two possibilities; either he was familiar with the *Mishnah* and saw nothing wrong in applying its categories to Christian churches, or he arrived at his conception independently of it but quite logically, since he began with the same premiss. The premiss was the idea of a specially holy temple set apart for worship. The Roman Catholic understanding and its affinity with that of Judaism are thus very clearly demonstrated.

If we move on towards the end of the period we are now surveying, we find the same outlook prevailing. Indeed Pugin, in *The Present State of Ecclesiastical Architecture in England*, 1843, shows that he was acquainted with the work of Thiers and speaks of him in the most laudatory terms.[7] Pugin supported Thiers' attack upon the sale of goods in church porches, and at the same time reveals that it was still going on in the middle of the nineteenth century:

> It cannot be urged in palliation of this great abuse, that the things sold are intended for holy purposes. The church has decreed that *nothing whatsoever shall be sold, either under the porches or within the edifice.* The dovesellers, whom our Lord cast out of the temple, traded only in *offerings*; and the profanation of the holy place is equally great by the traffic in candles, from which abuse so much scandal continually rises. We cannot, however, hope for any improvement in these respects from our foreign brethren, while they have so little feeling for the sanctity of the temple of God as to erect shoe stalls between the buttresses, and heap filth against the entrances, of the most glorious monuments of Christian antiquity. But we trust that English Catholic churches will at least be preserved from these horrible profanations.[8]

The reference in this paragraph to 'the sanctity of the temple of God' shows that Pugin accepted the prevailing Roman Catholic attitudes. Elsewhere in the same work he speaks of the sanctuary as the 'holy of Holies'; he discourses on the chancel screen and

I · The Christian Basilica: S. Sabina, Rome, 422–32

II · The Agape: Stucco Decoration in the Catacomb of S. Callisto, Rome, third century

III · The Agape: A Sculptured Relief in S. Ambrogio, Milan, ninth century

IV · A Cathedral Built for Defence: Albi, France, begun in 1277

V · The Classical Temple: The Temple of Cybele on the Palatine, 191 B.C.
Relief from a wall in the Villa Medici, Rome

VI · The Renaissance Temple: The Church at Maser by Palladio, 1580

VII · Baroque Theatrical Architecture: Michaelskirche, Berg-am-Lain,
1691–1766

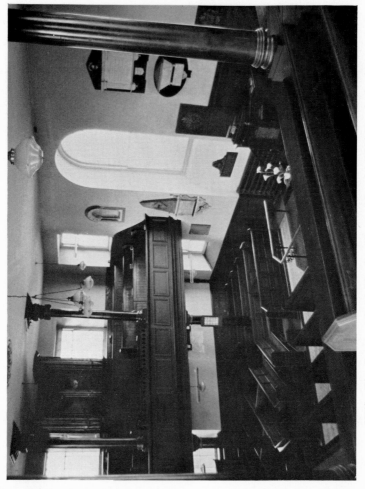

VIII · The Congregational Meeting House: Norwich 'Old Meeting', 1693

declares that 'from the earliest ages there has been a separation between priest and people, between a sacrifice and the worshippers, in every church'; indeed he calls the chancel 'the place of sacrifice, the most sacred part of the edifice'.[9]

Nearly forty years after Pugin published his work, another scholar was endorsing the same view. In 1881, A. Kempseneers issued *Le type des églises*. This was entirely devoted to proving the questionable thesis that the Jerusalem Temple and Christian churches belong to the same class of buildings and that the latter were derived from the former. Roman Catholic thought has thus remained largely unchanged for over 1,500 years, although its origins lie in the fourth century and not in the period of the pre-Nicene Church and of the New Testament. Nevertheless, criticisms of this general view are currently being voiced and there are those Roman Catholic writers who are prepared to affirm that churches must not be regarded as replicas of the Jerusalem Temple.[10] Indeed one can state: 'The New Testament puts us on our guard against a pagan conception and even against the pre-exilic Jewish conception of a habitation of God in a temple. The Lord cannot be circumscribed in a dwelling place made by the hand of man.'[11]

The official Anglican attitude was also inherited from the Middle Ages. It, too, continued to regard churches as holy shrines to be preserved from profanation. It is important, however, to note that this outlook was influenced not a little by that adopted by the Puritans. The more they attacked churches, and indeed they did not stop short of deliberately misusing them, the more Anglicans supported what had become the traditional concept. It is this Puritan onslaught, which will be considered below, that explains both the large number of statements and treatises on this subject and their increase as the clash moved towards its climax in the decade immediately preceding the outbreak of the Civil War.

The royal and episcopal injunctions issued during the opening stages of the English Reformation were concerned, *inter alia*, to prevent the desecration of churches, but the first comprehensive statement of the Anglican position was contained in the second *Book of Homilies* published under Elizabeth. These sermons, appointed to be read out during the service, were the product of the needs of the age. Because of the iconoclasm that had followed the reformed attack upon images, etc., and because of the disruption in English religious life, many people were now absenting themselves from the services of the Church and those who did attend were apparently guilty of unseemly and irreverent behaviour. The homily on 'The Right Use of the Church or Temple of God, and of the Reverence due to the Same' was written to cope with this situation. Its principal thesis is that a church is a holy place and must therefore be treated with respect. It begins by acknowledging that God does not dwell in temples made with hands and that the true temple is the community of Christians, but it goes on to assert that nevertheless a church is rightly to be understood as the house and temple of the Lord. This is supported by a series of biblical quotations, all of which are used on the assumption of the identity of temple and church, and passages referring to Jerusalem are applied to church buildings. A church is defined as a place where the word of God is read and taught, and this is based upon Jesus' own teaching in the Temple. The finding of the boy Jesus among the rabbis by Mary and Joseph is also used and the comment is made:

if we lack Jesus Christ, that is to say, the Saviour of our souls and bodies, we shall not find him in the market place, or in the guild hall, much less in the ale house or tavern amongst good fellows (as they call them), so soon as we shall find him in the temple, the Lord's house, amongst the teachers and preachers of his word, where indeed he is to be found.

It is clear that the author is aware that there may be some objections to this exegesis, and these he seeks to anticipate. So he quotes from II Cor. 6, about Christians being the temple of God, and says:

which sentence, although it be chiefly referred to the temple of the mind of the godly, yet, seeing that the similitude and pith of the argument is taken from the material temple, it enforceth that no ungodliness, specially of images or idols, may be suffered in the temple of God, which is the place of worshipping God.

The author is also prepared to admit that the Jews honoured their Temple superstitiously, but he seeks to turn this point by arguing that many of his contemporaries go to the opposite extreme and do not pay their temples sufficient respect. As to the behaviour which Christians should adopt in church, the homily quotes Lev. 19.30— 'Fear you with reverence my sanctuary'—and Psalm 5.7—'I will worship in thy holy temple in thy fear'—to inculcate reverence and humbleness of mind and uses the story of the Cleansing of the Temple to stress the need to keep churches free from 'wicked talk and covetous bargaining'.

There is another homily that is entitled 'For Repairing and Keeping Clean and Comely Adorning of Churches'. This is very much in the same vein as the one just considered. It bases its exhortation upon Old Testament precedent and in particular upon the accounts of the repairs done to the Temple. It asks: 'Why then ought not Christian people to hold their temples and churches, having as great promises of the presence of God as ever had Solomon for the material temple which he did build?' It acknowledges that 'the church or temple is counted or called holy, yet not of itself, but because God's people resorting thereunto are holy, and exercise themselves in holy and heavenly things'. If we enquire what these holy and heavenly things are, we are told the honouring of God, the hearing of his word and the celebration of the sacraments. Churches, therefore, are 'dedicated and appointed to these godly uses, and utterly exempted from all filthy, profane, and worldly uses'. A church instead is 'the house of prayer, not the house of talking, of walking, of brawling, of minstrelsy, of hawks, of dogs'.

Before finally leaving this second book of homilies, we must take note of another address on 'The place and Time of Prayer'. This argues that the parish church is the proper place, and so it can even say that the tabernacle in the wilderness was 'as it were the parish church', and of the Temple it declares that it too 'was the parish church, the mother church of all Jewry'. This anachronistic identification is supported by a catena of Old Testament passages about the Temple and its cultus applied to churches and their services.

The position outlined in these statements is a cautious one. That the Church, as the Christian community, is the primary reality is stressed; that the temple is also, in the first instance, the body of the faithful is recognized. Further, it is acknowledged that a church is not holy in itself, but has a derived holiness from both the people who use it and the sacred uses to which they put it. In later Anglican utterances this judicious discrimination was not always to be observed, although, as is to be expected, Richard Hooker wrote along the same lines.

According to Hooker, 'solemn duties of public service done unto God must have their places set and prepared in such sort as beseemeth actions of that regard'.[12] He then proceeds to argue that this principle can be illustrated from the building of the Temple. He acknowledges that the early Christians had no special places but contends that this was on account of the persecutions, and that when they could build, they did so; hence, after the conversion of Constantine, 'temples were in all places erected'.

To appreciate Hooker's position further we have to take account —even though this is an anticipation—of two Puritan objections which he chose to counter. The Puritans were scornful of dedication ceremonies and they were critical of the plans of contemporary churches on the grounds that they imitated Solomon's Temple and therefore were evidence of a lapse into Judaism. Hooker sought to answer the first point by affirming that dedication ceremonies had a long history and were in themselves unobjectionable. Further, he asks, 'Can we judge it a thing seemly for any man to go about the building of an house to the God of heaven with no other appearance, than if his end were to rear up a kitchen or a parlour for his own use?' Services of dedication, according to him, are 'to testify that we make them places of public resort, that we invest God himself with them, that we sever them from common use'. To the charge of Judaism, he replies that a church is not exactly the same as the Jerusalem Temple because the latter had far more divisions and sections; but, in any case, 'so far forth as our churches and their temple have one end, what should let but they may lawfully have one form?' On the sanctity of churches, Hooker had this to say: 'churches receive as every thing else their chief perfection from the end whereunto they serve. Which end being the public worship of God, they are in this consideration houses of greater dignity than any provided for meaner purposes'. Hence, while worship can be offered anywhere, churches are the normal places which by their 'very majesty and holiness' assist devotion.[13]

The Anglican attitude, at the beginning of the seventeenth century, can therefore be summarized to this effect; a church is a house
of God; it is a holy place; it is primarily for worship; it should be
preserved from profanation by not being put to secular use. This
was the view of William Laud, in contrast to that of the Puritans,
and the controversy to which it gave rise, as the Puritans increased
in numbers, centred in the position and railing off of the altar.

During the first years of Elizabeth it was customary to keep the
altar at the east end of the church, and to move it out into the
chancel for the communion service, the worshippers coming up
and grouping themselves about it when they brought their alms;
afterwards it was replaced in its previous position. Since, however,
Elizabethan communion tables were heavy objects, the tendency
was to leave them permanently in the middle of the choir. So in the
latter part of Elizabeth's reign and under James I altars were placed,
not only during communion but at all times, in the nave or at the
lower end of the chancel, and not near the east wall.[14] Only in the
Chapel Royal and in certain cathedrals did the altar stand permanently against the east wall, not even being moved for the
eucharist.

Laud was not happy about this general situation, since to his
mind it led all too easily to a disregard for the altar and to its profanation. As soon as he obtained a position of authority, he sought
to change the practice. So in 1616, immediately after being made
dean of Gloucester, he required the transference of the altar from
'the middest of the Quire' to the east end against the wall.[15] Being
in control, as dean of the cathedral, his order was executed, but he
had to wait several years more before he was in a position to exercise
any wider authority. When he became Bishop of St David's in 1621,
the way was open for him to take further steps throughout his new
diocese, and so the following year he included in his articles the
question: 'Whether is the same table placed in convenient sort within
the chancel; and whether it is so used out of time of divine service,
as is not agreeable to the holy use of it, and by sitting on it, throwing
hats on it, writing on it, or is it abused to other profane uses?'[16]

In 1626 Laud was translated to Bath and Wells and two years later
to London. His visitation articles for the latter diocese, in the year

of his appointment, contain the same questions.[17] But he was fully aware that, even after becoming Archbishop of Canterbury in 1633, he had no legal basis for the implementation of his wishes regarding the location and railing in of the altar. Even as late as 1636 we find him writing to the king in his annual account of his province and referring to the difficulty the Bishop of Lincoln was experiencing in putting the Laudian policy into effect. Laud comments:

Now because this is not regulated by any canon of the Church, his lordship is an humble suitor that he may have directions herein. And truly, I think for this particular, that people will best be won by the decency of the thing itself; and that I suppose may be compassed in a short time. But if your majesty shall think fit, that a quicker way be held, I shall humbly submit.

The king's reply was :'Try your way for some time.'[18]

Laud had in fact been trying more than this way ever since the decision in 1633 concerning St Gregory's-by-St Paul's. The dean and chapter of the cathedral had directed that the altar should be placed against the east wall; five parishioners objected and appealed to the Court of Arches. Laud had the case discussed by the Privy Council, which directed the Dean of Arches to confirm what had been done. So the way was open for steady pressure if not for legal enforcement. Determined efforts were now made by all the supporters of Laud to execute his plans. In 1634 Laud entrusted his vicar-general, Sir Nathaniel Brent, with a visitation of his province and gave him private instructions to command all churchwardens 'to place the Communion Table under the Eastern Wall of the Chancel, where formerly the Altar stood; to set a decent Rail before it to avoid profanation; and at the Rail the communicants to receive the blessed Sacrament'.[19] Pierce of Bath and Wells and Montague of Norwich adopted the same policy and Laud himself went steadily on. In his articles for the deanery of Shorham in 1637, we find him enquiring about the altar, whether there is any 'sitting, leaning, throwing of hats or writing thereon, and whether the parishioners make any assembly thereat, which is not agreeable to the holy end for which it was ordained'.[20] To the king he reported a very ill accident on Christmas Day 1638, when a dog seized the loaf off the altar at Tadlow 'by reason of not having the communion table railed in, that it might be kept from profanation'.[21]* But resistance was increasing. His account of his province of 1639 includes the observation that 'many that were brought to good order for receiving of the holy communion, where the rails stood before the table, are now of late fallen off, and refuse to come up thither to receive. And the same is now commonly fallen out in divers other dioceses.'[22]

The only remedy seemed to be to give the Laudian policy the force of law and so in 1640 a canon was passed declaring that a church is 'the house of God, dedicated to his holy Worship' and that

because experience hath showed us, how irreverent the behaviour of many people is in many places, some leaning, others casting their hats, and some sitting upon, some standing at, and others sitting under the Communion Table in time of Divine Service; For the avoiding of these and the like abuses, it is thought meet and convenient by this present Synod, that the said Communion Table in all Churches or Chapels be decently severed with Rails to preserve them from such or worse profanations.[23]

The subsequent downfall of Laud was to render this enactment of non effect.

What lay behind Laud's insistence in the face of mounting opposition? From one aspect the archbishop was simply concerned with the orderly and seemly celebration of the communion service, but his interest in this was based upon his concept of the holiness of a church building. His concept may be illuminated from his actions at the consecration of St Catherine Creed in 1630. According to the unsympathetic account of William Prynne the service began with the singing of 'Open, open, ye everlasting doors, that the King of Glory may enter in'. Laud then knelt and declared: 'This place is holy, and this ground is holy: In the name of the Father, of the Son, and the Holy Ghost I pronounce it holy'; and then he took up some of the earth or dust and threw it up into the air. Next there was a procession into and round the church, the singing of psalms, prayers and readings. Laud is then said to have gone to the altar and to have 'pronounced many curses upon all those which should hereafter in any way profane that Holy and sacred place, by any Musters of Soldiers, or keeping any profane Law-courts, or carrying burdens through it'. Each curse had a contrasting blessing; there was a sermon and a dedication of the altar and its vessels.[24] At his trial

Laud denied that he had thrown dust in the air and that he had uttered any curses, but he did roundly declare that he had pronounced the place holy,

and that was in the solemn act itself of the consecration, according to the usual form in that behalf. And no man will deny but that there is a derivative and a relative holiness in places, as well as in vessels, and other things dedicated to the honour and service of God. Nor is anything more common in the Old Testament; and 'tis express in the New both for place and things. I Cor. 11.[25]

Within the church itself Laud regarded the altar as the most holy object. So in 1637, at the trial of Bastwick, Burton and Prynne before the Star Chamber, he declared:

This is the misery, it is superstition nowadays for any man to come with more reverence into a Church, than a tinker and his bitch come into an ale-house. The comparison is too homely, but my just indignation at the profaneness of the times makes me speak it. And you, my honourable Lords of the Garter, in your solemnities, you do your reverence, and to Almighty God, I doubt not; but yet is it *versus altare*, 'towards his Altar', as the greatest place of God's residence upon earth. I say the greatest, yea, greater than the pulpit; for there it is *Hoc est corpus meum*, 'This is my Body'; but in the pulpit it is at most but *Hoc est verbum meum*, 'This is my Word'.[26]

Pierce of Bath and Wells, who supported Laud, was inclined to use less theological and more practical arguments. He contended that with the altar at the east end there is more room in the chancel for the communicants and that the minister is more audible. But he also argued that 'there should be some difference between the placing of the Lord's Table in the Church, and the placing of a Man's Table in his House'.[27]

The pamphlet war was now hotting up. In 1637 John Pocklington published his *Altare Christianum*. He was prepared to argue that

the Church of God set itself to comply with the Church of the Jews in erecting, dedicating, consecrating Churches and Altars, ordaining of Priests and Levites, appointing and receiving of oblations, offering Sacrifices, and conforming Christ's Church to the true pattern thereof showed to Moses in the Mount, and lively presented in the Tabernacle and Temple.[28]

He was even ready to contend that Christians had their holy places from the very beginning:

Churches, I am well assured, they had in the Apostles' time, for the Saints of God to meet in at least every Lord's-day: made at first of private houses, dedicated by the Owners; and in such sort consecrated by the Apostles, and Bishops their Successors, to the Lord's service; that they could never more return to their former common use, to eat and drink, to lie down and sleep in; but were employed only for the worship of God.[29]

Pocklington's argument was of course historically incorrect, but it was taken up by others as the Anglican attitude hardened. In 1638 Joseph Mede issued his *Churches, that is, Appropriate Places for Christian Worship, both in, and ever since, the Apostles Time.* Apart from his lengthy and specious appeal to patristic precedent, Mede also put forward theological arguments, affirming that

as the divine Majesty itself is most sacred and incommunicable . . . so it is likewise a part of that honour we owe unto his most sacred, singular and incommunicable eminency, that the things wherewith he is served, should not be promiscuous and common, but appropriate and set apart to that end and purpose.[30]

In a second work—*The Reverence of God's House*, 1638—he stressed the similarity of church and Jerusalem Temple and went on to assert that

the House of God is the place set apart for his worship and service, and so hath peculiar Relation unto him: wherewith being invested, it becomes sacred and holy, not only whilst divine duties are performed therein, as some erroneously affirm, but as long as it is for such use.[31]

In the first of *Several Discourses concerning the Holiness of Churches* Mede took his argument about relation further. According to him there are three kinds of holiness: 1. Essential holiness, which belongs to God alone. 2. Holiness of integrity, which is a condition of righteousness and purity from sin. 3. Relative holiness, which is 'a state of Relation of peculiarity to Godward, either in respect of presence or propriety and dominion'. Churches have this third holiness; their holiness is relative since by consecrating them to God 'the propriety thereof becomes so his, as it is no longer ours'.[32]

On 8th September 1638, at Kingston-on-Thames, William

Hardwick delivered a visitation sermon, and this contained the following passage:

> There is a conclusion highly cried up amongst us and which hath oftentimes been objected to me, and it is this: That Churches are none other than ordinary and common places, but only in time of Divine Service. For my part, I confess ingenuously, I cannot but blush to hear such an unsavoury assertion to proceed from any mouth which makes a profession of Christ and Christian Religion. O Beloved! Shall we who are Christians belch out that against the House of God which never any pagan did against the Temple of his feigned Deity? Blessed Brethren! Are not these houses always separated to a holy use, set apart to a holy employment?[33]

Meanwhile Richard Montague of Norwich was prefacing each section of his visitation articles with a biblical quotation to emphasize the holiness of churches and their similarity to the Temple of Jerusalem. In connection with churches and churchyards he cited Haggai 1.4: 'Is it a time for you yourselves to dwell in your cieled houses, while this house lieth waste?' With reference to churchyards he used Joshua: 'Put off thy shoe from thy foot; for the place whereon thou standest is holy'.[34] He raised the question: 'Do your parishioners at their entrance within the Church doors use that comely and decent deportment which is fitting for God's house?'[35]

Montague's attitude to churches and their immediate surroundings was indeed typical of the leading Caroline divines. In the *Preces Privatae* of Lancelot Andrewes (d. 1626), first published in 1648, the prayer upon entering church is a skilful mosaic of Old Testament passages about the Temple.[36] This was to remain the general understanding after the Restoration. One example will suffice. In 1716 T. Bisse preached a sermon at the Rolls Chapel, in the course of which he said of the sanctuary:

> Now this is the most honourable place in the house of God, and is therefore separated from the lower and inferior part of the Church, answering to the Holy of Holies in the Jewish Tabernacle, which was severed by a veil from the Sanctuary: and the holy Table or Altar in the one answers to the Mercy-seat in the other.[37]

In the early nineteenth century Anglicans were convinced that a church is essentially a building set apart for worship. This became very evident in the course of the agitation from 1810 to 1818, which resulted in the passing of an act of parliament to finance and authorize those buildings which came to be known as the Commissioners' Churches. The Church of England, with its teaching on religion and morals, was regarded by many as the great bulwark against revolution, now much in the air because of the events in France. But the Industrial Revolution had led to a great increase in population and housing without a corresponding increase in church accommodation. So in 1815 a memorandum was addressed to the Prime Minister which spoke of 'the danger to which the constitution of this country both in church and state is exposed from the want of places of public worship, particularly for persons of the middle and lower classes'. It went on to argue that 'parliament alone can do it; and we conceive one of its chief duties to provide places of worship for the members of the established religion'.[38] The 1818 Act, under which the Church Building Commission was established, required the Commissioners to see that in every church erected under their authority 'the character be preserved, both externally and internally, of an ecclesiastical edifice for divine worship according to the rule of the united Church of England and Ireland'.[39]

The apotheosis of the sacralizing attitude was attained some twenty years later by the supporters of the Gothic Revival. To them a church is a temple and is a direct descendant of the one in Jerusalem. So they speak of the 'analogy between Jewish and Christian Institutions not only on matters of doctrine, but on minor points of arrangement and ceremonies'.[40] Of the sanctuary they can say: 'this part of the Christian temple answers to the Holy of Holies in the Jewish, being that of the immediate presence of Divinity, even beyond the rest of the consecrated structure'.[41] Hence 'there are two parts, and only two parts, which are absolutely essential to a church: chancel and nave'.[42] This overruling consideration determines the function and interior arrangement. 'We believe that the parting off of a Holy of Holies by the symbolical veil is the main characteristic of the Tabernacle; and this type is preserved in the Rood-screen of a Christian church.'[43] Nevertheless the ecclesiologists were not in favour of altar rails, but their reason for rejecting them exemplifies

their attitude also. They acknowledged that they had been introduced by Laud but commented that

the horrible profanities which occasioned that injunction having ceased,
there seems no reason why we should not return to the primitive arrangement, leaving the Altar to be defended by the reverence of the worshippers
rather than by so ugly and inconvenient a fence.[44]

Above all a church, to the ecclesiologist, is a shrine of the divine
presence. So churchwardens are reminded of their privilege 'in being
allowed to watch over God's earthly dwelling-place'. They are
warned against the 'sin of ill-using God's chosen abode';[45] indeed
the 'unnecessary mutilation of the building is an offence against' God
himself,[46] for a church is 'the House of Him who gave us all we
have'; it is 'the holy House where God Himself deigns to dwell';[47]
it is 'the glorious Throne on earth of the Most High'.[48] The ecclesiologists were therefore prepared to repudiate one aspect of previous
Anglican teaching, viz. that the holiness of a church is relative and
derives from its use by a holy people. They declared instead: 'surely
the presence of a congregation cannot make the place holy: but He
is always present, in Whose sight even angels hide their faces'.[49]

In common with the Roman Catholics, they accepted degrees of
holiness, and so the chancel is 'the most sacred part of the edifice'.[50]
Indeed 'that no layman *ought* to enter altar rails or chancel either, is
plain from ancient canons and immemorial usage'. So the influential
American architect, R. A. Cram, an ardent supporter of the Gothic
Revival, was prepared to affirm:

I need hardly say that the chancel and sanctuary are not only the most
sacred portions of a building consecrated to the service of God, but also
almost *the* church, the nave being but an adjunct of more or less size
provided for the shelter and convenience of worshippers.[51]

This attitude was the natural corollary of their basic position. To
the ecclesiologist every religion produces its own peculiar architectural style and the style that expresses the true nature of Christianity is the Gothic of the Decorated Period.[52] Further, only a
convinced Christian, holding the true faith, can be expected to pro-
duce or reproduce this style; indeed 'there cannot be a more painful
idea than that a separatist should be allowed to build a House of

God'.[53] The profession of church architect is as holy as the buildings he designs, and ideally he should not defile himself by undertaking secular ones. Since 'religion enters very largely into the principles of church architecture, a religious *ethos*, we repeat, is *essential* to a church architect'.[54] So the entire theory and practice of church building is placed firmly within the exclusive sphere of the holy. There is a sacred style for a sacred building planned by men set apart for this task and devoted to a sacred calling. The separation of sacred and secular could not be carried to more extreme lengths.

The ecclesiologists were nothing if not consistent in their ideas. They sought to rule out every activity other than the performance of the cultus. To churchwardens they said: 'Take care also to hinder parish-meetings from being held either in the vestry or in the church itself. The way in which holy buildings are sometimes profaned by those who never go into them at other times, is enough to make the very stones cry out.'[55] Not even school teaching was to be accommodated, since 'it is turning a consecrated edifice to a profane use. The fabrick of the church should be reserved only for the holiest associations.'[56]

Amidst this united chorus only one discordant note was sounded and this was soon drowned. In the third volume of the *Ecclesiologist* (New Series), there was printed an article on 'The Uses of Churches'.[57] The author shares most of his contemporaries' views. He is convinced that the chancel is the most sacred place and is not to be profaned; he is emphatic that daily prayer and the celebration of the sacraments are the principal activities to take place in the building. He objects to oratorios, contending that they turn 'the House of God into a mercantile speculation', and he suggests that the way to displace them is to restore choral services of beauty. Nevertheless, he points out that in ages past the nave was the scene of a variety of activities and that those that 'can be traced to a praiseworthy or innocent original should not be put aside because they bear a strange appearance now'. So he can commend 'Councils, Synods, Convocations, Visitations, trials for ecclesiastical offences and (we would suggest) meetings of a more modern and familiar kind, when such are conducted exclusively by members of the

Church, and for objects solely of religion or charity'. His final plea
is as follows:

> May we not conclude on the whole, that, theoretically speaking, our
> churches might be used for other purposes than those to which we now
> confine them, and if in any of those things which may be generally
> acknowledged to be right, the objection be interposed, that our manners
> and customs are unsuitable, what is wanted, but that we should pursue
> these good objects, with more of reverence and recollection, and more
> habitually keep present in our minds the remembrance of the Presence in
> which all acts are performed? A feeling which could not fail to be strength-
> ened by the other and purely sacred uses to which the building has been
> dedicated. While the prayers and the blessing with which all such assem-
> blies should be begun and closed, suited to the sermon or the ecclesiastical
> proceedings, or the religious meeting, would render the view complete, by
> showing the business or the teaching to be only as it were one act of the
> service, while the direct appeal to religion would shed a hallowing influence
> over the whole proceeding.

It is quite astonishing to find such an essay published in the
*Ecclesiologist*, since it runs so counter to the official opinion. Its
challenge was avoided by simply ignoring it—always the most effective means of dealing with anything that questions or might disturb
the *status quo*. The pontifications of the ecclesiologists were accepted
and Anglicans adopted a uniform attitude to churches. They
accepted the view that 'a church is a building in which to do work,
and the work to be done there is to carry out the distinctive worship
of the body to which it belongs'.[58] J. C. Jeaffreson spoke for all when
he said that his contemporaries assumed that churches were required
solely for the purposes of public worship:

> We regard any introduction of secular interests within the walls of our
> churches as an act of impiety. . . . We forbid our temples to be used for
> any but religious purposes and spiritual ends. . . . In our commendable
> zeal to protect our holy places from profanation, we attach such sanctity
> to their very precincts as to think them no fit spots for mere diversion.[59]

This Anglican attitude, as previously noted, arose in part from an
initial reaction to that of the Puritans who, in their turn had been
influenced by the ideas of Calvin. The Puritan position, as far as it
affected church buildings, was based upon three principles: first,
any practice, other than what is explicitly prescribed in Scripture, is

heathenish; second, any survival of pre-Reformation ritual and ceremonial is popery and is therefore abominable idolatry; third, any
imitation of Judaism is to be condemned. Since they could find no
reference to consecrated Christian buildings in the New Testament,
they were led by their first principle to reject them. Their refusal to
continue any practice from the Middle Ages meant that they condemned consecration rites. Their concern about the reintroduction
of Judaism made them repudiate any connection between church
buildings and the Jerusalem Temple, or, alternatively, to declare
that if there was any connection this proved that church buildings
should be destroyed.

The Puritans were neither always consistent nor reasonable in
their arguments. They would have nothing to do with the Church-
ing of Women because 'it smelleth of Jewish purification',[60] and yet
they were prepared to transfer the entire Jewish sabbath legislation
to the Christian Sunday. Their insistence upon scriptural precedent
for everything they taught or did failed to take account of the historical conditioning of the documents they regarded as authoritative. Yet at the same time one cannot deny that in certain respects
they were nearer to the original meaning of the New Testament than
many of their opponents. So they refused to accept a dichotomy
between worship and life. They will maintain, reports a seventeenth-
century writer, that 'there is no more holiness in the church than in
their kitchen, nor in the Lord's table than in a dresser-board'.[61]

The Puritan attitude to the church, its furniture and the ceremonies associated with it may be illustrated both by word and deed.
In the letter of Thomas Beza, appended to the *Admonition to Parliament* of 1572, we find the statement: 'they ought to have considered, that the abolishing of the Ceremonies of Moses by little and
little, was not to set them up again in time by another pretence'.[62]
From this standpoint they questioned the consecration of churches,
which in any case they deemed houses of idolatry. According to
Beza again:

A simple and common furniture pleased them not, nor was agreeable,
therefore they sought out marble, they gilded walls, they provided vessels
of gold and silver, and their ministers began to be attired in precious and
Bishoplike, yea, and Emperorlike garments, and all forsooth to honour

the sacrament with all. As so forthwith these were the means and instruments to foster and cherish riotousness, to neglect true charity, and to be short, to bring in foolish and stagelike furniture.[63]

So we find them attacking the use of a font. Thomas Cartwright argued that it was not mentioned in Scripture, that it had popish associations and had indeed been 'invented by Pope Pius'.[64] Those of his persuasion among the Anglican clergy studiously refused to employ the font for baptisms and substituted basins—throughout the Elizabethan period they were under constant attack from the ecclesiastical authorities for this defiance of the royal injunctions.[65] The Puritans, however, steadfastly refused to endorse the concept of specially holy objects or spaces. We find this being put into practice, for example, by a Puritan layman named James Brooke.

James Brooke had a house behind the church of St Martin in Coney Street, York, next to the churchyard. Wishing to carry out some repairs and alterations to his property, he asked the vicar and churchwardens if some carpentry might be done in the churchyard. The wardens were agreeable but the vicar only gave qualified assent. In 1635–6 Brooke was cited before the Chancery Court for desecration and was in fact condemned. He, of course, saw nothing untoward in his action, while the Anglican authorities, whose approach was different, regarded him as guilty of profanation.[66]

Some five years after the hearing of this case, in 1641, the Puritans, now moving towards their ascendance, drew up a series of charges against the Caroline divines. In these their attitude finds very clear expression. The Anglican leaders are accused of

attributing special holiness to places and things by their appointment and consecrations: as if without their consecration all things were unclean, nothing fit for holy uses: and being consecrated they may never admit of common uses, though lawful, publick, necessary and inoffensive; or, if by such polluted, they must be re-consecrated ere used.

Attributing distinct degrees of holiness to several things by special consecrations. . . . To places, viz. to churchyards one degree, to churches more, and of churches, the Mothers or Cathedrals holier than others, the Metropolitans yet more holy: and in each church the navis or body holy, the chancel more, the place of the altar with the altar holiest of all.[67]

So the Anglicans were charged with holding a view identical with that of the Roman Catholics, in particular as enunciated by Thiers and previously quoted, and the Puritans, by implication, assumed a position at the opposite extreme.

No sooner had they seized power in England than they vented their spleen upon the existing church buildings. At first this was aimed at separate items of the furniture, and it is not surprising to find that of those who went to fight the Scots in 1640, many of the Puritan-minded soldiers took the opportunity to enter churches and drag the altar rails outside.[68] The font was equally an object to be mishandled or otherwise disdained, and so in 1644 we hear of a Captain Beaumont and soldiers christening a colt in the font of Yaxley Church (Huntingdon).[69] Determined to show that no building can be regarded as more sacred than another and that they had no respect for consecrated churches, the Puritans deliberately used them for the most menial purposes. The Earl of Essex, who had espoused the Roundhead cause, defaced the cathedral of Worcester on 24th September 1642, stabled his horses in it and kept fires alight and companies of guards in the nave. At Lichfield the soldiers amused themselves by hunting a cat with hounds daily through the cathedral. At St Asaph, the postmaster kept his horses and oxen in the nave, his calves in the choir and removed the font to his garden to serve as a hog trough.[70] Churches became prisons: on the lead font of Burford (Oxon.) are scratched the words 'Antony Sedley, Prisner, 1649'.[71] The following year Durham cathedral was a prison for the Scots, 4,500 being confined there and most of them dying before their release.

These are of course all examples of secular uses, but they do not really fall within the scope of this survey, since they have no direct bearing upon the question of the relationship of the sacred and secular uses of church buildings. Unlike the medieval Christians, who united sacred and secular within their churches, the Puritans denied any relationship between them and expressed their attitude by actions which were deliberately offensive, not to say crude. The importance of these facts is simply that they are evidence of the Puritan attitude to consecrated buildings—what they preached, they practised, and in the *Directory for Public Worship* for 1644 they also formulated it:

As no place is capable of any holiness under pretence of whatsoever Dedication or Consecration, so neither is it subject to such pollution by any superstition formerly used and now laid aside, as may render it unlawful or inconvenient for Christians to meet together therein for the publique worship of God. And therefore we hold it requisite that the places of publique assembling for worship among us should be continued and imployed to that use.[72]

This statement represents a more balanced view than that held by their forebears in the sixteenth century. Then the Puritans had attacked churches as centres of idolatry and many had argued that to avoid a resurgence of this it was necessary to destroy buildings. John Knox, for example, is reported to have said that the best way to prevent rooks returning is to pull down their nests.[73] Now at least the Puritans were aware that the obverse of their view that places cannot be made holy was the equally valid concept that they cannot be desecrated.

Sharing the same platform on this issue with the Puritans were other Protestant groups in England, in particular the Brownists and the Quakers. One of the first of the former, who were later to be known as the Independents and as the Congregationalists, was Henry Barrow. Barrow wrote his *A Brief Discoverie of the False Church* in the Fleet prison in 1589–90 and it was published immediately at Dort in the Netherlands. A long section of this treatise is devoted to church building, and from this we see that Barrow shared the Puritan concept. He begins his attack by comparing Anglican churches with Jewish synagogues and with the Jerusalem Temple:

These synagogues are built altogether to the form of the old temple of the Jews, in a long square east and west, with their holy court walled round about, commonly called the churchyard, which is holy ground, and serveth for christian burial, being altogether exempt from civil use; yet it is lawful for the young men and maids to play there together upon their Sundays and holy days. But whoso smiteth any in that holy ground, by statute is to have his hand cut off therefore. These synagogues have also their battlements, and their porch adjoining to their church, not here to speak of the solemn laying the foundation; where the first stone must be laid by the hands of the bishop or his suffragan, with certain magical prayers, and holy water, and many other idolatrous rites. They have unto it their folding doors and an especial Levite, the parish clerk, to keep the

key. They have at the west end their hallowed bells, which are also baptized, sprinkled, etc. They have their aisles, and their body of the church:
they have also their cells to the sides of the walls, their vestry to keep the
priests' ministerial garments, where they are to attire and dress themselves before they go to their service: they have their treasury. All the
cathedral or mother churches also have their cloisters for their dean,
prebendaries, canons, petty canons, singing men and singing boys, etc.
within their precincts and wall to abide and dwell, that they keep the
watch of the temple, and their hours of orisons. Again they have in the
body of their church the hallowed font, to keep the holy water wherewith
to baptize, all other vessels and water to the use of baptism being by
express law forbidden. They have also their holiest of all, or chancel,
which peculiarly belongeth to the priest and choir, which help the priest
to say and sing his service. They have their roodloft as a partition between
their holy and holiest of all. The priest also hath a peculiar door into his
chancel, through which none might pass but himself. Now this church
thus reared up, is also throughly hallowed with their sprinkling water,
and dedicated and baptized into the name of some special saint or angel,
as to the patron and defender thereof, against all enemies, spirits, storms,
tempests, etc. Yet it hath within also the holy army of saints and angels in
their windows and walls, to keep it. Thus I think no doubt can be made,
but that the very erections of these synagogues (whether they were by the
heathens or papists) were idolatrous.[74]

So Barrow accepted and applied the second and third of the Puritan principles, viz. the identification of medieval survivals with
idolatry and the rejection of Jewish precedent. He then went on to
apply the first principle, viz. that that which is not approved and
certainly that which is condemned by Scripture is wrong, arguing
that since these churches are centres of idolatry, as defined by him,
they come under the condemnation of false worship so widespread
in the Old Testament.[75] Barrow was not primarily interested in
theological argument; his entire rejection of church buildings and
his appeal to have them destroyed arose out of his experience of the
facile restoration of Roman Catholic worship within those same
buildings under Mary. They were, to his mind, buildings erected
for a particular purpose, which he described as idolatrous worship;
they were therefore both a standing invitation to renew that worship
and a hindrance to what he regarded as true Christian devotion. He
perceived clearly the close connection between function and the
architectural provision made for it. He did not consider whether

the wholesale destruction he demanded was at all practicable in the circumstances.

The attitude of George Fox to church buildings was much more theological. Writing in his Journal under the year 1646, when he describes his early life and his divine call, Fox says:

> At another time it was opened in me, 'That God, who made the world, did not dwell in temples made with hands.' This at first seemed a strange word, because both priests and people used to call their temples or churches, dreadful places, holy ground, and the temples of God. But the Lord showed me clearly, that he did not dwell in these temples which men have commanded and set up, but in peoples' hearts; for both Stephen and the apostle Paul bare testimony, that he did not dwell in temples made with hands, nor even in that which he had once commanded to be built, since he put an end to it; but that his people were his temple, and he dwelt in them.[76]

Throughout his long and adventurous ministry Fox was to return time and again to this initial concept, and in his Journal the references are many. In 1651 he was at Mallon:

> The steeple-houses and pulpits were offensive to my mind, because both priests and people called them the house of God, and idolized them; reckoning that God dwelt there in the outward house. Whereas they should have looked for God and Christ to dwell in their hearts, and their bodies to be made temples of God; for the apostle said, 'God dwelleth not in temples made with hands.'[77]

Shortly afterwards he was at a town near Pickering and he referred to churches as 'idol temples', and in the course of an address he declared that 'the apostles going into the Jews' synagogue and temples, which God had commanded, was to bring people off from that temple, and those synagogues'. He was emphatic that 'that piece of ground was no more holy than another piece of ground. . . . I was sent of the Lord God of Heaven and earth to preach freely, and to bring people off from their outward temples made with hands, which God dwelleth not in; that they might know their bodies to become the temples of God and of Christ.'[78] At Patrington, where a professor bade him leave the church, he replied: 'Dost thou call the steeple-house the church? The church is the people, whom God hath purchased with his blood, and not the house.'[79]

The following year, at Dent, 'I opened to the people that that ground and houses was no holier than another place; and that that house was not the church, but the people, whom Christ is the head of.'[80] The same year, at Firbank Chapel, he preached on a hill:

I was moved to open to the people, that the steeple-house, and the ground whereon it stood, was no more holy than that mountain; and that those temples, which they call the dreadful houses of God, were not set up by the command of God and of Christ. . . . but that Christ was come, who ended both the temple and its worship. . . . I declared unto them that the Lord God had sent me to preach the everlasting gospel and word of life amongst them, and to bring them off from all these temples.[81]

Thirteen years later he was still maintaining the same position. In 1665 he had a discussion with a Dr Cradock:

'What dost thou call the church?' 'Why,' said he, 'that which you call the steeple-house.' Then I asked him, 'whether Christ shed his blood for the steeple-house; and purchased and sanctified the steeple-house with his blood? And seeing the church is Christ's bride and wife, and that he is the head of the church, dost thou think the steeple-house is Christ's wife and bride, and that he is the head of that old house, or his people?' 'No,' said he, 'Christ is the head of the people, and they are the church.' 'Then,' said I, 'but you have given the title, church, which belongeth to the people, to an old house, and you have taught people to believe so.'[82]

Although the attitude of these English Protestants was partly the result of their own study of the New Testament, they, and in particular the Puritans, were not uninfluenced by the ideas of the continental Reformers and it is to them that we must finally turn. We begin with Luther, as having chronological precedence, although Calvin had the most direct effect upon thinking in England.

Where Barrow was quite unrealistic in his demand for the destruction of all existing churches, Luther's attitude was based upon common sense. This is apparent from one of the earliest of the few passages in his voluminous works that he devoted to the subject, in his *Treatise on Usury* of 1520:

We would not prevent the building of suitable churches and the adornment of them, for we cannot do without them, and the worship of God ought rightly to be conducted in the finest way; but there should be a limit to it, and we should have care that the appointments of worship should be pure rather than costly.[83]

To Luther the question of church buildings was not primary; obviously some were needed for worship, but they were never the centre of his concern. Nevertheless the concept of holiness was a vital one for him, and in one of his sermons on this subject we can discover how he related this to the architectural setting of word and sacrament. The sermon opens with a description of the threefold division of the tabernacle into the holy of holies, the holy place and the forecourt. Luther then goes on:

This is doubtless the original form of our churches, which we also divide into three parts, viz. the forecourt, the church, and the chancel; of these the chancel is the most sacred, then the church, then the forecourt.[84]

So in 1521 Luther accepted the traditional idea of the origin of church plans and seems to have endorsed degrees of sanctity and the idea of a holy place; but in fact, as the development of his sermon makes clear, he was merely doing this as a didactic device, i.e. he started where the people were; he began with what was familiar to them; by the end of the sermon he had made it quite clear that he himself had no reverence for holy places but only for holy people and that he rejected the outward show for the inner reality:

All these matters are outward works, confined to clothes and places. . . . This shows how much their consciences are concerned with outer things, and how little with questions of moral values. . . . It has gone so far on account of certain blind teachers, that no layman dare actually touch the chalice. . . . No matter of clothes, food, places, or holy days makes anyone into a godly man.[85]

Luther therefore condemned those who found their religion in 'food and vestments, in holy places and holy days'. He spoke of humility, gentleness, peace, love, etc., and commented: 'These things have no necessary connection with food, clothing, holy places, holy days or personal position.'[86] The didactic device, on which the sermon is based, is the presentation of the threefold division of the tabernacle to illustrate three aspects of life, and Luther's thesis was that the forecourt is really outward show, the holy place may be no more than a mockery and that Christians must live in the holy of holies, i.e. under the daily guidance of the Holy Spirit.

It is further evident from this sermon that Luther was opposed to the consecration of objects and to the idea of specially holy things or places. So in the *Formula missae*, he accepted vestments as a matter of indifference, but objected to blessing them since he did not agree that this made them any more holy than other garments.[87] Entirely consistent with this was his later condemnation of the dedication of churches and altars as liable to corrupt the Christian faith.[88] Calvin, like Luther, began from a common sense point of view:

> As God by his word ordains common prayers for believers, so also ought there to be public temples wherein they may be performed . . . this is the lawful use of temples.[89]

Nevertheless, Calvin considered that there was a superstitious attitude towards churches which had to be counteracted in the interests of Christian truth:

> We must guard against taking them to be God's proper dwelling places, whence he may more nearly incline his ear to us—as they began to be regarded some centuries ago—or feigning for them some secret holiness or other, which would render prayer more sacred before God. For since we ourselves are God's true temples, if we would call upon God in his holy temple, we must pray within ourselves. Now let us leave this stupidity to Jews or pagans, for we have the commandment to call upon the Lord, without distinction of places, 'in spirit and in truth'. At God's command the temple had indeed been dedicated of old for offering prayers and sacrificial victims, but at that time the truth lay hidden, figuratively represented under such shadows; now, having been expressed to us in living reality, it does not allow us to cleave to any material temple. And not even to the Jews was the temple committed on the condition that they might shut up God's presence within its walls but in order that they might be trained to contemplate the likeness of the true temple.[90]

To Calvin, therefore, churches were necessary because of the need to provide for a community assembly, but he did not regard them as especially holy and they were certainly not, to his mind, to be called houses of God. Their importance then lay in their being places where the word could be preached; they are places where God makes himself known 'in the mirror of his teaching':

> Whatever temples the Gentiles built for God on any other principle were a mere profanation of his worship. To a degree the Jews fell into this, though not with such equal grossness. Stephen upbraided them in

the words of Isaiah: 'God dwells not in temples made with hands'. By his word, God alone sanctifies temples to himself for lawful use.[91]

Thus Calvin regarded churches as necessary in order to fill a certain function, i.e. to make provision for worship, with preaching as its central act. At the same time he was not prepared to countenance lavish expenditure upon such edifices, since any surplus money a Christian might have should go to the poor. This led him to condemn contemporary Roman Catholic practice as he saw it:

So far are they from taking due care of living temples that they would rather let many thousands of the poor die of hunger than break the smallest cup or cruet to relieve their need . . . they induce people by superstition to apply what should have been distributed to the poor, to constructing churches, erecting statues, buying vessels, and providing sacred vestments. Thus are daily alms consumed in this abyss.[92]

Hence the true centre of the Christian life is not to be sought in bricks and mortar. Worship is vital, but it is not dependent upon the buildings in which it is held. The presence of God is in the community and not in anything outside it. 'Where is the temple of God?' asked Calvin. 'There is Jesus Christ who fills the world, he is with us, and even dwells in our souls. . . . Our God does us the honour of appointing us to be sanctuaries and temples . . . each Christian bears the exalted title of sacrificer.'[93]

Calvin's theological understanding of a church logically allowed its use for secular purposes, and indeed in Switzerland itself, although not outside, Reformed churches have been employed for secular activities down to the present day.[94] But there were two other aspects of the Calvinist system that militated against this. The first was the minute regulation of everyday life which ruled out entirely the continuance of certain practices which had found a place in churches previously; the second was the definition of a church building entirely in terms of its liturgical function.

In the *Draft Ecclesiastical Ordinances* of 1541 there were condemned 'games forbidden by the law and scandalous dances and similar dissoluteness'.[95] In the *Ordinances for the Supervision of Churches in the Country* of 1547 there were forbidden 'carousels . . . songs that are unworthy, dissolute or outrageous . . . and spinning wildly round in the dance, or the like'.[96] The presentation of plays, too, was not in favour. The complete prohibition of these activities at any time and in any place, inside or outside church, immediately made an inroad upon the list of what took place in the medieval ecclesiastical buildings. Calvin further laid great emphasis upon sermons. He directed that there were to be sermons in the three main Geneva churches every Sunday at daybreak, at 'the usual hour' and at 3 p.m. On working days, there were to be three sermons, on Mondays, Tuesdays and Fridays in St Peter's, and two other addresses elsewhere during the week.[97] In country churches sermons were also prescribed and the 'buildings are to remain shut for the rest of the time in order that no one outside the hours may enter for superstitious reasons'.[98] So a Calvinist church was essentially a preaching house, although of course Calvin himself was also in favour of encouraging a regular celebration of the communion. With its function so clearly and narrowly defined, while a church could be used for legitimate non-liturgical activities, it was unlikely to be so, unless social conditions demanded it. To this day, Reformed churches, outside Switzerland, have remained exclusively centres of worship. The *temples* of the French Reformed Church, for example, are only open at the time of service and are never occupied or used for any other activity. With their precise system of discipline, the Calvinists were able to achieve what the medieval bishops had attempted in vain—the restriction of churches to liturgical gatherings. Although the theories were opposed, the practices that obtained or were envisaged became identical.

## 2. BUILDINGS

A church building is the product of many factors, liturgical, social, cultural, economic, etc. To examine all these would be to give a complete history of church architecture, and this is neither my intention nor does it lie within the scope of this study. But there is one influence to which attention must be given and that is the influence exercised by the attitudes outlined in the previous section. Those attitudes were not only formulated in books and pamphlets; they were also given architectural expression. Consequently, they can be

illuminated further by a description of some of the church buildings
of the centuries following the Reformation.

The Renaissance was a rebirth of classical culture, based upon a
careful study of the writings and ruins of ancient Rome coupled
with an imaginative recreation of that past era as a 'Golden Age' in
which consolation and refreshment could be sought.[99] The theoretical corner-stone of Renaissance architecture was laid by Leon
Battista Alberti (1404–72) in his *de Re Aedificatoria Libri Decem*. The
seventh book of this work is devoted entirely to churches, and from
both this and Alberti's own buildings we can discover the Renaissance attitude to churches and the forms that that attitude produced.
Alberti accepted without question the view that a church is a sacred
edifice. 'As for the temple,' he wrote, 'who can doubt that to be
sacred, as well for other reasons, as chiefly because we there pay the
due reverence and honour to God for those infinite obligations which
mankind has towards him?'[100] It should therefore not be profaned
by any secular use. 'As there is nothing in nature can be imagined
more holy or noble than our sacrifice, so I believe no man of sense
can be for having it debased by being made too common.'[101] As a
corollary of this Alberti declared that a church must be the most
beautiful of all the buildings in a city:

In the whole compass of the Art of building, there is nothing in which
we ought to employ more thought, care and diligence than in the laying
out and adorning a temple; because, not to mention that a temple well
built and handsomely adorned is the greatest and noblest ornament a city
can have; it is moreover the habitation of the Gods: and if we adorn and
beautify the house where a king or any great man is to dwell, with all the
art we are masters of, what ought we to do to those of the immortal Gods?
Whom we expect, when invoked, to be present at our sacrifices, and to
give ear to our prayers. And though the Gods may despise those perishable
things which we most highly value; yet men are moved by the purity of
beautiful materials, and raised by them to reverence and devotion for the
deity to which they are sacred. It is certain that temples may be of great
use for stirring up men to piety, by filling their minds with delight, and
entertaining them with admiration of their beauty. The ancients were
wont to say that piety was honoured when the temples were frequented.
For this reason I would have the temple made so beautiful that the
imagination should not be able to form an idea of any place more so; and
I would have every part so contrived and adorned, as to fill the beholders

with awe and amazement, at the consideration of so many noble and
excellent things, and almost force them to cry out with astonishment:
This place is certainly worthy of God![102]

Alberti also accepted the view that a church is a temple and that
consequently the temples of pagan Rome could be taken as models
for and prototypes of Christian buildings. He therefore devoted a
great deal of space to a description of these temples, of their proportions, their materials and their furnishings. He noted that archi-
traves were the norm and therefore inclined to have no arches in
church buildings.[103] He compared the pagan altars with the Christian ones. He sanctioned the display of objects of beauty within
churches to excite wonder and reverence by citing such examples as
the hanging up of Cupid's dart in the temple of Diana at Ephesus.[104]
Temples, as Alberti observed, could be either quadrilateral or circular, the latter embracing all those figures, such as octagon and
hexagon, that can be contained in a circle; hence churches should
have the same plan, although he favoured the centralized disposition,
because 'it is manifest that nature delights principally in round
figures'.[105] Since God is the creator of nature, the implicit idea is
that he has revealed his preference for the circle and hence the form
of his earthly habitation should be round.

Alberti was not only a theorist, he was a practising architect, and so
was able to implement his ideas. In S. Sebastiano, Mantua, begun in
1460, we have a completely centralized building, breaking with the
Gothic tradition of an elongated plan, and even S. Andrea, which
was started twelve years later, is really a centralized composition at
its east end with two bays added at the west to provide further space
and to present the shape of the Greek cross. Moreover, according to
Alberti himself, this latter building was based upon his own recon-
struction of an Etruscan temple, and writing to his patron Ludovic
Gonzaga, on 19th October 1470, he described the shape of the
church as 'called, after the ancients, *Etruscum sacrum*'.[106] It is
noticeable that he suppressed the aisles, which were unusual in
pagan temples, and replaced them with a series of side chapels,
connected with the nave alternately by tall and wide and low and
narrow openings (Fig. 5).

So Alberti gave remarkable architectural expression to the attitude that a church is a sacred shrine, the locus of the divine presence, and therefore belongs to the same genre of buildings as the temples of ancient Rome, the main distinction being that the pagan temples housed false gods whereas the Christian temple houses the one true God. A further example of the physical embodiment of the same concept is to be found in the S. Maria del Miracoli (1480–9), designed by Pietro Lombardo at Venice. This is simply a Greek temple, consisting of a single aisleless nave, with barrel vault roof and a raised sanctuary. But even before Alberti we find a Florentine architect, Michelozzo di Bartolommeo designing, *c*. 1444, a circular chapel in exact imitation of a Roman temple.

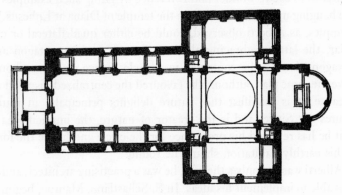

*Fig. 5   S. Andrea, Mantua, 1470*

If we move now to a later phase of the Renaissance, viz. to that known as Mannerism, and to the writings and work of Palladio we find essentially the same theory and practice. Like Alberti, Andrea Palladio (1518–80) published a treatise on architecture entitled *Quattro Libri dell'Architettura*, of which book four is entirely devoted to churches and to the study of the ancient temples. In his preface Palladio echoes Alberti in insisting that a church is the house of God and must therefore be of the greatest beauty:

If labour and industry are to be laid out upon any fabric, to the end that in all its parts it should have the exactest symmetry and proportion, this, without the least doubt, is to be practised in those temples wherein the most gracious and all-powerful God, the Creator, and giver of all things, ought to be adored by us; and in the best manner that our abilities may permit, be praised and thanked for such manifold favours as he continually bestows upon us. For if men, in the building of their own houses, use the utmost diligence to find out skilful and excellent architects, with other capable workmen, they are certainly obliged to be much more diligent in the building of churches; and if in the former their principal aim be convenience, so in the latter they ought to have regard to the dignity and greatness of him that in the same is to be invoked and worshipped.[107]

Palladio too shared Alberti's preference for the circular shape, because it is 'alone among all figures simple, uniform, equal, strong and most spacious . . . the extreme in every part being equally distant from the centre; it is, therefore, the most proper figure to show the unity, infinite essence, uniformity and justice of God'.[108]*

Palladio's buildings illustrate his theories. The façade of Il Redentore at Venice, begun in 1577, although it has certain original Palladian features, is recognizably similar to several of the temple fronts that he drew in his book. His little church at Maser (Plate 6) is circular and has the same proportions as the Pantheon; from its exterior it could easily be taken for a Roman temple.

Although Baroque architecture differs considerably from the classicism of the Renaissance, it too was influenced by the concept of the church as the house of God. But now, with the emergence of the national states, each with its own monarch having his court ceremonial and his magnificent apartments, the church became the divine palace. Since God is the King of Kings, ruler of heaven and earth, his residence has to display even more splendour than that which is lavished upon princes. Baroque was not simply the outcome of a taste for luxury which was to be seen in contemporary civic building; it was inspired by the desire to offer to God all the riches of the world, to gather together in the edifices consecrated to him and in which he resides all forms of beauty, sanctified by the sacred character of their function. The Baroque churches and cathedrals of Latin America, for example, were the direct product of this attitude. The mine and slave owners, who financed these buildings, were concerned to honour God by decorating his palaces with the greatest possible sumptuousness and at the same time to thank him for the treasures he had bestowed upon them. The liturgy itself was included within the same ambit of ideas. Just as an earthly king must be honoured daily by the pageant of court ceremonial, so also the heavenly King. The courtly atmosphere around him, as he was present in his churches, was to be provided by the liturgy, which, as many handbooks of the period actually say, was considered to be the 'etiquette of the great King'.[109] So worship was performed with a pomp, decorum and grandeur that corresponded to its architectural setting.

Nevertheless, if the Baroque architects considered the church to be a place set apart, a holy shrine to accommodate and to provide for the honouring of the heavenly King, this did not involve a complete divorce from secular culture. The chief artistic creation of that culture, and the most popular one, was the opera. Christians of the period sought to find a religious equivalent for this in the liturgy, and in the France of Louis XIV the Theatines were said to 'have sung a veritable opera in their church, to which the world goes with the intention of listening to the music'.[110] The buildings themselves came to resemble theatres in plan and decoration, so François Mansart copied the plan of the theatre of Marcellus.[111] S. Maria della Salute at Venice is a clear example. Designed by Baladassare Longhena and begun in 1631, it has the plan of an octagon surrounded by an ambulatory, thus showing the continued interest in a centralized disposition. Attached to this, but almost independent, is the sanctuary, beyond which is a third room, viz. a rectangular choir. Thus, while the altar remains the primary centre of the church, there is a scenic progression along the horizontal axis which derives from the stage (Fig. 6). S. Maria is in fact scenographic architecture and was the ideal setting for the liturgy as then understood. The church was the place for an 'occasion', similar to a *soirée* at court complete with a *divertissement* by Lully. The chief focus was no longer the mass but the exposition of the reserved sacrament. 'In the Presence of the Divine King, a kind of heavenly grand opera could be performed, with all the display of lights, jewels (mostly false), exquisite polyphonic singing and pageantry which commonly accompany a royal reception.'[112] In terms of the contemporary taste and culture, Baroque achieved the apotheosis of the architectural embodiment of the idea of a church as a shrine of the divine presence.

Neither the classicism of the Renaissance nor the exuberance of

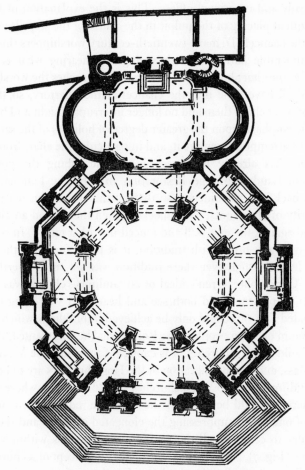

*Fig.* 6   S. Maria della Salute, Venice, 1631

the Baroque were to make a great impact upon Anglican church buildings, although the general attitude of the Church of England to churches was similar to that of the Church of Rome. For almost a hundred years after Luther had first sounded the call to reform, church building in England was virtually non-existent. Gothic buildings continued to be the norm, but were used with a recognition of the functional diversity of the parts. The one room, i.e. the sanctuary, served for the eucharist, and the other room, i.e. the nave, for the daily and occasional offices. This is the explanation of the not infrequent placing of the pulpit in the centre of the steps leading up into the chancel. To many twentieth-century worshippers this seems an intolerable barrier to their seeing and hearing what is taking place at the altar; but in post-Reformation churches the worshippers would all have gone into the chancel at the offertory, so that the pulpit was behind them and no longer interrupted sight and hearing.

The emphasis upon the greater degree of holiness of the sanctuary and the attempt to preserve it, and in particular the altar, from desecration, has already been recorded in describing the policy of William Laud. With the Restoration in 1660 the Laudian ideals came back into prominence, so that by the end of the century the majority of churchmen were shocked when they found an altar not placed against the east wall and fenced in with a rail.[113] In so far as there was any break with tradition, it is to be found in the Wren churches, although even there tradition was not really overthrown.

Sir Christopher Wren's ideal of an 'auditory' church was one in which all present could both see and hear what was going on. He estimated that this could only be achieved in buildings which held a maximum of 2,000 people. 'The Romanists,' he commented, 'indeed, may build larger Churches, it is enough if they hear the Murmur of the Mass, and see the Elevation of the Host, but ours are to be fitted for Auditories.'[114] So Wren churches should be places where liturgy and sermon could be followed; he therefore reduced their plans to that of one room, suppressing the elongated chancels and the aisles in order to comprise all the worshipping activities within a single volume (Fig. 7). Nevertheless, the medieval concept of a church still prevailed; the well-defined places for the various services were simply replaced by liturgical centres in an ascending order of importance—font, pulpit and altar.[115]

It cannot be said that any of these buildings embody the concept of a sacred space to the same extent as the churches of the Renaissance and Baroque architects. Contemporary records do show that they were regarded as holy shrines, but the determining factor in their planning was liturgical practice rather than a view of the location of the divine. Only in the nineteenth century did this attitude achieve visible expression and then not in the form that had become

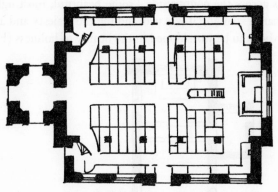

*Fig.* 7   St James, Piccadilly, 1684

traditional within Roman Catholicism. To the adherents of the Gothic Revival each religion produces its own supreme architectural form that best expresses its ethos and spirit. The temples of ancient Rome were not therefore to be imitated, since they were the expression of heathenism. Renaissance architecture, in so far as it looked back to these, was dismissed as 'pagan'. On the contrary it was Gothic that represented the full flowering and ideal embodiment of the Christian faith. A church then must be in the Gothic style and must be apart from all other buildings. It had to be divided into sections corresponding to the different degrees of holiness. So, according to Pugin, 'from the earliest days there has been a separation between priest and people, between the sacrifice and the worshippers, in every church'.[116] Hence chancel screens, corresponding to the veil in the Jerusalem Temple, were essential, as were elongated chancels. No new plan emerged from this—Victorian Anglican buildings are largely indistinguishable in this respect from their medieval predecessors. It was primarily because these were regarded as the sole proper form for a house of God that they were reproduced in their hundreds throughout the late nineteenth century. Accepting the medieval concept of sacred and secular, the Church of England was content with the medieval expression of these concepts. Hesitant to follow in the steps that Rome had logically taken, although starting from the same premiss, the Church of England indulged its romantic vision of the Middle Ages and spread a rash of two-roomed buildings across the countryside—some beautiful, most ugly—convinced that in so doing it was proclaiming the majesty and apartness of God who is to be worshipped in the beauty of holiness (Fig. 8).

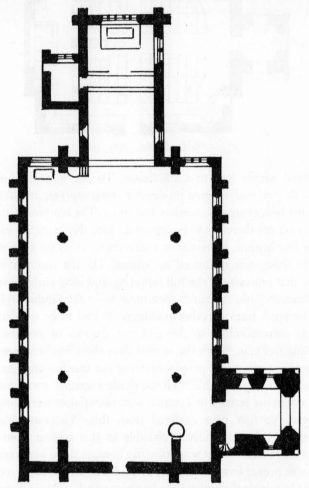

*Fig.* 8 St George, Oakengates, 1862

This apartness was emphasized by another aspect of the Anglican building programme, viz. the erection of church halls, which became common towards the end of the nineteenth century. Since the church is a sacred space from which all secular activities are to be excluded, if the Christian community is to perform any social services requiring rooms, the accommodation has to be provided outside the liturgical area. This is the rationale of the church hall. In parish after parish these large rooms were erected, and in new districts this meant building two halls: one for the liturgy and one for other activities. This has remained Anglican practice to the present day. A clearer expression of the division of sacred and secular could scarcely be found.

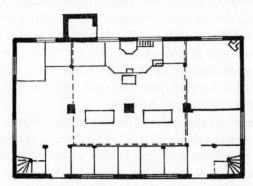

*Fig.* 9   Old Congregational Chapel, Walpole, Suffolk, 1647

Both historical circumstances and theological conviction led the English Separatists initially to adopt a very different style for their places of assembly. As a persecuted minority, like the primitive Christians, they met at first in private houses. During the Civil War (1642–9) there was little opportunity to build, although the Congregational Chapel at Walpole, near Halesworth in Suffolk, is said to date from 1647. In external appearance it looks like a country house and may indeed have been created out of two previously existing cottages.[117] Inside it had a pulpit, communion table, pews and, in course of time, a gallery (Fig. 9). Even under the Commonwealth the opportunity to erect special chapels was slight. The Act of Uniformity of 1662 was a renewed attack on Dissent, and it was not until the Declaration of Indulgence of 1671–2 that non-Anglican places of worship could be licensed. Over the next thirty years a large number of chapels was built, having a general similarity and their common characteristics show the steadfast refusal of their owners to accept the idea that a Christian place of worship is a holy shrine. Most of them are of a modest, retiring and domestic nature, without spires or obvious ecclesiastical features on the exterior. Brick was the usual material, with tiles for the roof. The doorways were like any others of the period and the windows had flat or semi-circular arches above them. The interior was planned as an auditorium, the design being rectangular without chancel, transepts or apse. Galleries were included in the larger buildings, simply to provide greater accommodation. The decorations were simple, even austere, with whitewashed walls and ceilings. The pulpit was large and prominent.[118]

Quaker buildings were equally simple, not even a pulpit was required for their gatherings, and the use of the term 'meeting house' indicates their acceptance of George Fox's critique of the churches of his day and their continued insistence that such holy places are not required by Christians.

Throughout the remainder of the eighteenth century and the first half of the nineteenth, meeting houses continued to be erected in a similar style and the same can be said of the Methodist chapels which belong to this period. Not a few were variants of Greek and Roman architecture, since the prevailing attitude was against the idea of a special Christian style and many suspected Gothic as too closely associated with the Roman Catholic past. But after the first decades of Victoria's reign, English Nonconformists began to Gothicize the exteriors of their chapels, probably in an attempt to remove their sense of social inferiority by making their buildings look like 'churches'. Inside, however, the arrangement was as before: central pulpit on a rostrum, galleries, etc. Yet there was also a tendency to follow the ecclesiologists, and hence the appearance of many buildings on the medieval plan with nave, aisles, transepts and chancels. It is difficult to tell, for example, the Congregational Church at Otley, as rebuilt in 1899, from Anglican churches of the same period. Social considerations had now replaced theological ideas. Whether they endorsed the view or not, many Nonconformist congregations appeared to have a sacred shrine. Moreover, the pressure of the majority view, represented by the Anglicans and Roman Catholics, was having its effect, so that not a few of the descendants of the Puritans and Separatists forgot the teaching of their ancestors and began to think of their churches as houses of God.

Of Lutheran church-building there is little to say that is relevant to our subject. To the first Lutherans a church was not a sacred space; it was a necessary shelter within which a large number of people could come together to hear the divine word and to worship. Luther did not concern himself with architecture, failing to see that it can make a proclamation as powerful, if not more so, because less consciously discerned, as the human mouth. He confined himself to saying that 'the altar cannot remain where it is' since the minister should always face the people at the eucharist as Jesus did at the Last Supper.[119] Some went further; for example, the Church of Hesse issued a regulation in 1526 to the effect that 'acts of worship will no longer be carried out in the choir but in the middle of the church . . . in concord and unity, for in Christ all are made priests'.[120] But in general the buildings taken over by Lutherans were used very much as they had been.

The most notable change came after the Thirty Years War when, owing to the destruction of so many churches, a full-scale building programme had to be undertaken. In the year after the devastation came to an end, Joseph Furttenbach, municipal architect at Ulm, published a book in which he condemned a one-sided stress upon the auditive nature of worship and sought to supplement it by emphasizing its visual aspect. He declared a preference for an oblong church, minus Gothic chancel, with a single space for conducting all the principal liturgical acts. 'The *Prinzipalstück*', he said, 'should be arranged at the east end as closely together as possible for the eye and the ear.'[121] Furttenbach's ideas were taken up by L. C. Sturm in two works of 1712 and 1718. Under the influence of the plan of the classical theatre, Sturm advocated the adoption of the *Zentralbau*, or the centralized auditorium, with *Prinzipalstück*. In so doing he was consistent with Luther's view that a church is a building with a function and that function is to provide as conveniently as possible for worship. The question of the relationship of the sacred and the secular is thus avoided and past history shows that when this is so the tendency is for the liturgical space to become sacralized. In other words, to define a church simply as a place for worship to the exclusion of other activities is to lay oneself open to the idea that a church is a holy shrine for the performance of religious exercises. This, as we have seen, has happened within English Nonconformity; it has also taken place within Lutheranism —to many of its contemporary leaders and congregations the church is something apart, something akin to, if not actually, a sacred area.

Calvinism, outside the country of its origin, has in the main reached the same position and by the same path. Unlike Luther, Calvin made determined efforts to rearrange the churches over which he had authority in accordance with his idea of worship. A comparison of the cathedral of St Pierre in Geneva before and after the Calvinist reformation shows what he was about (Fig. 10). The

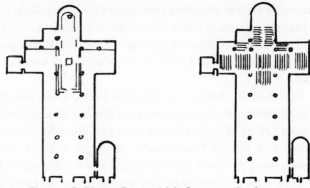

*Fig.* 10   St Pierre, Geneva (*a*) before 1541 (*b*) after 1541

medieval building, oblong with transepts, had the bishop's throne in the eastern apse, the altar in the centre of the choir and the pulpit on the same level as the rood screen separating the priests from the congregation. In 1541 Calvin had this altered. The rood screen and choir were demolished; the pulpit was moved to the first pillar on the left and the congregation was arranged in the form of a star in the front of the nave, in the transepts and in the ancient choir. So the community was gathered around the word of God. The table was brought in only on communion days and baptism was administered from a basin. The rest of the large edifice remained empty and un-used. An alternative method, adopted for Basel cathedral, was to leave the chancel unused, partitioning it off as an annex, and having the nave for the congregation with the pulpit in the midst.[122]

The disposition at both Geneva and Basel clearly demanded a

centralized plan, which was now becoming popular with the advance of the Renaissance. Consequently, when Calvinist churches were built, as distinct from the rearrangement of medieval ones, they often followed the circular plan, e.g. the *Temple du Paradis* at Lyons of 1564 (Fig. 11). In France at the end of the sixteenth century and at the beginning of the seventeenth, there were erected squares, rectangles, octagons, ovals and ellipses. These plans were the direct outcome of liturgical considerations.[123] Calvinist churches in Holland, Germany and Switzerland followed the same concepts, e.g. the numerous square, rectangular and polygonal ones in Amsterdam and Leyden. At the same time the conventional lay-out was also being reproduced, and in the nineteenth century Calvinism did not escape the influence of the Gothic Revival, unconscious of the fact that it did not accord with its original liturgical requirements. Calvinism sought to be 'religious' by adopting neo-Gothic imitations.

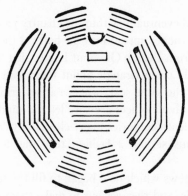

*Fig.* 11   Temple du Paradis, Lyons, 1564

According to Presbyterian theology, a church could be used for anything; in practice it was restricted to worship, and this practice spoke louder than the theory. So the churches became centres for religious activities and a separation from the secular was inevitable.

To whatever Christian communion we turn, with the notable exception of the Quakers, we find the same phenomenon. Churches either are deliberately built as sacred shrines, e.g. by Roman Catholics and by the Anglican ecclesiologists, or they become such in practice, e.g. among the Lutherans and the Reformed.

## 3. PEWS

There is one item of the furnishings of these churches which has a bearing upon our subject, and that is the pew. In the early Christian basilicas worshippers stood for prayer and indeed throughout the services. There was little in the way of seating, although occasionally a few wooden or stone benches were provided for the aged and infirm.[124] This was the practice until the thirteenth century, so that the spacious naves were free from any fixed objects that might prevent circulation or any activity in which Christians might wish to engage. Stone benches against the walls were not uncommon, as for example, in the fourteenth-century East Riding church at Patrington, which has a seat running round most of the nave, including the west end, but which left the central area free. There the parishioners could dance or act or, having brought in trestles and forms, consume their ales.

Seats were fixed eventually within the chantry parcloses and guild chapels and from thence spread into the body of the church, so that in 1287 we hear from Bishop Quivil of Exeter that 'the parishioners of divers places do often wrangle about their seats in church, two or more claiming the same seat; whence arises great scandal to the Church; and the divine offices are sore let and hindered'.[125] In the fifteenth and sixteenth centuries many churches were fitted up with wooden seats, thus setting a fashion that was to prevail to the present day.

Most of these pews which now began to fill the nave belonged to private individuals, and they set out to make them comfortable. As early as 1450 we hear of a chamberlain being instructed before his lord went to church, 'to procure all the things for his pew, and that it be prepared both cushion, carpet and curtains, bedes and book'.[126]

After the Reformation the custom of reserved pews was widespread, leading Bishop Corbett of Norwich, in a sermon preached in 1623, to lament:

Stately pews are now become tabernacles with rings and curtains to them. There wants nothing but beds to hear the word of God on; we have casements, locks and keys and cushions. I had almost said bolsters and pillows, and for these we love the church. I will not guess what is done with them, who sits, stands, or lies asleep at prayers, communion, etc., but this I dare say they are either to hide some vice, or to proclaim one; to hide disorder or to proclaim pride.[127]

Since these objects were in effect private possessions, their owners kept them under lock and key and arranged them at their will. Thus in the north aisle of Wensley church, Yorkshire, there is a pew belonging to the Scrope family which, under James I, was provided with a top or ceiling with pendants. Fireplaces were installed—there is a faculty of 28th November 1740 granted to Sir Jeremy Sambrooke to have a fireplace built, on the grounds that his pew is 'Situated below the Ground or Level of the Church Yard, so Cold and Damp, that it is truly Incommodious and Unsafe for Him and His Family, in the Winter Season to be there so frequently and so long as they are Required and Disposed to be'.[128]

Special compartments for pet dogs were inserted, as at Aveley, Essex, and Northorpe, Lincolnshire, and they accompanied their masters when they went up for communion, as we learn from a report of the parish of St Anthony in Cornwall of Whitsunday, 1640. On that day the church was hit by a storm and among the casualties was 'a dog at the feet of one kneeling to receive the cup'.[129] The occupiers set up their private libraries therein, as did Sir John Kederminster at Langley Marish, Buckinghamshire. Sometimes they had sofas and tables, and between the prayers and the sermon a liveried servant would bring sherry and light refreshments.[130]

To the ecclesiologists these pews, often derogatorily called 'pens', were anathema. They were arranged according to no set plan, so that many of the occupants sat with their backs to the communion table, and their walls were so high that the minister could see few of his congregation when he addressed them. In various numbers of the *Ecclesiologist* disdainful accounts were included. It was noted that at High Wycombe, Buckinghamshire, there was a pew with sash windows, carpet and rich velvet sofas, and at Hedsor, in the same county, there was one 'with the usual accessories of fire-place, carpet, cushions, and all the accommodations of a private apartment'.[131] After a sustained attack most of them were removed and replaced by open seats.

Quite clearly the filling of the nave with fixed benches limited the use to which it could be put. Any activity, other than those involving sitting and looking and hearing, became difficult, if not impossible. Moreover, the fact that they belonged to certain families meant that many of the parishioners had no seats or that they were crowded into uncomfortable corners and galleries. If to this be added the fact that after the Reformation many people wished to absent themselves from the services, either because they were Catholic recusants or adhered to other forms of dissent, it becomes apparent that the parish church was ceasing to be a centre of the life of the community as a whole, and this, too, contributed to a decline in its use for secular purposes.

Yet the pews themselves are evidence of a certain unity of the sacred and the secular, at least in the minds of their owners. They did not see why they should not be as comfortable in their parish church as they were in their own homes. Indeed, comfort was one reason for their original construction as indicated by a faculty issued in 1616 to a parishioner of Haverstock in Essex. He was allowed to erect a pew and to make it high with a wainscot or board in order 'to break and keep off the wind that cometh out of the chancel'.[132] The provision of sofas, cushions and even fireplaces stems from the same motive and at the same time indicates that they saw nothing unsuitable in making the house of God at least an attractive if temporary resting place. The inhospitality of many buildings today is something they would not have endured, and this is yet another example of the division of sacred and secular. An austere form of devotion is imposed upon all, if they are prepared to submit to it. This is but a further aspect of the restriction of churches to a single specialized use, viz. to the cult. The result of this historical process is self-evident:

> The final separation of the churches for Church services alone, desired by all the greater and more pious men who have served them, has been accompanied by a reduction of the fulness of their strength and meaning.[133]

But the history of that reduction has still to be concluded as we go on to review the secular use of churches in the post-Reformation period, considering first St Paul's as a specific example, and then outlining the continuation and final disappearance of those activities which were common in the patristic period and throughout the Middle Ages.

# 5

# Paul's Walk

IN THE YEAR 1554, the Lord Mayor of London issued a proclamation 'For the preventing of Profanation and Abuses offered to St Paul's.' The text of this mandate is as follows:

Forasmuch as the material Temples of God were first ordained for the lawful and devout Assembly of People, there to lift their Hearts, and to laud and praise Almighty God; and to hear his Divine Service, and most Holy Word and Gospel, sincerely, said, sung, and taught; and not to be used as Markets, or other profane places, or Thorough-fares, with carriage of Things: And for that (now of late years) many of the Inhabitants of the City of London, and other People repairing thither, have, (and yet do) commonly use and accustom themselves very unseemly and unreverently (the more the pity) to make their common Carriage of great Vessels full of Ale and Beer, great Baskets full of Bread, fish, Flesh and Fruit, and such other Things; Fardels of Stuff, and other gross Wares and Things, through the Cathedral Church of St Paul's. And some leading Mules, Horses and other Beasts through the same unreverently; to the great Dishonour and Displeasure of Almighty God, and the great Grief also, and Offence, of all good People; Be it therefore, for remedy and reformation thereof, Ordained, Enacted, and Established, etc. That no Person, either Free or Foreign, of what Estate or Condition soever, do at any time from henceforth, carry or convey, or cause to be carried through the said Cathedral, any manner of great Vessel or Basket, with Bread, Ale, Beer, Fish, Flesh, &c., or any other like Thing or Things, upon pain of forfeiture of losing for every such his or their first Offence, 3s. 4d., for the second 6s. 8d., for the third 10s., and for every other offence, after such third time, to forfeit 10s. and to suffer Two Days' and two Nights' Imprisonment, with Bail or Mainprise.[1]

This mayoral injunction is interesting for two main reasons. First, it illustrates the post-Reformation insistence that the function of a church is to be solely a place of worship. Indeed the mayor, although in office under a Roman Catholic monarch, Queen Mary, was giving voice to an attitude shared by Catholic and Protestant leaders alike. Second, this passage provides evidence of the secular use of St Paul's, and this particular cathedral can serve as an example for almost every conceivable secular activity. In our previous survey of the medieval material, we have already had occasion to cite St Paul's in connection with eating and drinking, the selling of goods, meetings, legal proceedings, financial transactions, storage and games.[2] We now hear of its continued use, after the Reformation, as a market and even as a main thoroughfare, but this is only the beginning of a story that reveals St Paul's as a microcosm of secular activities in all churches and cathedrals:

It was the fashion of those times—wrote Osborne in 1658 of the reign of James I—and did so continue till these . . . for the principal gentry, lords, courtiers, and men of all professions, not merely mechanic, to meet in Paul's church by eleven, and walk in the middle aisle till twelve, and after dinner from three to six; during which time, some discoursed of business, others of news. Now, in regard to the universal commerce, there happened little that did not first or last arrive here: And I being young, and wanting a more advantageous employment, did, during my abode in London, which was three-fourths part of the year, associate myself at those hours with the choicest company I could pick out, amongst such as I found most inquisitive after affairs of state; who being then myself in daily attendance upon a hope (though a rotten one) of a future preferment, I appeared the more considerable, being as ready to satisfy, according to my weak abilities, their curiosities, as they were mine; who, out of a candid nature, were not ordinarily found to name an author, easily lost in such a concourse, where his own report was not seldom within a few minutes returned to him for news by another. And these newsmongers, as they called them, did not only take the boldness to weigh the public, but most intrinsic actions of the state, which some courtier or other did betray to this society; amongst whom diverse being very rich, had great sums owing them by such as stood next the throne, who, by this means, were rendered in a manner their pensioners.[3]

Paul's Walk (Plate 10) was thus a promenade, a popular resort for London men about town to swap gossip and generally to pass their time in social intercourse, although this on occasion could involve open quarrels.[4] This was so under Elizabeth, and we hear how the

Recorder of London, Fleetwood, went there 'to learn some news' to convey by letter to Lord Burghley.[5] In 1592 Bacon described the cathedral as 'a place where people used to meet and confer',[6] while on 26th July 1600, Dudley Carton wrote to John Chamberlain: 'These great matters put Ireland out of talk, and there is nobody to talk with, for Paul's is as empty as a barn at midsummer.'[7]

Usually, however, it was thronged and was so common a feature of London life that Ben Jonson in his *Every Man out of His Humour*, which was first performed by Shakespeare's company at the Globe the year previously, i.e. in 1599, set the opening scene of Act III in 'the Middle Aisle of St Paul's'. This provides a vivid account of the manners and conversation of those who resorted thither. We meet two gallants, accompanied by their serving men, one leading a dog and the other carrying a cat in a bag. We see another character who brings his tailor to look surreptitiously at the suit of a fashionable dandy in order to copy it. We learn that the walk was known as *Insula Paulina*, that the south aisle was familiarly known as Mediterraneo and that the main area of the promenade was the west end of the nave. We discover that one of the reasons for attendance was to examine the bills or advertisements, and that by this means servants could be engaged and tutors hired.[8] Similarly, in the cathedral of Chartres in the Middle Ages, masons, carpenters and other craftsmen gathered in the nave waiting for a possible employer.[9] This practice was in vogue in London over a hundred years before Jonson. In the preface to his *Canterbury Tales*, Chaucer described the exemplary parson by saying:

> He set not his benefice to hire,
> And left his sheep encumbered in the mire,
> And ran to London, unto saint Paul's,
> To seek him a chantry for souls,
> Or with a brotherhood to be withhold;
> But dwelt at home, and kept well his fold.

To the same effect we find William Paston writing in 1479 to his servant Richard Lee in London to find an assistant curate for Oxnead by perusing the bills in St Paul's.[10] These bills were the *Si-quisses* of which Jonson provides two examples relating to secular employment:

If there be any lady or gentle woman of good carriage that is desirous to entertain to her private uses, a young, straight and upright gentleman, of the age of five or six and twenty at the most; who can serve in the nature of a gentleman-usher, and hath little legs of purpose, and a black satin suit of his own, to go before her in; which suit, for the more sweetening, now lies in lavender; and can hide his face with her fan, if need require; or sit in the cold at the stair foot for her, as well as another gentleman: let her subscribe her name and place, and diligent respect shall be given.

If this city, or the suburbs of the same, do afford any young gentleman of the first, second or third head, more or less, whose friends are but lately deceased, and whose lands are but new come into his hands, that, to be as exactly qualified as the best of our ordinary gallants are, is affected to entertain the most gentleman-like use of tobacco; as first, to give it the most exquisite perfume; then, to know all the delicate sweet forms for the assumption of it; as also the rare corollary and practice of the Cuban ebolition, euripus and whiff, which he shall receive or take in here at London, and evaporate at Uxbridge, or farther, if it please him. If there be any such generous spirit, that is truly enamoured of these good faculties; may it please him, but by a note of his hand to specify the place or ordinary where he uses to eat and lie; and made sweet attendance, with tobacco and pipes of the best sort, shall be ministered.

If we cannot assume a similar wit in every genuine *si-quis*, these examples at least give a hint of their possible contents.

Jonson also describes one of his characters as he who 'comes every morning to empty his lungs in Paul's'. Another, when accosted, proudly declares: 'I am known sufficiently in this walk, sir.' A third speaks of his presence in the form: 'I am come to spit private in Paul's.'

The evidence relating to this multi-use of the cathedral goes back farther than the closing years of Elizabeth's reign. An anonymous pamphlet of *c.* 1556 reveals that moneylending and business transactions were common. The writer, who is represented as being inside the cathedral, says: 'Had all promises been kept, I should ere this hour have seen a good piece of money told here upon the font; and as many indentures, obligations, and other writings sealed as cost me twice forty shillings for the drawing, and counsel.'[11] This particular quotation specifies two secular usages that can be illustrated from other sources, viz. payments at the font and legal transactions. As regards payment, we may cite the case of Thomas

Bedyll, in 1536. He was a prebendary of Massam in St Peter's Cathedral, York, who demised his prebend for fifty years at an annual rent of £36 13s. 4d., payment to be made at the font stone in the body of St Paul's between the hours of nine and eleven before noon.[12] As regards legal transactions, according to William Harrison: 'the time hath been that our lawyers did sit in Paul's upon stools against the pillars and walls to get clients'.[13] This was so common that St Paul's became the place for the making of new serjeants. Henry Machyn, in his diary, described this ceremony, which was held annually on 17th October:

> After dinner they went unto Pauls, and so went up the steps, and so round the choir and there did their homage, and so came into the north side of Paul's and stood upon the steps until four old serjeants came together and fetched four new and brought them unto certain pillars, and left them, and then did fetch the residue unto the pillars, and there was an oration read unto them by the old serjeants, and so done they went unto Gray's Inn.[14]

This custom still obtained a hundred years later, according to the witness of William Dugdale, writing in 1680:

> St Paul's Church, where each Lawyer and Serjeant at his Pillar heard his Client's Cause, and took note thereof upon his knee, as they do in Guildhall at this day: And that after the Serjeants' feast ended, they do still go to Paul's in their Habit, and there choose their Pillar, whereat to hear their Clients' cause (if any come) in memory of that old custom.[15]

To many churchmen all this amounted to desecration, and attacks, both direct and satirical, were launched against what was taking place. As far back as 1561 Bishop Pilkington of Durham had preached on this theme at St Paul's Cross and had denounced the activities in the cathedral, referring to 'taking, buying and selling, fighting and brawling there'.[16] Two years later it was necessary to defend the sermon and a tract, probably written by the bishop himself, affirms that 'the south alley was for usury and popery; the north for simony, and the horse-fair in the midst for all kind of bargains, meetings, brawlings, murders, conspiracies. The font for ordinary payments of money.' The pamphlet continues:

God's house must be a house of prayer and not the proud tower of Babylon, nor the pope's market-place, nor a stews for bawds and ruffians, nor a horse-fair for brokers; no, nor yet a burse for merchants, nor a meeting-place for walking and talking. And that if a convenient place to meet for honest assemblies could not be found, nor had conveniently otherwise, a partition might be had, to close up and shut the *praters* from the prayers, the walkers and janglers from well-disposed persons.[17]

Joseph Hall, who was later to become Bishop first of Exeter and then of Norwich, preferred the satirical approach, and in 1597 published these lines of verse:

> Saw'st thou ever Siquis patch'd on Paul's church door,
> To seek some vacant vicarage before?
> Who wants a churchman that can service say,
> Read fast and fair his monthly homily?
> And wed and bury, and make christen-souls?
> Come to the left-side alley of Saint Paul's.
> Thou servile fool, why couldst thou not repair
> To buy a benefice at steeple-fair?[18]

Mayoral injunctions and episcopal denunciations, however, made little difference. Paul's Walk was and remained a reflection of city life and what took place or did not take place there was a mirror of events in London at large. The extent to which this was so may be illustrated by an anonymous pamphlet published in 1604 with the title *The Meeting of Gallants at an Ordinarie, or The Walkes in Powles*. This takes the form of a conversation, the first half of which is in the cathedral and then the gallants repair to an 'ordinary' or eating house to continue their discourse. One of the characters, in the first section, remarks: 'Me thinks, Signiors, this middle of Paul's looks strange and bare, like a long-haired Gentleman new poled, washed and shaved, and I may fitly say shaved, for there was never a lusty Shaver seen walking here this half-year: especially if he loved his life, he would revolt from Duke Humphrey, and rather be a Wood-cleaver in the Country, than a chest-breaker in London.'[19] Paul's Walk was therefore unfrequented; only a few of the citizens were to be seen in its aisles. The reason for this was the plague which ravaged London in 1603 from May to December. As many as could sought escape in the country and the resulting acute decrease in concourse and circulation was reflected in the temporary disuse of the cathedral for social gatherings—the 'middle of Paul's looks strange and bare' to the few now beginning to return when the risk of infection had passed. The effect of the plague also manifested itself in another particular; it appeared that few people had bothered to buy new clothes—a more serious concern occupied their minds. Hence St Paul's was not, as at other times, the usual fashion parade. But the situation was being restored since 'Paul's is charged with Gallants, and those I saw come up in old Taffata Doublets yesterday are slipt into nine yards of Satin today'.[20] The pamphlet further provides evidence of the custom of friends meeting at a predetermined spot, since one of those present, seeing two acquaintances approaching, says: 'Let's encounter them at the fifth Pillar'.[21] Under normal conditions, of course, the cathedral was crowded, and so a satire of 1605 states: 'It is agreed upon what day soever St Paul's Church hath not, in the middle ile of it, either a broker, masterless man, or a penniless Companion, the usurers of London shall be sworn by oath to bestow a new steeple upon it.'[22]

In 1609 Thomas Dekker published his *Gull's Handbook*, which is a satirical account of how a young gallant should conduct himself. Advice is given as to his dress, his conduct in a playhouse or a tavern, and the fourth chapter is entirely devoted to the subject: 'How a Gallant should behave himself in Paul's Walk'. Dekker makes it clear that the nave of the cathedral was a fashionable rendezvous where up and coming young men of the early seventeenth century were bound to spend a not insignificant part of their time if they were to be in the social swim!

> Your mediterranean aisle is the only gallery, wherein the picture of your true fashionate and complemental Gulls are, and ought to be hung up. Into that gallery carry your neat body; but take heed you pick out such an hour, when the main shoal of islanders are swimming up and down.[23]

Dekker advises the dandy to take not above four turns and certainly not to stay after eleven, but he may appear again, in different attire, after dinner.[24] As regards dress:

> All the diseased horses in a siege cannot show so many fashions, as are to be seen for nothing, every day, in Duke Humphrey's Walk. If therefore you determine to enter into a new suit, warn your tailor to attend you in

Paul's, who, with his hat in his hand, shall like a spy discover the stuff, colour, and fashion of any doublet, or hose that dare be seen there; and, stepping behind a pillar to fill his tablebooks with those notes, will presently send you into the world an accomplished man.[25]

We also learn from Dekker that servants, too, collected for gossip, seating themselves on a block or bench near a particular pillar, that Paul's was the resort of creditors, that there was a *Si quis* door[26]* 'plastered with serving-men's supplications', that gentlemen of fashion were accustomed to go into the choir at festivals and distribute silver to the boys, and that an ascent of the steeple to admire the view was part of the habitual parade.

Attacks continued, and the laity entered the fray. In 1622 a freeman of London named Henry Farley published *Portland-Stone in Paules Church-yard*. In the course of this he asks:

> Was it not example, scurrilous and rude,
> At first to grant that traders should there intrude?
> Nay; are they not accursed that did yield
> To make God's Courts a merchandizing field?[27]

Yet so accepted a practice was this that in the same year that Farley issued his booklet, the Lord Mayor of London, Sir Edward Barkham, financed the erection of an inscription over the tomb of a former bishop of the capital. The lines run as follows:

> Walkers, whosoere you be,
> If it prove your chance to see,
> Upon a solemn scarlet day,
> The City Senate pass this way,
> Their grateful memory for to show
> Which they the reverent ashes owe
> Of Bishop Norman here inhum'd;
> By whom this City hath assum'd
> Large privileges. Those obtain'd
> By him, when Conqueror William reigned.
> This being by thankful Barkham's mind renew'd,
> Call it the Monument of Gratitude.[28]

What is especially noticeable about this verse is its opening word— St Paul's Walk was so much a part of social behaviour that the mayor thought it quite appropriate to address its frequenters directly as

'Walkers'. Barkham, with his reference to a 'scarlet day', had in mind the solemn processions to St Paul's of himself and his aldermen. These occasions could be quite spectacular. Machyn records how on 29th October each year, after he had taken the oath, the newly elected mayor went to Paul's, accompanied by various pageants—in 1553 there was a pageant of St John the Baptist—and they went about the choir blowing trumpets.[29]

In 1628 John Earle included a description of Paul's Walk in his *Micro-cosmographie*, which shows that matters remained much the same:

The noise in it is like that of Bees, a strange humming or buzz—mixt of walking, tongues and feet. . . . It is the great Exchange of all discourse, and no business whatsoever but is here stirring and afoot. It is the Synod of all parties politic. . . . It is the Market of young Lecturers, whom you may cheapen here at all rates and sizes. . . . It is the other expense of the day after Plays, Tavern, and a Bawdy House, and men have still some Oaths left to swear here. . . . The Visitants are all men without exception, but the principal Inhabitants and possessors are stale Knights, and Captains out of Service, Men of long Rapiers, and Breeches, who after all turn Merchants here, and traffic for News. Some make it a preface to their Dinner, and Travel for a Stomach; but thriftier men make it their Ordinary and Board here very cheap.[30]

Earle's reference to dinner directs attention to another aspect of our subject, viz. 'dining with Duke Humphrey'. The tomb of Sir John Beauchamp was erroneously thought to be that of Duke Humphrey of Gloucester, who in fact was buried at St Alban's. This tomb gave rise to the proverbial saying: 'dining with Duke Humphrey', which meant to go dinnerless. The tomb was also the scene of a ceremony on each St Andrew's Day, when a group would gather there and agree upon a breakfast or dinner 'assuming themselves to be servants, and to hold diversity of offices under the said Duke Humphrey'.[31] John Weever, who provides this last item of information, had further disclosures to make in 1631. He reported that the cathedral was being misused by 'beastly and unclean persons, to pollute and bedaub the walls of the place where God is to be worshipped, with piss or some other more nasty excrement; against the like irreverence to this goodly consecrated Edifice of Saint Paul, diverse prohibitions upon certain penalties have been, and are daily, published in print, and pasted up in divers places, in and about the Church. And anciently this Atheistical uncleanness (if I may so call it) was forbidden by a verse depicted at every door of this Church; some part of which at the great South door is yet remaining, which in my time might perfectly be read. Thus it runs:

> *Hic locus hic sacer est, hic nulli mingere fas est.*
> This house is holy here: unlawful tis
> For any one, here on her walls to piss.'

Weever also reports that 'strict orders were likewise published against Beggars, and bearers of burdens, in and through the Church: so these four lines were fixed to a pillar, over an iron box for the poor.

> All those that shall enter with the Church door,
> With burden or basket, must give to the poor.
> And if there be any ask what they must pay,
> To this Box a penny, ere they pass away.'

Weever finally expresses the pious hope: 'It could be wished, that walking in the middle Aisle of Paul's, might be forborne in the time of Divine service.'[32]

A year later an attempt was made to realize Weever's hope. In March 1632, the Attorney General and the King's Advocate were consulted as to the best way of remedying the profanation of St Paul's. The abuses are said to include 'walking there during Divine Service, and on Sundays and festival days the boys and maids and children of the adjoining parishes, after dinner, come into the Church and play as children use to do till dark night'. Shortly after this there were issued:

Articles by His Majesty's command to be observed by all persons in St Paul's.
  I. No man to walk in the Church during Divine Service.
 II. No man to profane the Church by carriage of burthens or baskets.
III. Parents and masters to forbid their children and servants to play in the Church.[33]

Yet in 1636 Laud had to order 'that due and diligent observance be made of all manner of profanation in your church and churchyard, and a particular thereof delivered unto us, that a remedy may be ordained'.[34]

With the outbreak of the Civil War and the consequent social disruption, St Paul's soon ceased to be a fashionable rendezvous. The ascendancy of the Puritans, with their antipathy to consecrated buildings, resulted in the cathedral being used as a cavalry barracks and stables,[35] and, in 1658, a new Exchange was built 'within the great Pillars at the West end of the Church'.[36] The situation had barely begun to improve with the Restoration when the Great Fire gutted the building and decades were to pass before Wren's plan for the new cathedral was realized. So we hear nothing of Paul's Walk, not even in the diaries of Samuel Pepys, who was always ready to play his part in the social round. It was not until 5th December 1697 that John Evelyn recorded that this 'was the first Sunday that St Paul's had service perform'd in it since it was burnt in 1666'.

Yet so great a hold upon people's memories had the former practice that within six years of the cathedral's reopening it was thronged again. In 1703 a pamphlet was issued containing a dialogue between Jest and Earnest:

JEST    Certainly you have never been at St Paul's. The flux of people there would cause you to make use of your handkerchief; and the largest Meeting-house in London has no proportion to it.

EARNEST    And what should I do there, where men go out of curiosity and interest, not for the sake of religion? You shop-keepers assemble there as at full 'Change, and the buyers and sellers are far from being cast out of the Temple. The body of the Church, every Lord's-day, contains three times the number of the choir.[37]

On 9th June 1710 members of the Royal Society were using the dome for experiments to show the attractive force of gravity.[38] In 1720 it was reported that the Stewards of the Sons of the Clergy were allowing 'persons from the Theatres to perform in their annual celebration in St Paul's', and further that during the *Te Deum*, the anthem and the sermon there were 'persons eating, drinking wine, laughing and talking'.[39] Once again, following a familiar pattern, the ecclesiastical authorities sought to intervene:

The custom of walking and talking in the nave of St Paul's cathedral had become so very prevalent in 1725, that the Bishop of London found it necessary, at his Visitation in that year, to declare his positive intention of enforcing the 18th Canon, and the Act of the First of William and Mary, by which transgressors forfeited 20*l.* for every offence.[40]

The Bishop was only wasting his efforts. More than a century later, Sydney Smith was giving evidence before the Select Committee on National Monuments in 1841. He declared:

The whole Cathedral, excepting the choir and those assembled in it for divine service, is converted into a lobby for fashionable loungers; hundreds of persons come together for no other reason than to make an exhibition of this description; so that what with the pacing of feet, the murmur of voices, the gadding to and fro of figures, every Church-like notion is driven from their minds; the whole thing resembles more a promenade in a ball-room than a congregation in the house of God.[41]

St Paul's was, of course, not unique; in the eighteenth century the naves of York Minster and Durham Cathedral were similarly fashionable parades,[42] despite a vigorous attempt, several decades previously, by a residentiary canon of the former to have it stopped.[43] But the records of Paul's Walk are so vivid and so full that it must be regarded as an outstanding example of how a consecrated edifice could be used for secular activities. Against the background of the Elizabethan period this use is readily intelligible. It was one of the few spacious buildings in the capital; it provided shelter from the weather and, in contrast to the ordure-choked thoroughfares outside, it provided a pleasant area of social intercourse. William Harrison, who has left us a description of England for the decade from 1577 to 1587, had his own explanation: 'As the number of churches increased, so the repair of the faithful unto the cathedrals did diminish: whereby they are now become, especially in their nether parts, rather markets and shops for merchandise, than solemn places of prayer, whereunto they were first erected.'[44]

The continuation of Paul's Walk over the centuries is explicable as due partly to the conservatism of habit, and partly to an attitude which saw in the cathedral a building for general use. But Sydney Smith's complaint did not fall upon deaf ears. The ecclesiologists were campaigning for a renewal of worship on the basis of an understanding of the church building as a sacred shrine. Their views were accepted as authoritative, and Paul's Walk became a thing of the past.

From the microcosm of Paul's Walk, we must next pass to the macrocosm of church buildings in general in the post-Reformation era.

# 6

# Secular Activities in the Post-Reformation Churches

ALTHOUGH THE Roman Catholic and Protestant attitudes to churches in the post-Reformation era were antithetical, in practice they each resulted in the same progressive disuse of them for secular activities. The Roman Catholics, accepting the medieval identification of church and temple, viewed their buildings as holy shrines which were to be preserved from profanation. With the greater discipline and the more tightly knit organization consequent upon the Counter-Reformation, they were able to repeat the episcopal injunctions of the past centuries prohibiting plays, games, the sale of goods, etc., and, what is more important, they were able to ensure that that which was thus declared illegal was steadily eradicated. So the rules that had been mainly dead letters in the Middle Ages were now put into effect.

The Anglican leaders largely shared the same attitude and, with considerable State backing, which because of the strong centralized government of the Tudors was now effective, were also able to achieve success in banishing non-liturgical activities. The articles and injunctions, royal, episcopal and archidiaconal, between 1550 and 1640, number well over two hundred separate series. If a particular course were not adopted these visitation articles would return to it again and again, year after year, until both notice and action had been taken. The visitation courts sat weekly to deal with presentations and to compel obedience. What is remarkable is not that secular uses eventually ceased, but that so many were sufficiently tenacious to survive for so long. If plays were more or less banished by the year 1600, church ales managed to persist until at least 1640, and elections, meetings and teaching even persisted to the beginning of the nineteenth century.

The attitude of the Lutherans and Calvinists to churches was that they were functional buildings for worship, with the preaching of the word as the central element in that worship. Churches had no other necessary function. Hence while they were not regarded as in any sense holy ground, they ceased to have an important role to fulfil apart from the liturgical assembly. The story of post-Reformation secular activities in all Churches is therefore one of progressive cessation.

### Living and Sleeping

(i) *Incubation*. The practice of living and sleeping in churches in order either to be healed or to be vouchsafed a prescription that would effect a cure, which was so widespread in the patristic period and, to a lesser extent, in the Middle Ages, continued after the Reformation but upon a diminished scale. In countries where the Reformation had made its way, the cult of the saints was largely if not entirely eliminated, and consequently men no longer turned to them for assistance in regaining health. There were of course isolated survivals; e.g. the church of St Hildersferthe at Swanscombe in Kent was one to which, in 1570, 'such as were distracted ran for restitution of their wits'.[1]

Methods of healing, too, were changing; not only was medical knowledge advancing, which meant that a fellow human being was as likely to be as helpful as a glorified saint, but some churchmen were substituting a different technique for that of incubation. So the abbey of Rigny, near Varmenton in France, preserved a tooth of St William of Bourges, which was believed to have the property of neutralizing the effect of a snake bite. The two Benedictine monks who visited the monastery in 1717 reported as follows:

Every day from the region round about there come folk who are very swollen. . . . They are first of all pricked with a silver needle on the spot where they have been bitten by the snakes. A few drops of blood are squeezed out. The affected part is then washed with water and wine specially blessed and the remainder of the blessed wine and water is drunk. Immediately they are relieved, and in a day or two are entirely healed.[2]

Nevertheless, in parts of Eastern Europe incubation has had a continuous history down to the present day. When Le Bas visited the church of the Maritza Monastery in the northern Peloponnese in 1840, he encountered in a church a woman with her child; a bed had been placed in front of the altar and the woman intended to pass the night there in the hope of a cure.[3] At the same epoch children lay on mattresses before the altar in the church of St Michael in the village of Ulubad on the river Rhyndakos in northern Asia Minor.[4] Further, in her study of incubation, Mary Hamilton records evidence from churches she visited in Boetia, Arcadia and Argolis.[5] Indeed, on 5th March 1906, fifteen thousand went for this purpose to the church on the island of Tenos in the Aegean.[6] On Corfu, on Crete, and in Sardinia, similar scenes are to be witnessed.[7] In the church of the Assumption at Isnik, on the site of the ancient Nicaea in Bithynia, lunatics are brought for a three days' stay, while in the church of the Pangra Phaneromena at Ghemelek, on the Sea of Marmara, people remain for periods of forty days.[8] In the northern districts of Persia, it is still the custom of Nestorian Christians when sick to spend a night in a vault beneath their parish church and, according to reports, some thirty people each year seek healing in this way. In Italy incubation could be witnessed in the neighbourhood of Naples, while sick pilgrims occupied the church of the Madonna of the Baths near Scafati, throughout the week after Ascension Day.[9] But in western Europe generally, where a shrine has continued to be or has become a centre of healing, the tendency is to erect special shelters for the visiting sick, e.g. at Lourdes.

(ii) *Sanctuary*. With the emergence of national states, each having a comparatively strong monarchy, and with the repudiation by a number of them of papal authority, the way was open for a more strict regulation of the right of sanctuary. Although it had been of some value in a period when disputes could quickly lead to bloodshed and it had allowed tempers to cool and a reasonably fair trial to be held, the development of the legal system rendered it less necessary, and indeed it could easily become an obstacle to the proper processes of the law. In England the right was progressively limited. In 1540 Henry VIII restricted it to seven cities only throughout his kingdom. In 1566 a bill was introduced into parliament to deny sanctuary to debtors—but this was not passed.[10] However, in 1603, under James I, sanctuary for crime was entirely abolished, although it lingered on for civil processes.

A reference to it can be found as late as 1687. On Good Friday, 28th March, of that year John Evelyn went to worship in St Martin's; in his diary he recorded this incident:

During the service a man came to near the middle of the church, with his sword drawn, with several others in that posture; in this jealous time it put the congregation into great confusion; but it appeared to be one who fled for sanctuary, being pursued by Bailiffs.

However, in 1723 all rights of sanctuary were finally declared null and, with its passing, one cause for the inhabitation of churches ceased to exist.

Indeed in Anglican churches generally there were some, but not many, who now lived and slept. Chapels of ease were at times used as lodging houses, e.g. the chapel at Sutton.[11] In the reign of Elizabeth there was a large increase in the population of London and accommodation was scarce. Not a few churches supplemented their budget by meeting this need. In 1577 at St Matthew, Friday Street, a man was permitted to build a room over the porch and, previously part of the vestry had been leased to a parishioner. In 1589 the vestry of St Margaret, Lothbury, let a room behind the belfry to one James Lambert.[12] The watching of the sepulchre, as in St Helen's, Abingdon, Berkshire, in 1557 and 1559, was but a relic of a medieval devotion that was soon swept away as the Reformation advanced.[13] The placing of a bed in the belfry and the renewing of a bar in the grate in Ludlow church in 1620 was an isolated incident.[14] Nevertheless, memories were long: as late as 1830 there was a tradition at Grantchester, near Cambridge, that parishioners without a house could take up residence in the church porch[15]—clearly a survival of the idea that the church itself could provide living accommodation for those in need.[16] Moreover, when there was need, nothing was allowed to stand in its way, as when three hundred pallets were laid out for the sick in the aisles of St Paul's in the plague year.[17]

## Eating and Drinking

The long and chequered history of the *agape* continued into the post-Reformation period, still associated with funerals, weddings and baptisms. First there is the will of Margaret Atkinson, dated 18th October 1544:

> The Sunday next after her burial, there be provided two dozens of bread, a kilderkin of ale, two gammons of bacon, three shoulders of mutton, and two couples of rabbits, desiring all the parish, as well rich as poor, to take part thereof, and a table to be set in the middle of the church with everything necessary thereto.[18]

Over one and a half centuries later, in 1698, an inhabitant of Sherborne, Dorset, left money for a bell to be tolled at his passing and for jugs of beer, bread and cheese to be given to the people in the church.[19] Yet such consumption in church was on its way out in England.[20]* In the 1680's John Aubrey records how it was the custom at burials at Amersden, Oxford, to bring one cake and a flagon of ale to the minister in the porch;[21] this is evidently a relic of the funeral *agape* pushed out of the church and now confined to a single person. Not that funeral *agapes* have ceased to exist—to this day a meal is commonly provided after the rites of burial, but the venue is the home of the chief mourner and no longer the church building itself.

The feasting on the anniversary of a death also continued, but here the idea of charity for the poor, rather than a meal of fellowship, was uppermost; nor is it possible to say that the distribution of food in churches in this connection necessarily always involved its immediate consumption—some of it could have been taken home. In 1580 one Peter Symons left money to the parish of All Hallows, Lombard Street, for an annual gift after morning service on Whitsunday of a penny and a packet of plums to sixty boys from Christ's Hospital.[22] In 1639 a similar bequest is to be noted, viz. that of Francis Pynner of Bury St Edmund's, who directed that a twopenny wheaten loaf be given to each of forty poor parishioners of St Mary's, in church on the last Friday of every month.[23] At Biddenden in Kent, in the seventeenth and eighteenth centuries, following the afternoon service on Easter Day, six hundred cakes, two hundred and seventy

loaves of three and a half pounds each and cheese were presented—
most of this must have been taken home.[24] Alderman Fletcher's
Charity at Yarnton provides a nineteenth-century example. On 7th
January 1855, a schedule of directions was drawn up and this
included the item: 'If the Alderman's Burial Day, 4th January, fall
on a Sunday it is our opinion that the Bread and Cakes shall be
distributed in the Yarnton Aisle or Church Porch'.[25]

A remainder of the marriage *agape* was the continued use of the
maser or bowl, filled with wine and small cakes and given to the
bride and bridegroom at the end of the ceremony. Thus in an inventory of Wilsdon parish church, *c.* 1547, we read of 'two Masers that
were appointed to remain in the church for to drink at Bride-ales'.[26]
There are notices of these bowls at Talaton, Devon, in 1595 and
1601,[27] and the practice still obtained in several French dioceses in
the eighteenth century,[28] in particular the diocese of Rouen.[29]

For a survival of the refreshments connected with baptisms, we
may turn to the description of the initiation of the son of Sir Thomas
Chamberlayne in 1559 at St Benet's, Paul's Wharf—'The church
was hung with cloth of arras, and after the christening were brought
wafers, comfits and divers banqueting dishes, and Hypocras and
Muscadine wine to entertain the guests.'[30] Yet these are but linger-
ing traces—the marriage breakfast was soon to find a home in the
private house or the public inn and similarly the christening party.

The holy loaf, i.e. the distribution of blessed bread after the morning service, was more tenacious. The English Reformers sought to
stamp out the practice and the accounts of St Laurence, Reading,
state that in 1551 a payment of five pence was substituted for the
money previously received for the holy loaf.[31] Under Mary, former
precedent reasserted itself and so at Stanford-in-the-Vale, Berkshire, the parish was divided into sectors, each was financially
assessed, and the parish clerk was charged with collecting the money
as part of his salary and with providing weekly a holy loaf as a *quid
pro quo*.[32] The accession of Elizabeth did not put a stop to this
revival. The accounts for Melton Mowbray of 1560 and 1588 and of
Mere for 1590 contain references to the holy loaf,[33] while there are
continuous entries in those of St Mary's, Reading, from 1566 to
1618, when the payment was merged with the charge for seats.[34]

In France both bread and wine were consumed. To the liturgiologist Bocquillot this was the *agape* continued, and, writing in 1701, he commented: 'Thirty years ago it was still to be seen in the majority of parishes in certain dioceses.'[35] In 1718 de Moléon described an *agape* in one of the chapels of St Marie de Rotunde, Rouen, on Holy Thursday; wine was being served in ancient silver goblets. On Easter Day itself in all the parish churches of Rouen an *agape* was distributed in the centre of the nave; each person received 'pastry cakes as large as two fists and as thick as a copper coin', a cup of wine and a napkin to wipe the mouth.[36] The offering of the firstfruits also ended with a kind of *agape*. On 6th August grapes were blessed and then eaten, e.g. at Angers, Tours, Rheims and Orleans, while on 14th September new wine was blessed, some of it being used for mass and the rest given in spoonsful to those who wanted to drink it.[37]

A deliberate revival, in contrast to a survival, of the love feast was undertaken by the Moravians. In 1727 their colony under Count Zinzendorf at Herrnhut re-introduced a common meal for social intercourse and religious rejoicing. Their missionaries took the custom with them to America and it was there on 8th August 1731 that John Wesley first encountered it in Savannah.[38] The following year Wesley was in Germany, where he had further experience of the Moravian love feast and decided to introduce it into his societies. The first Methodist love feast was held at Fetter Lane on 31st December 1738—henceforth it became a normal feature of Methodism. Dr F. Baker, who has traced its history very thoroughly, shows how it was celebrated in chapels throughout England, the food varying from bread or biscuits to semi-sweet buns and the drink being usually water and occasionally tea.

Wherever Methodism spread it took with it the love feast—to Wales and Ireland, to the United States, to the West Indies, to South Africa, New Zealand and the Fiji Islands. Throughout much of the nineteenth century there were quarterly love feasts, though increasingly restricted to the leading churches. But by the beginning of the twentieth century it had come to be regarded as a quaint survival rather than a normal church activity. This was largely due to the fact that it had previously been associated with personal testimony and the movement of revival and the change of atmosphere affected its observance. Nevertheless, it still continues, although mainly in remote country villages conservative in their outlook.

The battle against church ales was less easily won in England than that against funeral and marriage *agapes* and the holy loaf. Indeed, in the first decades of the Reformation these wakes were left undisturbed, but they proved far from acceptable to the Puritans of Elizabeth's reign. The first attempt to suppress them was made by Edmund Grindal when Archbishop of York. In his injunctions of 1571 he declared that there should be 'no feasts, dinners, common drinkings kept in the church'.[39]* Grindal's theology was moderately Calvinistic and he had strong sympathies with the Puritans, which led eventually to his suspension in 1577. The inspiration of his injunction is therefore evident. The Puritan attitude was very clearly expressed by Philip Stubbes in 1583; he was opposed to ales, not because they involved a misuse of churches but because they were examples of intemperance:

In certain Towns where drunken *Bacchus* bears all the sway, against a *Christmas*, an *Easter*, *Whitsunday*, or some other time, the Churchwardens (for so they call them) of every parish, with the consent of the whole Parish, provide half a score or twenty quarters of malt, whereof some they buy of the Church-stock, and some is given them of the Parishioners themselves, every one conferring somewhat, according to his ability; which malt, being made into very strong ale or beer, it is set to sale, either in the Church, or some other place assigned to that purpose. Then, when the *Nippitatum*, this Huf-cap (as they call it) and this *nectar* of life, is set abroach, well is he that get the soonest to it, and spend the most at it; for he that sitteth the closest to it, and spends the most at it, he is counted the godliest man of all the rest. . . .

They repair their Churches and Chapels with it; they buy books for service, cups for the celebration of the Sacrament, surplices for Sir John, and such other necessaries; And they maintain other extraordinary charges in the parishes besides.[40]

In the same year that Stubbes published his work, Marmaduke Middleton of St David's enquired: 'whether any of your parishioners have kept either their marriage-dinners or other drinkings or tipplings in your church, churchyard or chapel used for Divine

Service ?'[41] Two years later, possibly influenced by Stubbes's tirade, John Mullins enquired in his archdeaconry of London about 'any banquets or common drinkings'.[42]

In general, however, church leaders were not much concerned about these matters.[43]* It was only when the civil authorities seized the initiative that they began to take notice. At the Quarter Sessions in the County of Devon, July 1595, church ales were forbidden on Sundays. Four years later in January, 1599, the further step was taken of declaring them unlawful at all times.[44] This lay initiative was given episcopal support by canon 88 of 1603 which declared that 'the churchwardens or questmen, and their assistants, shall suffer no plays, feasts, banquets, suppers, church-ales, drinkings . . . to be kept in the church'.

There now followed a whole series of episcopal and archidiaconal visitations and injunctions by means of which an attempt was made to ensure the observance of this canon, its wording being almost exactly reproduced again and again. Extended quotation is unnecessary, but a list will illustrate this concerted effort: the articles of Thornborough of Bristol 1603;[45] those of Archbishop Bancroft of Canterbury 1605 and of Babington of Worcester two years later; the articles of the Archdeacon of Norfolk 1608 and of Archbishop Abbot *c.* 1611, and of King of Lincoln 1612. In 1616 Abbot again issued articles and so did Andrews of Winchester in 1619, Howson of Oxford in the same year and Harsnet of Norwich in 1620. William Laud, when Bishop of St David's, enquired into the matter in 1622; Kent, Archdeacon of Sudbury, in 1624; Williams of London, in 1625, and Neile of Winchester in 1628. Eland, Archdeacon of Bedford, included feasts in his visitation articles of 1629 and Curle of Bath and Wells specified 'feasts, banquets, church ales, drinkings' in 1630 and repeated this in 1633 when he became Bishop of Winchester. Meanwhile, Robert White, Archdeacon of Norfolk, was making the same enquiry in 1632; Lindsell of Peterborough in 1633; Archbishop Laud for Norwich in 1635 and Williams of Lincoln in the same year. In 1636 Wren of Norwich was followed by Kingsley, Archdeacon of Canterbury, and in 1640 by Juxon of London and Bostock, Archdeacon of Suffolk.

To this ecclesiastical onslaught was added further civil action. At

Easter, 1607, another order for the suppression of church ales was issued. In 1615 the Exeter Assize Court, in an area that was constantly opposed to church ales, repeated the condemnation. At Exeter again in 1627, before barons Walter and Denham, wakes were forbidden and in 1631 before Richardson for Somerset.

It was at this juncture that Laud decided to intervene and wrote to the Bishop of Bath and Wells to enquire how the annual dedication feasts were kept and how free they were from disorders. William Pierce replied:

First, that they have been kept, not only this last year, but also for many years before, as long as they have lived in their several parishes, without any disorders. Secondly, that upon the feast-days (which are for the most part everywhere upon Sundays), the Service of the Church hath been more solemnly performed, and the church hath been better frequented, both in the forenoons and in the afternoons, than upon any Sunday in the year. Thirdly, that they have not known or heard of any disorders in the neighbouring towns, where the like Feasts are kept. Fourthly, that the people do very much desire the continuance of those Feasts. Lastly, that all these ministers are of opinion, that it is fit and convenient these Feast-days should be continued, for a memorial of the dedications of their several churches, for the civilizing of the people, for their lawful recreations, for the composing of differences by occasion of the meeting of friends, for the increase of love and unity, as being feasts of charity, for the relief of the poor. . . . I find that throughout Somersetshire, there are not only Feasts of Dedication, but also in many places church-ales, clerks'-ales, and bid-ales. The Feasts of Dedication are more general, and generally they are called Feast-days; but in divers places they are called revel-days. . . . Concerning *church-ales* I find that in some places the people have been persuaded to leave them off; in other places they have been put down by the Judges and Justices, so that now there are very few of them left: but yet I find, that by church-ales heretofore, many poor parishes have cast their bells, repaired their towers, beautified their churches, and raised stocks for the poor; and not by the sins of the people (as some humorists have said), but by the benevolence of people at their honest and harmless sports and pastimes; at which there hath not been observed so much disorder, as is commonly at fairs and markets.

Touching *clerk-ales* (which are lesser church-ales) for the better maintenance of parish-clerks, they have been used (until late) in divers places, and there was great reason for them; for in poor country parishes, where the wages of the clerk is very small, the people, thinking it unfit that the clerk should duly attend at church, and lose by his office, were wont to send him in provisions and feast with him, and give him more liberally than their quarterly payments would amount unto in many years. And since these have been put down, some ministers have complained unto me, that they are afraid they shall have no parish-clerks, for want of maintenance for them. There is another kind of public meeting, called a *bid-ale*, when an honest man decayed in his estate is set up again by the liberal benevolence and contribution of friends at a Feast: but this is laid aside almost in every place.[46]

This unfortunate bishop was to suffer for his judicious reply, since when he was impeached in 1642 one of the articles against him was that he had profaned the Lord's Day by approving of wakes and revels.

The triumph of the Puritans marked the end of ales in churches. It is true that when the series of injunctions began again after the Restoration, there were two that enquired about 'feasts, banquets, church ales, drinkings', i.e. those of Layfield, Archdeacon of Essex, and of Pory, Archdeacon of Middlesex, both in 1662,[47] but they give the impression of unintelligent reproductions of pre-Commonwealth articles without consideration having been given to the actual situation in the 1660's. No other articles from 1662–1710 refer to church ales and we must dismiss this apparent evidence for them as simply an archaism, yet in his *Ex-ale-tation*, published in 1671, Peter Mew included the quotation:

> The churches must owe, as we all do know
> For when they be drooping and ready to fail
> By a Whitsun or Church-Ale up again they shall go,
> And owe their repairing to a pot of good ale.

But there is the occasional mention of church ales held elsewhere than in churches. In 1785 there was one at Greatworth.[48] In 1816 there was a Whit-ale at Bicester in a barn and another on Lammas Day at Kirtlington[49] and in the early nineteenth century one used to be held in a barn at Kingsutton.[50] Yet, further away from the centres of authority, something very like church ales persisted. As recently as 1750 it was a custom for people to gather to eat and drink in a church in the islands of Orkney[51] and the inhabitants of Lewis, one of the western islands, came to the church of St Mulway, at All

Saints, each with his provisions and a peck of malt that they brewed into ale in the church.[52]

Eating and drinking in churches in the Middle Ages was also associated with audits. At St Martin-in-the-Fields in 1531 eighteen pence was spent on bread, cheese and ale consumed 'in the church' when passing the accounts.[53] At St Mary's, Cambridge, in 1602, two shillings were paid for a bottle of sack 'which was drunk in the Chancel of the Auditors and others at the giving up of the last Churchwardens' accounts', and in 1603 the cost was two shillings and four pence 'for wine at the audit in the chancel'.[54]

Indeed, in the first half-century after the Reformation in England, eating and drinking continued as before. There are, for example, these three entries in the accounts of St Margaret's, Westminster:

1546   Paid on Ascension-even, for bread, ale, beer and wine,
       for the prebendaries and choir of the minster, after mass
       was done                                                    1s 2d.
1553   Paid for bread and drink on Ash-wednesday, to the
       ringers at victory and overthrow of Wyat and his
       adherents                                                      8d.
1554   Paid for bread, wine, beer and ale for Mr Deane, the
       prebendaries and the choir, when they came in pro-
       cession to our church                                     1s. 8d.[55]

In 1558 four gallons of ale and four pence in cakes were consumed in St Margaret's, Leicester.[56] Indeed, a church or chapel was regarded as a suitable dining-room. So in 1531 the Serjeants' Feast was held in Elie House, in the presence of King Henry and Queen Katherine, and since there were too many for the hall, some of the knights, esquires and gentlemen were seated 'in the Cloisters Chapel and gallery'.[57] While in 1554 at Rogationtide, the priest of Queen Mary's chapel went in procession to St Martin's 'and there a sermon was preached, and mass sung, and the company drank'.[58] The Guild of St George, Norwich, held its feasts in the chapel of the common hall of the city which had been formerly the church of the Dominican convent. In the late seventeenth century 'a barrel of good Ale' was brought into the church at Curry-Yeovil, Somerset, on St Nicholas's Day.[59] Even in the nineteenth century, churches were the scene of the partaking of refreshment. Thus in Hentland church, Ross, cakes and a cup of beer were offered. Sometimes this happened in the vestry, as at Romford, where, after the charity sermon had been preached, a table was covered with a large white cloth and bottles of port and sherry with plates of almonds, raisins and biscuits were provided for the clergy and their friends.[60] But in Sellack church, Hereford, on Palm Sundays, the churchwardens gave to all present in the nave buns and horns of cider; they then said: 'Peace and good neighbourhood' and the eating and drinking began.[61] There is too a report of 1843 which tells how the 'governors' of the church of Crediton 'used to dine together at stated times in one of the Chapels, their wine, etc. being kept in the church'.[62]

In former days the eucharist itself was seen more as a meal than as a token of it. In 1561 one gallon of wine was consumed by one hundred and eight communicants in St Peter Cheap on 25th October, and one pint for twenty-two on 13th April. At Easter in 1614 at Hartland, Devon, twelve gallons one quart of Canary were used,[63] and in 1622 in St Julian's, Shrewsbury, thirteen quarts. The comment of the Victorian Vaux upon this, after recording it, is typical of his era and show how the ideas prevalent in that period were severing the sacred and the secular. He says: 'well instructed Church folk . . . are accustomed to partake only a few drops from the chalice . . . The idea of more than three gallons being consumed . . . reveals a dreadful state of things'.[64] Indeed, in the nineteenth century the emphasis upon the holiness of the church building was even more pronounced than previously. This may be illustrated by what happened at St Briavel's, near Coleford, Gloucestershire. It was the custom to bring bread and cheese for distribution in the church on Whitsunday; but *c.* 1850 these items were thrown to those who wished to scramble for them from the church tower; shortly after this the point of distribution was the churchyard gate and finally in 1879 it ceased altogether.[65] The everyday life of the parishioners, represented by food and drink, was not to be allowed to intrude within the sacred precincts.

## Dancing

Dancing in churches, which had been a regular feature of medieval life, did not cease with the Reformation, even in Protestant countries, although in view of the prevailing climate of opinion, it was in-

evitably under attack in the latter. In 1544 a document was issued
with the title: *A Supplycacion to our moste Soveraigne Lorde Kynge
Henry the Eyght*. Among the items which it besought his majesty to
suppress was the 'keeping of church ales, in the which with leaping,
dancing, and kissing, they maintain the profit of their church'.[66] So
the story of the suppression of the church ales, which has been told in
the previous section, is also that of the condemnation of the dancing
which accompanied them. But besides these feastings, there was
also Morris dancing, for which we may cite as examples St Ives
and St Columb Major, Cornwall, in 1595.[67] In 1612 the churchwardens of Great Marlow, Buckinghamshire, derived part of their
income from the hiring out of their stock of Morris dancers' coats
and bells.[68]

Episcopal injunctions provide evidence of a sustained campaign
against this form of jollification in churches. Archbishop Grindal
appears to have made the first move, as he did in relation to church
ales. In his articles for York of 1571 he enquired about Morris
dancers coming 'unreverently into the church, or churchyard, and
then to dance'.[69] William Chaderton asked a similar question in his
articles for the diocese of Chester in 1581 and so did Overton of
Lichfield in 1584; we find the same in regard to Chichester and
Hereford, both in 1586.[70] In the opening decades of the seventeenth
century there was a steady flow of such enquiries: Bristol, 1603;
Lincoln, 1604; Oxford, 1619; Winchester, 1628; Bedford, 1629, and
Norfolk, 1632.[71] After the Restoration there are only two enquiries
—by Morley of Winchester in 1662 and Archbishop Sancroft for
Lincoln in 1686[72]—but these may be reproductions of previous
articles and are not necessarily proof of the continuation of Morris
dancing in churches. Yet in the late seventeenth century in Yorkshire country churches, on Christmas Day after service, the parishioners are reported to have danced to the singing of 'Yole! Yole!',[73]
while down to the end of the nineteenth century the villagers at
Spelsbury and Chipping Warden, Oxford, had Morris dancing on
the church towers.[74]

For Europe, and particularly for Roman Catholic areas, the evidence is more plentiful. At Aix, where dancing took place in the
Middle Ages, it was still going on in the cloisters of St Mary Mag-

dalen in 1647, despite previous condemnation by a diocesan synod in 1601. In St Stephen's in the sixteenth century there was dancing, too, after which the participants went to the chapel of St Martin's for food and drink.[75] In 1551 the provincial court of Narbonne tried to stop dancing in the cathedral and similar synodal statutes were issued in Lyons in 1566 and 1577.[76] An attack from the Protestant side was launched by Thomas Kirchmaier, whose work was translated into English by Barnabe Googe in 1570. He scornfully recounts the Christmas Day practice of placing a wooden doll on the altar 'about which both boys and girls do dance'.[77] But at Besançon, from 1582 to at least 1738, the *bergeratta* was danced in St Mary Magdalen after nones on Easter Day, in the cloisters or, if raining, in the nave.[78]

Up to the beginning of the seventeenth century there were dances in the churches of Bohemia[79] and in Paris at the same period clergy and singing-boys were to be seen dancing on Easter Day.[80] In 1682 when de Menestrier published his *Des ballets anciens et modernes suivant les règles du théâtre*, he noted in his preface that he had himself witnessed dancing in numerous Parisian churches to the singing of the prose *O filii et filiae*. At Barjols, in Provence, a triple dance was performed at mass on St Marcel's Day, and there is evidence for it down to 1913.[81] As late as 1749 a Basque bishop allowed male dancers and tambourine players to enter the church on Christmas Day and his permission was also extended to the festivals of the patron saints.[82] At Echternach in Luxemburg the medieval dance survived into the nineteenth century.[83] At the end of that century the dance known as *El Baile de Pifano* was performed in the churches of the mining districts of Chile, the men moving from cross to cross and altar to altar.[84] In Abyssinian churches and in the Azores, Whitsunday dancing has not yet died out,[85] while at Pola there is the *Guglia de San Paolino* on 26th June in honour of the patron saint.[86] In Breton chapels of the seventeenth and eighteenth centuries dancing was common,[87] while on 17th May, the feast of St Pascal Baylon, people still dance in front of his altar at Calatayud and at Manilla.[88]

Of all the dances, that of Los Seises at Seville is probably the most well known. Said to have been instituted by Cardinal Ximenes

(1436–1517) when he restored the Mozarabic rite at Toledo and Seville, it is performed on the feasts of Corpus Christi and the Immaculate Conception, during the octaves of these two, and the three days of carnival. Twelve choirboys, divided into groups of six, wear medieval costumes with castanets in their hands and dance before the Reserved Sacrament in the presence of the Cardinal Archbishop and his clergy.[89] Although closely linked with religious devotion, it is clearly a survival from a time when churches were centres of recreation, as well as of liturgical worship.

## The Sale of Goods

One of the features of Paul's Walk, to which many objected, was its use for the sale of merchandise; but this was not peculiar to that cathedral. Anglican visitation articles again provide evidence of a widespread attempt to stamp out this practice from all ecclesiastical buildings. As early as 1549 in *A Draft for Visitation Articles* the churchwardens were bidden to 'suffer no buying or selling, in church or churchyards, especially during common prayer, the sermon, and reading of the homily'.[90] The year following, Nicholas Ridley applied this to his London diocese, and John Hooper was so concerned about it that the item appears in his articles, in his interrogatories and in his injunctions of 1551–2,[91] although in this last he permitted it if there were a real need at times other than when services were being held. In 1557 Richard Barnes of Durham sought to prohibit pedlars from selling their wares 'in any churches, church-porches, or church yards' and Marmaduke Middleton of St David's in 1583 wanted to know 'whether any disturbance by fairs or brawling has been used in your church or churchyard'.[92] In 1603 Thornborough of Bristol enquired about 'fairs, markets or selling of wares' and Chalderton of Lincoln in 1604 about pedlars.[93] It is clear, however, that this practice was not as widespread in English churches as other secular activities. Not only is there no specific mention of it in the canons of 1603, but the series of injunctions makes much less reference to it than, for example, to church ales or dancing. Yet the evidence is extant and there have been survivals. In 1566 the 'dead men's bones' were cleared out of the vault of St Christopher le Stocks and it was leased as business premises for 5s a year. In 1581 a sempstress was allowed to hang her wares on the vestry wall of St Michael's Church, London.[94] In 1677 a shepherd was selling ale in the church of Thorpe-by-Newark.[95] There was also a quaint reminiscence of the connection of church and commerce in the middle of the nineteenth century at Lawton, Cheshire. The parish clerk there was named Briscall, and he was also the village cobbler. Clients who wanted their boots mended were accustomed to place them under the bench near the stove and close to the entrance; Briscall would collect them and bring them back repaired the following Sunday.[96]

In Roman Catholic countries selling was not immediately discontinued in the sixteenth century. Kirchmaier, whom we have already had occasion to quote, speaks of the selling of fish in church on St Ulric's Day, 4th July:

> Amid the church there sitteth one, and to the altar nigh,
> That selleth fish, and so good cheap, that every man may buy.[97]

But this was frowned upon by the ecclesiastical authorities, who had been waging a constant battle against the sale of goods in churches throughout the Middle Ages. By the end of the sixteenth century they had largely obtained their victory. In France the synod of Boulogne-la-Grasse of 1566 forbade the selling of goods in churches and porches and in Italy the fifth synod of Milan under Charles Borromeo in 1578 issued the same injunction.[98] Over the next century there appeared further prohibitions, but now they all concerned church porches, i.e. having expelled commerce from the nave, the struggle continued to push it out of appendages and so even further away from the sacred shrine. In 1579 the mayor of Loeins forbade stalls and booths and the display of goods in the cloisters and porches of Chartres cathedral. In 1628 the chapter issued a regulation forbidding shops in the cloisters near the steps, but allowed them elsewhere if they caused no inconvenience. In 1675 the mayor of Loeins prohibited 'the opening of shops and the sale of all kinds of merchandise, as well as lotteries and draws, teeth extractors, singers and vendors of songs', but excepted such articles as rosaries, medals, Chartres shirts and food for pilgrims, although two years later the chapter itself forbade the sale of anything.[99] The mayor had the future on his side, for to this day Roman Catholic churches and cathedrals frequently have stalls either at the rear of the nave or in the porch for the sale of postcards, rosaries and other objects of devotion—commerce has continued but is mainly confined to articles with religious associations.

## Meetings

Neither the Reformation nor the Counter-Reformation affected the use of churches for meetings of all kinds.

(i) *Councils.* In England, convocation, removed by Wolsey from St Paul's, found a home in Henry VIII's chapel at Westminster. In 1562, for example, there were thirty-six sessions, some in the chapter house of St Paul's and the remainder in the abbey. In 1564 the chapel was still the scene of the gathering. In 1603 it began at St Paul's on 20th March and adjourned to Westminster on 6th November.[100] But the outstanding example of modern times, which is still fresh in people's minds, is the Second Vatican Council which occupied St Peter's for month after month. Provincial and diocesan synods also used churches, but to some this was a desecration since the ecclesiastics present tended to litter the altar 'with skull caps, handkerchiefs, spectacle cases, snuff boxes, and many other things of the same nature'.[101]

City councils continued their medieval habit of having their sessions in churches. In 1582 the Head Court of the borough of Elgin met in the parish church and in 1590 there was an assembly of the common council before the mayor in the chancel of St George's, Doncaster.[102] At Cartmel, near Windermere, in 1597, the affairs of the town were managed by a body known as the Twenty-four Sidesmen; they met in the church. In 1676 the burgesses of Sheffield were similarly using the parish church.[103]

(ii) *Elections and Appointments.* The medieval custom of electing churchwardens and mayors in churches was not interrupted in any way. The former practice can be illustrated very fully by a description which was included at the end of the accounts for 1667 in the records of St Margaret's, Westminster. There had been a dispute about the election and so it was deemed necessary to give a statement of the procedure for future reference:

The churchwardens are chosen according to the ancient customs at the said parish (time out of mind) the Thursday immediately before Whitsunday, after the manner following:

There is a bell appointed to be tolled, by which the parishioners have notice, and thereupon do repair unto the church, to see the church-wardens which be going out of their office deliver up their accounts and balance moneys; and also to understand who be chosen churchwardens for the year ensuing. Then they have a table set in the chancel, at which the doctor or minister of the parish, and the rest of the vestry-men do sit, and thither the churchwardens in being bring their accounts fairly engrossed, and bound up in vellum, together with the balance moneys; the ancient vestry-men at the upper end of the table receiving the same, and inspecting at least the total sums of what has been received, what paid, and what remains to adjust the said churchwardens' accounts. Then they order and appoint some that have already executed the same office of churchwardens to audit the said accounts and within one month to make report thereof unto them. This being done, the vestry-men adjourn from thence into the vestry-room, and there take out of the records of the names of former overseers of the poor, the names of eight or ten persons, and set them down after this manner:    A.B.

C.D.

always setting down the younger of the present churchwardens first: then they debate the fittest man for that office; and so every one crossing those whom they judge the most meet, they that have the most crosses carry it. As soon as this is done, they give the paper into the hands of the minister, who immediately goes therewith into the reading-pew, and there in the open church, and in the audience of the parishioners present, publishes and declares the names of the persons elected churchwardens, to the end that they may have notice of the same. After this the churchwardens expired do use to invite the doctor or minister, together with the vestry-men, and other ancient inhabitants of the parish, to a supper at the charge of the said churchwardens.

NB   The churchwardens chosen after this form were adjudged to be the right churchwardens, by a decree of the commissary Dr Exton, and afterwards by a court of delegates, against Baker and Edwards, who were chosen by some of the inhabitants in the church porch.

The year following, i.e. 1668, Samuel Baker and Thomas Edwards had to pay £20 6s 8d to defray the legal costs incurred in this dispute.[104]

Whereas at Westminster the business was conducted partly in the chancel and partly in the vestry, at Codrington the election took place in the sanctuary, where the folk sat smoking and drinking. In

1692 this was declared to have been the custom for the past sixty years.[105] It was further the general practice for the rector or vicar to swear in the newly elected wardens in front of the congregation at Morning or Evening Prayer on the Sunday immediately following the meeting.[106]

The election of beadles was also held in churches, and in his *Sketches* by *Boz* Charles Dickens has provided a graphic description. The election was in two stages: first the nominations and then, at a later date, the voting. According to Dickens the first step should have been taken in the vestry, but on the occasion he describes the number of interested parishioners was so great that it had to be held in the church. The proposers of the two rival candidates expatiated on their merits to the accompaniment of cheers and boos. At the second session the polling was held and one of them was duly elected.[107]

Elections for civic offices are particularly well documented for the county of Kent. In Lydd church there is a monumental brass of Clement Stuppeney, who died in 1608. It lies on a large altar-tomb in the middle of the north chancel, although it was formerly in the south chancel. It was around this that the jurats of Lydd elected their town bailiff each St Mary Magdalen's Day. In New Romney church there is a similar tomb (Plate 11) erected in 1622 by another Clement Stuppeney in memory of his great-grandfather Richard; around this the jurats annually elected their mayor. The inscription reads:

Here lyeth buryed the bodye of Richard Stuppenye jurate of this towne in the first yeare of K. Hy. viij. who dyed in the xviij yeare of the sayde kynges reigne of whose memorye Clement Stuppenye of the same port his great grandsonne hath caused this tombe to be new erected for the use of the auncient meeting and election of maior and jurats of this port towne. June the 10th. Anno Dm. 1622.[108]

At Sandwich until 1683 the mayor was elected in St Clement's; at Fordwick near Canterbury the church was used until the early eighteenth century, and at Derby the north aisle of All Saints' until the early nineteenth century.[109]

The mayoral procession to a church after his election is often an indication that the church had originally been the place where he was appointed. At Norwich from 1772 to 1835 the mayor and corporation went in this way to the cathedral, preceded by whifflers, swordsmen, musicians, standards of blue and silver, crimson and gold, the councillors in their robes, the mace bearer, the city waits, the marshalmen and the civic authorities, with the sword borne erect. They went through the nave and were met at the entrance to the choir by the dean and chapter.[110]

In Dover in 1583 they began to elect the mayor and the town's parliamentary representatives at the communion table in St Mary's, because St Peter's, where they had previously assembled, was in a bad state of repair, and it was not until 1826 that the elections were moved to the town hall. This election of members of parliament was common in churches. In 1679, for example, the one for Southwark was held in St Mary Overy.[111] In 1825 it was taking place in Cirencester church,[112] but the following year a bill was introduced into the House of Commons to forbid it. Speaking against the motion, Sir Charles Banbury stated that he could see no good reason why members of the house, as well as the officers of a town, should not be elected in churches:

Sir, our pious and rational ancestors contented themselves with this mode of election, why are we to put the counties and boroughs to the expense they must necessarily be at, if this bill pass into law? Nor do I see why the electors themselves should not meet in a church when those elected themselves meet in a chapel.[113]

Sir Charles's argument was not accepted and the bill became law.

In one particular the post-Reformation period did witness a development in elections, or rather appointments. The vestry was becoming more and more an organ of local government as the parish, previously an area of ecclesiastical jurisdiction, was recognized by the State as an area for civil administration. To it fell the task of appointing constables and surveyors of highways. So at Denton, near Grantham, from *c.* 1450 to the early eighteenth century, there were meetings in the church to elect town officers and constables.[114] In 1662 it was ordered that wardens and constables or tithingmen were to appoint the surveyors of highways 'with the advice and consent of the major part of the inhabitants' in church after Morning Prayer on Tuesday in Easter Week.[115] At Adlingfleet, near Goole, the church became a polling booth for the election of the Commissioners of Drainage in 1767,[116] while according to William Hone, writing in 1826, St Thomas's Day, i.e. 21st December, was the day when 'the guardians of the inquest' are chosen 'in church'.[117]

(iii) *Discussions and Lectures.* That a church should be used for theological debate will no doubt seem reasonable to most people. In the seventeenth century, when Puritanism was a fierce bone of contention in England, we find several instances of such discussions. Under James I the Bishop of Peterborough held a two-day disputation in the cathedral with those of his clergy who were of the Puritan persuasion.[118] During the Commonwealth such scenes were not infrequent. At Henley-in-Arden the orthodox Presbyterian minister argued in his church with five self-styled preachers—a nailer, a baker, a ploughwright, a weaver and a baker's boy—on the subject of 'preaching with or without call'. At Kendal, a baptist named Thomas Taylor debated with three Presbyterian divines in the parish church and was deemed to have established his case against infant baptism, whereupon his followers ran up the high street crying: 'Mr Taylor hath got the day!'[119]

Sometimes the discussion related to the general running of the church. For example, in 1536 certain of the inhabitants of Morebath, Somerset, had failed to pay their agreed contribution towards the salary of the parish clerk and so the vicar was without assistance. A dispute ensued, and four men were chosen under order at a visitation. On a Sunday in church the parishioners were asked if they would accept the four men and abide by their decision. Twenty-six agreed and five dissented, so because of the lack of unanimity a second meeting was called for the Sunday before Rogation week and the parishioners were again asked to assent. 'All that were in the church said yes.' Details of the payments were then agreed, the clerk's duties were itemized and the matter was settled.[120] In 1573 another matter of community concern was discussed in the Dutch church in London. The congregation was suspected of being a hotbed of Puritanism and received a letter from the lords of the council about this. Accordingly they assembled in church where the letter was read out and a suitable reply was framed.[121]

The most common discussions however were of an entirely secular nature. The parish vestry, as we have already noted, was now becoming the organ of local government; all aspects of community life, therefore, could be and were argued about throughout the year in the parish churches. At Royston, Hertfordshire, the vestry minutes affirm that 'all meetings to be at the church at toll of bell, and adjourn as they think proper'. At St Martin's, Leicester, the parish meeting was in the side chapel built by the Corpus Christi Guild.[122] So we have a meeting in the church of Holme Cultram, Cumberland, in 1718 to agree upon the provision of a house for the schoolmaster.[123] We have meetings about the poor rate, e.g. 24th July 1720, when the chancel of Tunstall church, Kent, was the scene of a gathering to determine the rate. The overseer of the poor, Thomas Banister, was charged with producing a schedule and this was presented on Sunday, 7th August, 'at which time the parishioners being again assembled in the chancel (the place where the parish meetings are usually held)' reached a common mind.[124] In 1773 at Mountstone, Salop, the vestry met in the church to consider an individual case relating to the maintenance of a poor boy.[125] In 1822 there was a public meeting in the parish church of Leeds to decide upon the demolition of Middle Row,[126] while until 1816 it was the custom for the villagers of Puxton, Somerset, to be called together to the church to draw lots for the division of Dolmoors Common.[127]

These meetings did not necessarily confine themselves to local matters. In 1815 the Greenwich vestry denounced the new Corn Bill; the following year it condemned the Property or Income Tax; in 1820 it welcomed Queen Caroline and criticized the conduct of the king. At Brighton in 1831 we find the meeting supporting the Reform Bill.[128]

The attendance could be very large indeed. In June 1828 three to five thousand people were in Leeds parish church to determine the property rate for poor assessment.[129] Moreover, the debates were frequently very heated; this was often the case in the Collegiate Church (now the Cathedral) of Manchester. 'When the Churchwardens and Constables appeared in the old Collegiate Church to pass their accounts and took their stand by the old "parish table", they would occasionally have to face a howling mob of several thousand persons, who filled the whole building, perched themselves on every coign of vantage, and vigorously applauded the speeches of their champions.' Indeed in 1820 the radical forces in the town rallied their supporters by printing handbills.[130] Not infrequently the altar was used as the chairman's table and at small gatherings those present would sit around it, much to the disgust of a contributor to the *Ecclesiologist* of 1843 who reported this behaviour in a parish church 'not four miles from Cambridge'.[131]

There is a vivid picture of the goings-on in an account of 1838, which, though fictional, is based upon contemporary incidents. At three miles' distance from the church of Welbourne, where one of the heroes of the narrative was the incumbent, there was a large centre of population known as Ashdale. The incumbent decided it must have a church, but the inhabitants of Ashdale, who are represented as an irreligious mob, would have none of it. A vestry meeting was summoned to levy a church rate and the Ashdale people came in a body to oppose it. The vicar rallied the members of his congregation and at noon on the day of the meeting they came together. The Ashdalers then appeared 'walking in a body three and three abreast straight up the middle of the village, followed by a crowd of boys from the factory, and carrying a flag, borrowed from an adjoining borough, bearing inscribed on it in large letters: "Civil and religious liberty"'. The crowd was so great that a meeting in the vestry was out of the question, 'so there was no alternative but to make use of the body of the church, much to Herbert's regret, who grieved to see the holy place made the scene of ungodly contention'. The vicar then read the notice of the meeting and the churchwardens gave their estimate. The opposition was led by a Mr Stubbs, said to be the principal shopkeeper at Ashdale, who stood on one of the pews and, assisted by the applause of his supporters, declared that he would not be a party to imposing a tax for an Anglican building upon Dissenters. Whereupon up stood a Dissenter and declared that since he had recently bought a house subject to a certain deduction for the Church rate, he would be acting dishonestly if he did not pay it. His contribution to the discussion won the day and the rate was agreed, those for being three times as many as those against.[132]

Besides these somewhat riotous proceedings must be set the more solemn occasions when churches were used as lecture halls. So, for example, *c.* 1584, a lectureship in mathematics was established in the chapel within the Leaden Hall, London. In 1588, because the chapel was taken over as a storage for goods from a captured Spanish galleon, the lecture was given in a private house.[133] In the early seventeenth century many churches had lectureships attached to them, but these were really Puritan inspired attempts to ensure that the people heard more sermons, rather than lectures.

(iv) *Financial transactions.* The evidence adduced in the previous section of vestry meetings also serves to illustrate one of the financial transactions conducted in churches, viz. the auditing of accounts, and there is no need to detail further examples. Attention, however, must be directed to the briefs, of which there were an abundance in the post-Reformation period. Briefs were letters patent issued out of Chancery on petition giving authority for a collection for a specific purpose. The following is a representative selection:

1571, Kingston, a mother and daughter allowed to collect because of the death of the husband at the hands of the 'Wylde Iryshe'.[134]

1611, Great Wigston, Leicestershire. 'Gave the men coming from Jerusalem, having the admiral's license for the ransoming of their seven sons'.

1626, Great Wigston. 'Given to Waterless Burnstable, in the county of Devon, which town was burnt down with fire, which seemed to come from heaven, which burnt 400 houses and above; where was burnt 7 score and 14 persons, and 8 women in their beds, and 500 more women that lost goods, by estimation amounting to 200,000 pounds'.[135]

1655, London. 'There was a collection for the Persecuted Churches and Christians in Savoy'.[136]

1686, London. 'A Brief was read in all churches for relieving the French Protestants who came here for protection from the unheard of cruelties of their King'.[137]

1690, Springthorpe, Lincolnshire. A collection for Teignmouth which had suffered destruction at the hands of the French.

1700, Ormskirk. A brief for the poor slaves in Sully, on the west coast of Morocco and a stronghold of slavery.[138]

This practice, however, became an abuse and four decades before the last example Samuel Pepys had expressed his dissatisfaction. '30th June 1661. To church, where we observe the trade of briefs is come now up to so constant a course every Sunday, that we do resolve to give no more to them.' In 1705 parliament sought to regulate the abuses and in 1825 finally abolished the practice.

Samuel Pepys is also witness to another financial transaction, viz. the collection of salaries. On Sunday, 6th January 1660–1, he noted: 'To church again, where, before service, a long Psalm was set that lasted an hour, while the sexton gathered his year's contribution through the whole church.' The church also was the place where the High Constable rendered accounts to the Justices of the Peace. So in July 1612 we have the statement that 'Tho Jackson, one of the High Constables of Hang East, shall repair to the Church of Pattrick Brompton on Monday next, to render account to Sir Comers Darcy and Sir Arthur Dakins of all moneys received by him for bridges or other matters'.[139]

(v) *Degree Congregations.* The two churches of St Mary in the universities of Oxford and Cambridge continued to be the scene of degree congregations. In recording this for the decade from 1577 to 1587 Harrison remarks that the occasion is termed an 'Act' at Oxford and 'Commensement' at Cambridge.[140] Not quite eighty years later John Evelyn described the Act at Oxford on 10th July 1654:

In the afternoon I tarried out the whole Act in St Mary's, the long speeches of the Proctors, the Vice-Chancellor, the several Professors, creation of Doctors by the cap, kiss, ring, etc. those ancient ceremonies and institutions being as yet not wholly abolish'd. Dr Kendal, now Inceptor amongst others, performing his Act incomparably well, concluded it with an excellent oration, abating his Presbyterian animosities, which he withheld not even against that learned and pious divine Dr Hammond. The Act was closed with the speech of the Vice-Chancellor, there being but 4 in Theology, 3 in Medicine, which was thought a considerable matter, the times being consider'd.

On 9th July 1669, however, Evelyn was at Oxford again for the opening of the Sheldonian Theatre. He continued:

This being at the Act and the first time of opening the Theatre (Acts being formerly kept in St Mary's Church, which might be thought indecent, that being a place set apart for the immediate worship of God, and was the inducement for building this noble pile) it was now resolv'd to keep the present Act in it.

So the 'holiness' of the church building had cut it off from direct association with academic assemblies.

## Legal Proceedings

We have previously considered legal proceedings in churches in connection with ecclesiastical courts, the ordeal, secular courts and inquests, and the payment of dues, either in cash or in kind. In the period after the Reformation all these uses continued.

One type of case was not infrequent in the latter half of the sixteenth century, viz. that concerned with presumed heresy. In 1548 some Anabaptists were tried on this score in St Paul's.[141] A few years later, with Mary on the throne, it was the anti-papalists that were the accused. In 1555 Latimer, Ridley and Cranmer were tried in St Mary's, Oxford, and condemned to the stake. In the same year one John Rogers was tried in St Mary Overy, Southwark; one Cardmaker, sometime vicar of St Bride's, in St Paul's,[142] and one Richard Taylor 'in the Arches at Bow Church'.[143] With the accession of Elizabeth it was Puritanism that was suppressed. In 1574 two adherents were cited to the church of Kirkby-in-Ashfield. This particular venue was apparently selected to avoid publicity, and indeed one of the defendants protested that the archdeacon 'did not well to call him to such an hole as Kirkby church is, where was so small an audience'.[144] Two years later another Puritan was sentenced by the Dean of Norwich sitting in St George's church.[145]

Churches remained the normal places for visitation courts, unless some untoward circumstances arose. When in 1582 a riot broke out in the bishop's court in Lichfield Cathedral, he had it transferred to his palace.[146] At Oxford the episcopal court was held in All Saints', while the archdeacon's had its sessions in St Martin's; the latter took place weekly, usually on Fridays and Saturdays.[147] All over the country churches were being used in this way. In 1591 St Andrew's, Holborn, was so employed.[148] In the same year, at Woodbury, Devon, there was a visitation court to assess the malt tax for the maintenance of the church. By 1631 the assessment had proved insufficient and another court met in the church to resolve what each individual should contribute.[149] In 1594 the Commissioners for Ecclesiastical Causes sat in the chancel of the Collegiate Church of

Southwell to give judgment in a dispute about the election of church-wardens at Mansfield, Nottinghamshire.[150] The archdeacon's court at Taunton sat in St Mary Magdalen, and the records extant for 19th September 1623 to 9th April 1624 show that during that period there were eighteen sessions, which were usually at fortnightly intervals on Fridays from 9 to 11 a.m.[151] Laud, in his orders for the cathedral of Norwich of 1635 and in those for Peterborough of the same year, required provision for consistories at the west end of each.[152]

It might be supposed that the ordeal had long since disappeared, and indeed in the form of the hot iron it had lapsed after the Lateran Council of 1215 had forbidden clergy to take part in it. But we encounter a peculiar relic of it in 1759 at Wingrive, near Aylesbury. A woman had been accused of bewitching a spinning wheel so that it would no longer turn. Her husband insisted that she be tried by the church bible—she went to the parish church, stripped to her shift and was weighed against the bible; since she was the heavier she was acquitted.[153]

The holding of secular courts in churches is mainly indicated by the injunctions against the practice. In 1565 a synod at Naples forbade secular business and law courts in churches, and a synod of Viterbo in 1614 made the same pronouncement. There would seem to have been the same processes as we have previously noted in connection with fairs. These European synods at first concentrated on moving secular legal proceedings out of the church; then when this had been accomplished they made a further effort to relegate them from the porches. So statutes of Evreux in 1664, of Agen and Soissons in 1673 and of Sens in 1678 only mention the hearing of suits in church porches.[154] Thus in the fifty years between 1614 and 1664 this particular battle had been won.

In England a similar movement was afoot. The Anglican Reformers did not immediately turn their attention to law courts; their first preoccupation was church ales, then fairs and plays. So we hear how in Holy Trinity, Chester, in 1540, a suit was brought about certain hides belonging to a shoemaker, and cases were heard in St Nicholas, Aberdeen in 1549, 1562 and 1613.[155] But in 1608 the archdeacon of Norfolk attacked 'leets and lay juries'[156] and from then on, with the addition of 'temporal courts', the onslaught was constant up to the outbreak of the Civil War. Injunctions relating to them are to be found dated 1611, 1619, 1624, 1625, 1629, 1632, 1633, 1636 and 1640.[157] They reappear in Pory's articles for Middlesex of 1662, but these, as we have previously noted, are probably an anachronism.[158] Hence in 1703 Bishop William Nicolson of Carlisle noted that there was a tradition at Ravenstondale that the benches in the choir had previously been used by the Steward and Jury of the Manor for trying capital offences.[159]

Nevertheless there were a few survivals. In the churches of Derbyshire in the seventeenth century inquests were still being held. A coroner's citation of 1689, for example, orders the constables of Bradborne, Brassington, Kniveton and Parwich to summon 'four-and-twenty honest and lawful men of your several liberties to be and appear before me, or my sufficient deputy, at the church of Bradborne tomorrow, being Sunday, the tenth day of November instant' at 11 a.m.[160] In 1763 at Ashover there were prosecutions in the church for felony and larceny[161] and Ritson in his *Jurisdiction of the Court Leet* published in 1791 asserted that in many churches courts were still held. In the Isle of Man the annual Tinwald Court sat in the chapel of St John, the building dating from 1847 on the site of a previous chapel.[162]

The evidence for payments in churches is most plentiful for the decades immediately after the Reformation, being perhaps best regarded as a left-over from the Middle Ages, although information regarding later centuries is not entirely lacking. In 1543 the Earl of Argyle granted the revision of certain lands upon the payment of two hundred marks at the altar of Our Lady in the church of Strathlachan. In 1551 Sir Robert Urquhard paid a mortgage of £30 at the altar of St James in the cathedral of Dornoch, and in 1554 a bond of £100 was settled at the high altar of the church of Chapel-en-le-Frith, Derbyshire. In 1580 a mortgage payment of £304 was made in Eyam church, also in Derbyshire.[163] In the same year all the London clergy were required to go to Christ's Church and there to pay one-sixtieth of the value of their benefices towards the rebuilding of a church in Denbigh which had been ruined.[164] In 1628 five people who had received loans from the churchwardens of Pittington,

Durham, returned the various sums in the chancel.[165] The
fathers of bastard children paid the money to the mothers for their
weekly maintenance, e.g. at Richmond in July 1625, it was decreed:
'the father of a bastard child to pay the mother thereof 4d a week
until the child be 7 years old, the payment to be made week by week
in Catterick Church on the Sunday, before noon'.[166]

Rents, too, were paid in churches and it was not until 1846 that the
incumbent of Caister, Lincolnshire, managed to stop the practice.[167]
Tithes also could be rendered in kind in the church, as in 1762 when
butter and cheese were brought to the chancel of Zennor church,
Cornwall.[168] We must note finally that until the end of the last
century the sale of land in the Isle of Portland was not held to be
valid until it had been confirmed before the altar.[169]

## Publishing of Notices

The worldly concerns of a congregation can often be gauged by
the subject matter of their public notices. Whereas at the present
day most of these are ecclesiastically centred, in former centuries
any and every community concern was given an airing. So in a
series of visitation articles of 1630 the parish clerk is required to give
notice, 'touching any goods strayed away or wanting, or of any Leet
court to be held, or of common-days-work to be made'.[170] When the
holding of courts in churches began to decrease, it was still customary to give notice from the pulpit of the meetings of secular courts,
e.g. in 1656 at Hathersage, Derbyshire, the convening of the Court
Baron was announced.[171] Other items of public interest might be of
a political nature, as the notice heard by John Evelyn on 2nd September 1683. 'This morning was read in the Church, after the office was
done, the declaration setting forth the late conspiracy against the
King's person.'

Individuals availed themselves of this means to enquire after
goods they had lost—there is an example from 1709.[172] Charity
commissioners made public their plans to see if any objections
would be raised—so at Sutton Bonington, Nottinghamshire, in 1731,
where some charities had been amalgamated and there was a pro-
posal to buy a cottage and land with the money, the residue to be
distributed to the poor; since no one questioned this, the purchase

was effected.[173] Details of legislation were proclaimed—so at Normanton-on-Soar, Nottinghamshire, in 1770, the text of the Enclosure Act was read immediately after the service.[174] The minister could use this means to show his interest in the everyday life of his flock, as in 1807 at Mayhole, Scotland. There had been a great deal of rain which jeopardized the harvest; on one Sunday it cleared and the minister took it upon himself to declare in church that he conceived 'the favourable change of weather might be used of to save the harvest on that day, without violating the sabbath'. He was later arraigned before the synod of Glasgow and Ayre for breaking the fourth commandment, but was acquitted.[175]

About 1816 a parish clerk was used to invite the tradesmen in the congregation to tender for the supply of bread to the poor[176] and from 1825–35 in a church near Welbeck Abbey the clerk announced the date of the Duke of Rutland's rent day.[177] According to Sir Walter Scott it was common for the traders in cattle near Hexham, 'which business is carried on to a great extent, to carry all letters received in course of trade to the parish church, when the clerk reads them aloud after service, and answers them according to the circumstances'.[178] Another clerk, of Belton, Suffolk, was in the habit of issuing appeals for help in finding a strayed horse and announcing the discovery of lost sheep.[179] In the same year that this man died, 1837, Victoria came to the throne and a statute was passed forbidding the publication of these secular matters. Yet another step had been taken in isolating the parish church from the concerns of the parishioners.

### Storing

The keeping of valuables and documents in churches is not well attested after the Reformation. An occasional early reference is no more than a witness to the slow abandonment of medieval habits. So the Guild of Lench's Trust in Birmingham in 1540 kept its papers in a chest in St Martin's.[180] Again, when the Bishop of Ely in 1575 kept his milk pans in the chapel in Downham Park 'in the heat of the summer, for two or three days in time of thunder',[181] he was only acting in the same way as those ecclesiastics who had used the church to store hay or barley. Further, we have few notices of animals, although in 1550 an Essex vicar sheltered his sheep in his church during a particularly heavy fall of snow.[182] Into some churches animals were introduced for an annual blessing, e.g. horses in Hertfordshire and also in Bavaria.[183] But the main items stored can most properly be described as those intimately connected with community life.

At Puxton, Somerset, the chain for measuring the common land was kept in the church until 1825. Its length was checked each year at a meeting in the nave by placing 'one end thereof at the foot of the arch, dividing the chancel from the body of the church, and extending it through the middle aisle, to the foot of the arch of the west door under the tower, at each of which places marks were cut in the stones for that purpose'.[184]

Fire-fighting appliances were also stored and were increasing in their variety and complexity. In 1628 there were one hundred and ninety buckets in the four churches in Northampton. Four years previously six wooden scoops were listed in St Bartholomew Exchange, and St Botolph, Aldersgate, in 1632–3 had 'one Brasse Squirt'.[185] Some churches had complex machines, as we learn from an entry in the accounts of St Margaret's, Westminster, for 1661, when six shillings were paid 'for bringing back the engine from Whitehall when the fire was there'.[186] The intimate association of church and fire fighting is shown by a quatrain in Dryden's description of the Great Fire of London:

> Now streets grow throng'd and busy as by day:
> Some run for buckets to the hallow'd quire,
> Some cut the pipes and some the engines play,
> And some, more bold, mount ladders to the fire.

In 1843 the *Ecclesiologist* recorded with disgust that 'at Great Shelford a fire-engine is kept in the church (a common but scandalous practice), and the walls adorned with rows of black buckets'.[187]

The store of parish armour was also increasing. The best surviving collection in England, with pieces ranging from 1470 to 1600, is at Mendlesham, Suffolk, but we also find arrays in the churches of Langwathby, and Great Salkeld, Cumberland; Over Peover, Cheshire; Higham Ferrars, Northamptonshire; Wimbledon, London, and in Norwich cathedral.[188] These of course had to be kept in trim and in 1568 the Queen ordered a survey and her commissioner was authorized to enter all churches, castles and houses in order to accomplish this.[189] In 1579 at St Margaret's, Westminster, there was an outlay 'for scouring of the armour and shot against the muster in Totehill Fields': the inventory of the church seventeen years before included seven sheaves of arrows and six daggers.[190] The storage of arms sometimes required special provision as when a frame was erected in the church of Cheddar, 1632, to keep the arrows. Sometimes it could be hazardous, as when the church of Basingstoke was 'much torn' in 1646 by an explosion, accidentally set off.[191]

This does not exhaust the list of items stored. There were ducking-stools for scolds; there were stocks for those condemned of petty crimes; there were even ploughs. This last implement was used on the Monday after Epiphany, Plough Monday, when the young men of the parish yoked themselves and went from house to house to collect money. Those who refused to contribute had the ground before their doors ploughed up. Such a plough, for example, was bought by the wardens of Cratfield in 1547.[192] At Wartinbury, Kent, they had the 'Dumb borsholders'—this was a club with iron spikes borne by the head man at the annual court leet; he was charged with seeking out goods unlawfully concealed and his mace served to break down doors if necessary; it was used down to 1748.[193]

There were also appliances for dealing with vermin. So great was the damage to crops through their depredations that numerous acts of parliament were passed requiring churchwardens to keep nets and traps in church to be loaned out for use. The wardens had further to pay for the head of every prescribed bird or beast brought into the church. So at Pittington, Durham, in 1628: 'It was agreed upon by the gentlemen and twelve of this parish that whosoever shall take any fox or badger in this parish and bring the head to the church shall have twelve pence paid by the churchwardens.'[194]

These were all matters involving the community; it was only occasionally that individuals availed themselves of the church for storage, as when Widow Warde at Great Bricett kept 'divers poles and tressels' in the chancel at fair time in 1597[195] or the parish clerk of Itchingfield, Sussex, who, in 1637-8, laid his faggots in the belfry, and Susan Cook of Little Badow, Essex, who 'laid her linen in the church to dry'.[196]

Just as medieval churches fulfilled in part the function of a modern museum, so curiosities were on show in ecclesiastical buildings in the post-Reformation period. With our twentieth-century facilities for travel and our knowledge of oddities old and new, it is difficult for us to appreciate the keen interest of our ancestors in a whole range of things that they found unusual. Something of their spirit may be recaptured from the pages of John Evelyn's Diary. On 22nd October 1684, 'I went with Sir William Godolphin to see the Rhinoceros, or Unicorn, being the first that I suppose was ever brought into England. . . . At the same time I went to see a Crocodile, brought from some of the West Indian Islands.' In the light of this, we can understand why there was 'hanged up for show' in St Lawrence in the Jewry a huge shank bone of a man and a massive tooth.[197] We can appreciate the interest in the wax effigies of the kings and queens of England which were kept in wainscot presses above the Islip Chapel in Westminster Abbey and attracted visitors from the fourteenth to the nineteenth century to see what was vulgarly known as 'The Play of the Dead Volks'.[198] A similar display in Beauvais cathedral equally attracted tourists.[199]

## Teaching

The Renaissance, with its emphasis upon human learning, gave an immense impetus to the foundation and organization of schools. In this section, however, we are not concerned with the great foundations but with the more humble, but none the less important, classes conducted in parish churches. Nor is our concern primarily religious teaching—which would embrace the development of the Sunday School—but with secular learning, with teaching the children their three R's. To provide a list of all schools occupying church buildings would be both tedious and unnecessary. What is needed is a sufficient number of varied examples to illustrate how extensive the practice was. That it was extensive is immediately evident from the fact that it gave currency to a quasi-proverb. In *Twelfth Night* Shakespeare describes Malvolio as one 'like a pedant that keeps a school i' the church'.[200]

In 1547 there was a school in the Thurstone chantry at Wakefield.[201] At Lathbury, Buckinghamshire, Anthony Cave endowed a school in 1552 to be kept in a chapel in the churchyard.[202] In 1573 at Wragley, Yorkshire, there was a pew where school 'was and at this period is accustomed to be kept'.[203] At Ilkley, Yorkshire, there was a grammar school in the church from 1592 to 1635 when a voluntary rate was levied and a special house built.[206] In 1593 Mr Edward Rogers held his class in St Margaret's, Lothbury, during the hot weather 'for the better keeping of his scholars in good order'.[205] At Amersham, Buckinghamshire, in 1621, there was a free grammar school in the church until a school house was erected.[206] In 1617 a house was built at Snaith, Yorkshire, for a school that had been in the church for a generation previously.[207] At Attelborough, Norfolk, a chapel was used as a school in 1623.[208] The diarist John Evelyn was taught during 1624 'at the church porch of Wotton'. In 1634 the parish clerk of St Mary Colechurch was presented to keep a school in the church, 'he behaving himself well and honestly'.[209] In 1636 the chancel and vestry at Patrington were used as a school and are said to have been occupied for this purpose for twenty years.[210] Later in the century we hear of a school in the church at Curry-Yeovil, Somerset.[211]

Thanks to the visitation of the Carlisle diocese in 1703–4 by Bishop William Nicolson and to the very full notes he made, we can obtain a clear picture of the situation at the beginning of the eighteenth century. The bishop visited one hundred and one churches; in nineteen of these schools were being held, as well as in two chapels of ease, i.e. a fifth of all the churches was in use as a school. In ten of them teaching took place in the choir, in three in the south aisle, in two at the west end, in one in the vestry and in another in the nave; in four cases the exact location is unspecified.[212] In general there were no objections to this secular activity on the grounds that it involved the profanation of a sacred building, although in 1625 William, Bishop of Lincoln, and in 1629 Eland, Archdeacon of Bedford, had included schools with the feasts and temporal courts they wished to exclude from churches.[213] Never-theless, Bishop Nicolson was anxious wherever possible to move the schools into their own quarters, his reason being the damage to the fabric that was often inseparable from the high spirits of the pupils. The kind of pranks to which they were prone may be illustrated by the scholars in Cawthorne parish church nearly a hundred years before Nicolson in 1618. When there was a wedding, these boys would barricade the bride's party inside the church and refuse to allow exit until a ransom had been paid, either sixpence or the bride's left shoe.[214]

Nicolson himself makes a number of caustic comments on school-boy behaviour. Writing of Farlam, he says that 'the Teaching of Children in the Quire (a General practice) is a great inconveni-ence'.[215] At Westward the boys were in the chancel, 'tho' I could have wish'd to have seen them elsewhere . . . and spoiling Mr Barwis's monument (at the West-end of the Church) with writing their copies upon it'. Of Wigton church he notes that the seats and pavements have been 'somewhat abused by the Scholars'. Referring to Holme he mentions 'the Mischief commonly done by such Inmates'. Of Irthington he notes that 'the Quire is here (as before) miserably spoil'd, on the floor, by the Schoolboys'; of Ousby, 'the Body of the Church is such a Condition as is usual when boys are taught in it'; of Shap, 'the Floor, Seats and Communion-Table are miserably abus'd by the Scholars that are taught in it'.[216]

In view of these conditions it is understandable that attempts should have been made to transfer the teaching to other buildings. Bishop Nicolson himself, for example, suggested at Shap that the school might go into the newly built town hall which was only in use occasionally for the Manor Court.[217] Yet this could be achieved only gradually and notices of schools in churches continue through-out the next century. For example in 1718 there was a school in the choir of Holme Cultram, Cumberland.[218] There was a Dame's school in a corner of the belfry in Davenham church.[219] In 1842 the chancel at Long Stanton, Cambridge, had green curtains across the arch to provide an area for teaching. A grate had been inserted in the north wall of the chancel, with a huge red brick chimney behind it; the master sat within the altar rail, with his chair against the table.

A visitor to Ashford by Melton noted that the altar had twenty writing and copying books, seven slates, a master's cane and sundry pens upon it; there was also a teacher's desk and a jug of ink.[220] In various numbers of the *Ecclesiologist*, from 1843 to 1847, there are notices of schools in churches, the journal calling attention to them as abuses and examples of profanation. So it lists schools in the north transept of San Creed; in chapels in the church at Gaddesby, Leicestershire, and the cathedral of St Alban's, as well as in St Mary Redcliffe, Bristol; All Saints, Milton Ernest, Bedfordshire; SS. Peter and Paul, Leintwardine, Hereford; in the aisles of St Luke, Spratton; St Denis, Kelmarsh; Ewell, Kent; Cliffe-at-Hoo, St Helens; and in the former chantries in SS. Peter and Paul, Rothersthorpe, Northamptonshire, and Long Melford, Suffolk; and at the west end of St Nicholas, Thanington, Kent. Of Quy it reports that 'the school children are allowed to sit with their ever-restless feet on the fine Brass which yet exists in the Nave'.[221] Up to 1850 there was a school in the south aisle of Hornsea in East York-shire[222] and over twenty years later Parson Kilvert recorded how at Glascum 'the belfry is the village school, fitted up with desks, forms and master's desk and a fireplace'.[223]

Churches were also used and are used for school assemblies. In 1825, after the annual Spital sermon had been preached in Christ-church, Newgate Street, London, a report was read 'of the number of children, and other persons maintained and relieved in these establishments', viz. Christ's, St Bartholomew's, St Thomas's, Bridewell and Bethlehem Hospitals.[224] In 1964 at Plymstock, near Plymouth, the parish church was used for the annual school prize-giving, so the connection between church and teaching has not been completely severed.

## Libraries

The post-Renaissance emphasis upon learning, which found expression in the foundation of schools, also gave an impetus to the creation of parochial libraries, and the invention of printing had its contribution to make. In the decades immediately following the Reformation in England there were two works that were considered to be of particular value, viz. Foxe's *Book of Martyrs* and the writings of Bishop Jewel. So on 11th January 1571–2 the vestry of St Michael, Cornhill, London, agreed 'That the book of Martyrs of Mr Foxe and the paraphrase of Erasmus shall be bought for the church and tied with a chain to the Eagle brass'.[225] These were of course kept in the worship area, but the libraries in churches at Leicester, 1586–7, and Newcastle, 1597, occupied adjoining rooms.[226] At Cartmel, Lancashire, however, the accounts for 14th July 1629 refer to the enlargement of the churchwarden's pew 'in the body of the church' to provide more space for the books that had been donated. In 1651 Humphrey Chetham left two hundred and two volumes to Manchester Cathedral to be kept chained in the Jesus chapel. At Melton Mowbray there was a library in the north transept and at Salford, Lancashire, in 1684, books were bequeathed by Humphrey Oldfield to be placed in the chancel.[227]

The value of libraries was now attracting the attention of a number of individuals, so that on 15th February 1684 Evelyn complained in his diary that the city of London had no library facilities and added a comment that there ought to be a library 'at St Paul's; the West end of that church (if ever finished) would be a convenient place'. The following year Barnabas Oley required his executor to give sixteen volumes to each of ten poor vicarages in the diocese of Carlisle, and Bishop Nicolson in his visitation discloses where some of them were kept. At Burgh by Sands they were in a chest in the choir; at Orton the east end of the north aisle had lately been cut off for a library; at Kirk-Bampton the bishop ordered 'a Cupboard to be fitted up in the Quire for the depositing of B. Oley's Books'.[228]

The great enthusiast for libraries was of course Thomas Bray (1656–1730), and in a pamphlet issued in 1704 he declared: 'I would recommend the having a book press with a lock and key, fixt in the vestry, or chancel of every Church.'[229] His activities were in part responsible for the passing of an act on 4th March 1708–9 'for the better Preservation of Parochial Libraries in that Part of *Great Britain* called *England*'.[230] Bray was also a member of the committee of the Society for Promoting Christian Knowledge and this did much to assist the establishing of collections of books in churches. Episcopal and archidiaconal visitations now concerned themselves with the matter, e.g. Canterbury and Norwich 1716, Oxford 1722, Bristol 1735 and Oxford again in 1759.

In 1735 the Lady Chapel of Chichester Cathedral was converted into a library[231] and we hear of another in the body of the churches at Denchworth, Feckeham, Hereford All Saints' and Oakham.[232] But by the second half of the eighteenth century public lending libraries of modern books were being established and this led to a gradual neglect of the parochial collections—a number still survive, but with little or no additions of new works.

### Distribution of Poor Relief

The suppression of the monasteries, which had been great centres of poor relief in the Middle Ages, meant that charity had to be organized on a large scale if the impoverished were not to be left to starve to death. This did not of course prevent the activities of private benefactors who continued to show a concern that the poor should be remembered at their funerals nor did they forget them in their wills. The obsequies of Lady Chamburlayne on 5th May 1557 were typical of the Elizabethan period; the poor who attended received a liberal dole.[233] The Puritans spoke out against this practice in their *Admonition to Parliament* of 1572, but to little effect.[234]

The distribution of poor relief in churches in fulfilment of bequests also continued. For example, Nicolas Almond of Thame, who died in 1653, vested in the clergy of Cuddington and Great Missenden, Buckinghamshire, a capital of £480 to defray the expenses of preaching the Easter sermon and 'immediately after the said sermon' the rest of the annual increment was to be divided among the poor.[235] In the eighteenth century we have the quaint bequest of Sir John Gayer. There was an annual thanksgiving service on 16th October in St Catherine-Cree and gifts were then distributed to the poor under Sir John's will, he having left £200 'in Memory of his deliverance from the Paws of a Lion in Arabia'.[236]

In the meantime the public authorities were recognizing their responsibility towards the poor. In 1546 orders were issued for their relief and 'the inhabitants were all called to their parish churches' where agreement was reached upon what each person should contribute weekly.[237] The following year Edward VI issued his royal injunction requiring the provision of a chest for alms:

They shall provide and have within three months after this visitation, a strong chest with a hole in the upper part thereof, to be provided at the cost and charge of the parish, having three keys, whereof one shall remain in the custody of the parson, vicar, or curate, and the other two in the custody of the churchwardens, or any other two honest men, to be appointed by the parish from year to year. Which chest you shall set and fasten near unto the high altar, to the intent the parishioners should put into their oblation and alms for their poor neighbours. And the parson, vicar or curate shall diligently from time to time, and specially when men make their testaments, call upon, exhort and move their neighbours, to confer and give, as they may well spare, to the said chest; declaring unto them, whereas heretofor they have been diligent to bestow much substance otherwise than God commanded upon pardons, pilgrimages, trentals, decking of images, offering of candles, giving to friars, and upon other like blind devotions, they ought at this time to be much more ready to help the poor and needy, knowing that to relieve the poor is a true worshipping of God, required earnestly upon pain of everlasting damnation: and that also, whatsoever is given for their comfort, is given to Christ Himself and so is accepted of Him, that He will mercifully reward the same with everlasting life: the which alms and devotion of the people the keepers of the keys shall at times convenient take out of the chest, and distribute the same in the presence of their whole parish, or six of them, to be truly and faithfully delivered to their most needy neighbours: and if they be provided for, then to the reparation of high ways next adjoining. And also the money which riseth of fraternities, guilds and other stocks of the church (except by the King's Majesty's authority it be otherwise appointed) shall be put into the said chest, and converted to the same use, and also the rents and lands, the profit of cattle, and money given or bequeathed to the finding of torches, lights, tapers and lamps, shall be converted to the said use, saving that it shall be lawful for them to bestow part of the said profit upon the repairing of the church, if great need require, and whereas the parish is very poor, and not able otherwise to repair the same.[238]

Cranmer's articles for the Canterbury diocese of 1548 included an enquiry as to whether or not the box had been provided[239] and the rubrics of the 1549 communion service direct the worshippers to place their money in 'the poor men's box' and then to tarry in the choir for communion itself.

Acts of Parliament were passed relating to the collection and dis-

IX · The Gothic Revival Two-Roomed Plan: St Chad, Nicholas Square, 1869

X · Paul's Walk: The Nave of Old St Paul's, 1658

HERE LYETH BVRYED THE BO
DYE OF RICHARD STVPPENYE
JVRATE OF THIS TOWNE IN T
HE FIRST YEARE OF K.H.VIIJ WHO
DYED IN TE XVIIJ YEARE OF THE
SAYDE KYNGES REIGNE OF WH
OSE MEMORYE CLEMENT ST
VPPENYE OF THE SAME PORT HIS
GREAT GRANDSONNE HATH
CAVSED THIS TOMBE TO BE
NEWERECTED FOR THE VSE OF THE
AVNCIENT MEETING AND ELEC
TION OF MAIOR AND JVRATS
OF THIS PORT TOWNE JVNE
THE 10TH ANNO.DM.1622.

XI · The Election of Civic Officials: The Stuppenye Brass in New Romney
Church, 1622

XII · The Distribution of Poor Relief: The Christmas Dole in 1854

XIII · Dancing in Church: The Black and White Minstrels rehearsing in
Coventry Cathedral, 1967

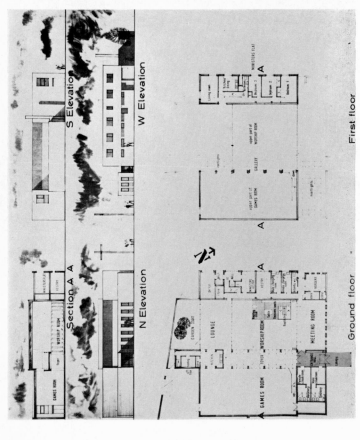

XVI · The Multipurpose Church: Plan and Elevation of the Baptist Centre,
Highgate, Birmingham, 1967

tribution, e.g. 5 and 6 Edward VI, c. 2 and 2 and 3 Philip and Mary
c. 5. Bishops included this in their articles, e.g. Ridley for London
in 1550 and Bulkeley for Bangor in 1551.[240] Town councils also
played their part, and so in 1588 at Leicester collectors were authorized to take up levies at churchings and weddings and they 'shall
thereof make account Quarterly and openly in Church'.[241] The royal
articles of Elizabeth of 1559 similarly concerned themselves with the
question.[242] In 1601 there was an act establishing Overseers of the
Poor, who were to be elected by each parish vestry and then confirmed in office by the Justices of the Peace at the Quarter Sessions;
they were to work in close association with the churchwardens.[243]
The overseers of the poor were required to meet at least once a
month on a Sunday in church following the afternoon sermon,
although not everyone observed this rule, e.g. in 1620 Edmund Hay
of Newton was presented in that 'he refuseth to meet monthly with
the rest of the Overseers of the parish at his parish church for the
relief of the poor, etc.'[244] The 84th canon of 1603 reproduced
almost verbatim the Edwardian injunction quoted above. Each
church now had its chest, e.g. St Margaret's, Westminster, in 1597
had 'a chest, covered with black leather, and barred with iron, with
locks and keys thereunto'. The same church previously, in 1553, had
purchased 'a footstool for them that distributed charity to the
poor'.[245]

Besides the chests for money, a number of churches had an almery
or dole cupboard. This was a receptacle for bread. The surviving
examples are similar in pattern, having a railed or pierced front to
allow a current of air. In a recess in the south transept of St Alban's
are three such cupboards, one of the time of Charles I and two dating
from the reign of Charles II. At Kingsthorpe, Northamptonshire,
there is another, as also at Ruislip, Middlesex.[246] Both in cash and
kind Christians provided in their churches for the relief of the poor,
and indeed used them for distribution. So the vestry book of the
parish of Pittington has an entry under 22nd April 1627 which refers
to 'money given to the stock of the poor of the parish of Pittington
and delivered to the Overseers of the same parish, and lent to the
parties whose names are here undermentioned. . . . The money was
paid in Pittington Church.'[247]

*Playing of Games*

The majority of the games played in churches after the Reformation were no more than the continuation of medieval festive practices. So we find evidence of the Feast of Fools, the Boy Bishop and
playing with balls for some time after the year 1530. At Aix, for
example, the Feast of Fools was observed until at least 1585. In
England, however, the Boy Bishop was forbidden by royal proclamation on 22nd July 1541. This condemned the gatherings of children
'decked and apparelled to counterfeit priests, bishops and women'
on the days of 'saint Nicolas, saint Catherine, saint Clement, the
holy Innocents, and such like'. Under Mary the custom was revived
in several London parishes, including St Andrew's, Holborn, and
St Nicholas Olave, Bread Street, but with the accession of Elizabeth
it fell into disuse.[248]

The ball game, which was so popular at Auxerre, and to which
Gérard Royer had demurred in 1471, was still being played in 1531.
In that year one of the canons, Laurent Bretel, criticized the game
and news of the ensuing dispute reached the king, Francis I. His
delegate, François Disque, attended the ceremony on Easter Day,
28th March 1535, and his report was considered by a commission
consisting of four members of parliament, four canons of Notre
Dame and four doctors of the Sorbonne. Eventually on 7th June
1538 the practice was condemned and so came to an end.[249] Yet in
England throughout Elizabeth's reign there were numerous edicts
against ball playing in St Paul's.[250]

The most tenacious game was that associated with the Lords of
Misrule and the Summer Lords and Ladies. According to Phillip
Stubbes, after the choice of the Lord of Misrule and the attiring of
his company in coloured livery,

then march this heathen company towards the Church and Church-yard,
their pipers piping, their drummers thundering, their stumps dancing,
their bells jingling, their handkerchiefs swinging about their heads like
madmen, their hobby-horses and other monsters skirmishing amongst the
route: and in this sort they go to the Church (I say) and into the Church,
(though the Minister be at prayer or preaching), dancing and swinging
their handkerchiefs over their heads in the Church, like devils incarnate,
with such a confused noise, that no man can hear his own voice. Then,

the foolish people they look, they stare, they laugh, they fleer, and mount upon forms and pews to see these godly pageants solemnized in this sort.[251]

According to Stubbes the election was elsewhere than in church, but in 1535 at Harwich the Lord of Misrule was actually chosen in the nave[252] and this was soon to attract the notice of the Reformers.

Edmund Bonner, in his injunctions for the diocese of London in 1542, forbade 'games' in churches,[253] but the main series of attacks came after the accession of Elizabeth. In 1569 John Parkhurst of Norwich instructed all churchwardens that

No person or persons calling themselves lords of misrule in the Christmas time, or other unreverent person at any other time, presume to come into the church unreverently playing their lewd parts, with scoffing, jesting and ribaldry talk.[254]

Archbishop Grindal, in 1571, added: 'Summer Lords and Ladies, or any disguised persons, or others, or at May games'.[255] Year in, year out, articles and injunctions returned to this theme with monotonous regularity, up to and including those of Archdeacon White of Norfolk in 1632.[256] Thereafter these games disappeared largely from view, but not without leaving their mark in the records of the visitation courts. So for example in 1584 there was a report of the 'evil rule done in the church of the Lord and Lady on Midsummer day' at Wootton, Oxford,[257] while at Blackthorn, during the sermon on the Tuesday in Whit week, a man had come into the nave 'with a painted cloth on his back', i.e. he was wearing the costume of a Lord of Misrule.[258] The Archdeacon's court at Oxford, which heard these cases, imposed suitable penalties.

Somewhat similar to these more or less innocent pastimes were the annual pageants in St Paul's. On 8th June 1557 Henry Machyn was there to see the parishioners of St Clement's in procession, with their banners, streamers and waits playing.[259] An alternative divertissement was the performance by the English acrobat William Pedel in November 1608 in Leyden. The authorities allowed him to display his gymnastic feats 'within the church of Bagynhogg within the city, provided he cease during the preaching of God's word, and that the poor orphans here have half the profits'.[260] Less attractive was the bear-baiting by the curate of Woburn in 1612, and in the thirties, the cock-fighting around the communion table at Knottingley on three successive Shrove Tuesdays.[261]

Sometimes games were promoted by the humour of a testator. According to the will of Dr Robert Wilde, who died in 1678, six boys and six girls were annually to throw dice on the communion table in St Ives church, Huntingdonshire, for bibles purchased out of his bequest. Reporting this on 24th May 1888 the *Strand* says that some years previously the bishop had directed the raffle to take place on a table on the chancel steps. Nor was this the only game to survive through the centuries. In 1757 the feast at Aix was still a popular event. This included a procession into the church with everyone singing, shouting, playing tambourines, fifes, flutes and trumpets and even firing muskets.[262] At Exton in Rutlandshire, at the beginning of the nineteenth century, children were allowed to play in the church on Innocents' Day, probably a relic of the Boy Bishop,[263] while at Charlton, Kent, as late as 1867, a king and queen were chosen on St Luke's Day and went in procession into the church wearing horns[264]—perhaps the Lords and Ladies of the Middle Ages or the *ludi de Rege et Regina* were not as dead as the Reformers would have hoped.

## *Acting*

In the previous description of plays in the medieval churches emphasis was laid upon the dramatic character of the liturgy itself. With the Counter-Reformation, while the mass was still understood in dramatic terms, the interpretation of these was totally different. The great cultural creation of the period, as previously noted,[265] was the opera, and the liturgy came to be regarded as its religious equivalent. This was not an atmosphere to promote the development of real drama within churches, and so the medieval plays gradually disappeared. Instead the taste was for displays and these did continue, even into the Romantic period with its antiquarian, but often ill-informed, nostalgia for the Middle Ages.

Kirchmaier's *Regnum papisticum* was first published in 1553, and in an English translation in 1570. One section of this is devoted to a

dramatic presentation on Ascension day, with a concluding reference to Pentecost:

> The block (i.e. image of Christ) that on the altar still, till then was seen
>    to stand,
> Is drawn up high above the roof, by ropes, and force of hand:
> The Priests about it round do stand, and chant it to the sky,
> For all these men's religion great, in singing most doth lie.
> Then out of hand the dreadful shape of Satan down they throw,
> Oft times with fire burning bright, and dashed asunder though,
> The boys with greedy eyes do watch, and on him straight they fall,
> And beat him sore with rods, and break him into pieces small.
> This done, they wafers down do cast, and singing Cakes the while,
> With Papers round amongst them put, the children to beguile.
> With laughter great are all things done: and from the beams they let
> Great streams of water down to fall, on whom they mean to wet.
> And thus this solemn holiday, and high renowned feast,
> And all their whole devotion here, is ended with a jest.
> On Whitsunday, white Pigeons tame, in strings from heaven fly,
> And one that framed is of wood, still hangeth in the sky.[266]

Some two and a half centuries later we find a similar dramatic
celebration still persisting and taking place at Dieppe on 15th
August. William Hone has provided a not entirely sympathetic
account and states that it is said to have been established in 1443.
A procession goes through the town and ends at the parish church,
where the mass begins:

> During the service, a scenic representation was given of the *Assumption
> of the Virgin*. A scaffolding was raised, reaching nearly to the top of the
> dome, and supporting an azure canopy intended to emulate the 'spangled
> vault of heaven'; and about two feet below the summit of it appeared,
> seated upon a splendid throne, an old man as the image of the Father
> Almighty. . . . On either side four pasteboard angels, of the size of men,
> floated in the air, and flapped their wings in cadence to the sounds of the
> organ; while above was suspended a large triangle, at whose corners were
> placed three smaller angels who, at the intermission of each office, per-
> formed upon a set of little bells the hymn of '*Ave Maria gratia Dei plena
> per Secula*' etc., accompanied by a larger angel on each side with a trum-
> pet. To complete this portion of the spectacle, two others, below the old
> man's feet, held tapers, which were lighted as the services began, and
> extinguished at their close; on which occasions the figures were made to
> express reluctance by turning quickly about; so that it required some

dexterity to apply extinguishers. At the commencement of the mass, two of the angels by the side of the Almighty descended to the foot of the altar and, placing themselves by the tomb, in which a pasteboard figure of the virgin had been substituted for her living representative (who had played the part in the procession), gently raised it to the feet of the Father. The image, as it mounted from time to time, lifted its head and extended its arms, as if conscious of the approaching beatitude; then, after having received the benediction, and been encircled by another angel with a crown of glory, it gradually disappeared behind the clouds. At this instant, a buffoon, who all the time had been playing his antics below, burst into an extravagant fit of joy; at one moment clapping his hands most violently, at the next stretching himself out as if dead. Finally he ran up to the feet of the old man, and hid himself under his legs, so as to show only his head. . . . Thus did the pageant proceed in all its glory. . . . the children shouted aloud for their favourite Grimaldi; the priests, accompanied with bells, trumpets and organs, thundered out the mass; the pious were loud in their exclamation of rapture at the devotion of the virgin, and the whole church was filled with a hoarse and confused murmuring sound.[267]

The official attitude of the Roman Church was not unfavourable to these presentations and the ruling of the Council of Compostella in 1565 may be taken as typical. This declared that dramatic performances could take place before or after mass as long as the leave of the bishop or chapter had been obtained.[268]

In England plays in churches survived the Reformation by several decades. There are notices of the following: 1532 Weybridge, Surrey;[269] 1533–4 Ashburton, Devon;[270] 1538 St Martin-in-the-Fields;[271] 1547 St Saviour's, Southwark;[272] 1549 Barnstaple;[273] 1551 St Martin's, Leicester;[274] 1557 Grey Friars, London;[275] 1560 Barnstaple; [276] 1562 Chelmsford;[277] 1564 King's College Chapel;[278] 1572 Bewdley;[279] 1576 Cranoe, Leicestershire;[280] and Chelmsford;[281] 1578 Hascombe;[282] 1584 Duns Tew;[283] 1592–3 Great Marlow, Buckinghamshire;[284] 1597 Romford.[285]*

By this date plays in churches had come under severe fire from the Reformers, although in the late 1530's Cromwell had deliberately fostered some to discredit catholic worship and morals by representing boorish clergy and a pompous liturgy, believing that 'nothing could more effectively drive out many of those abuses, which yet remained, than to expose them to the contempt and scorn of the people'.[286] It was partly in reaction to this, and in the line of the medieval episcopate, that Edmond Bonner, the last Bishop of London to die in communion with the see of Rome, issued injunctions against them in 1542.[287] The year following, an act was passed allowing 'plays and interludes for the rebuking and reproaching of vices and the setting forth of virtue' but forbidding such as meddled with 'interpretations of scripture, contrary to the doctrine set forth or to be set forth by the king's majesty'.[288] Some of the Roman party then used the Cromwellian device against the *Book of Common Prayer*, so the Act of Uniformity forbade interludes 'depraving and despising' it. In 1550 Ridley of London enquired about 'interludes, plays, songs, hymns' that 'declare or speak anything in depraving or despising the said book' while Hooper in 1551–2 once again forbade them.[289]

The Puritans were opposed to theatrical representations as such and in the *Admonition* of 1572 they attacked interludes in churches.[290] In the same year was published *An Answer to a Certain Libel* which censured the clergy for hurrying through the services because there is 'an interlude to be played, and if no place else can be gotten, it must be done in the church'.[291] In 1580 there appeared *A Second and Third Blast of Retrait from Plaies and Theaters*, which complained bitterly that actors were 'permitted to publish their mametree in every Temple of God, and that throughout England, unto the horrible contempt of prayer. So that now the Sanctuary is become a player's stage, and a den of thieves and adulterers.'[292] This attack had its counterpart in episcopal injunctions and in 1571 Grindal was enquiring about 'disguised persons . . . that play unseemly parts'.[293] Further enquiries or condemnations were made in 1575, 1577, 1585 and 1586.[294] The outcome of this was a number of cases in the visitation courts. For example, in 1576 Richard Hacky of Cranoe was charged with allowing in his church 'puppet plays and morris dancing',[295] while the churchwardens were presented at Romford in 1577 and pleaded that the proceeds of the two plays performed were only for the benefit of 'a poor man in decay'.[296] At Oxford in 1584 John Castell and Robert Mesie, churchwardens of Duns Tew, were presented 'for keeping interludes and plays in the church' in particular upon a Saturday in the evening after service.[297]

In the light of this situation we can appreciate the entry in the Systone register for 1602: 'Paid to Lord Morden's players, because they should not play in the Church'—i.e. the actors claimed some kind of prescriptive right to use the church but the wardens preferred to pay them off rather than risk being presented for allowing them to perform there.[298]

In the meantime play-houses were being built and with them, in London at least, the need to use churches for acting decreased, and after the opening of the seventeenth century we hear little or nothing of it. It was not until the present century that drama once again began to find a home in church buildings in England, although in Roman Catholic countries there has been a continuous tradition, e.g. in 1768 there was a play of the crucifixion in a convent church in Lisbon.[299]*

It remains now to assemble some examples of miscellaneous secular uses of churches in the post-Reformation period that do not fit conveniently into our previous divisions. In England the fortifying of churches was no longer deemed necessary, although some were employed for defence during the Civil War. In Europe, where international war was constant, there were numerous instances of churches being built for defence, particularly in Germany during the Thirty Years War. In the valley of the Werra in Saxe Meiningen there are a considerable number surviving, being strongholds enclosed with turreted walls, e.g. the church at Walldorf. Some of them, as at Quienfeld and Milz, had moats excavated around them.[300] However, as the nature of warfare changed and castles and forts became things of the past, so the church ceased to be regarded as an equivalent.

The previous survey of Paul's Walk has made us familiar with the church as a thoroughfare. St Paul's was not unique in this respect. In 1532, a visitation of the Priory of Eye, Norwich, revealed that there was a *communionem viam* through the church, cloisters and gardens.[301] In 1570 Archbishop Parker, in his injunctions for Canterbury cathedral, demanded that 'order be taken that the church and cloister be no highway or passage for market folks'.[302] In 1632 a slype was opened at the west end of Winchester cathedral to prevent its having to be left open as a common passage to the close and college. In 1634 Laud was enquiring about thoroughfares through Salisbury and Exeter cathedrals.[303] In 1740 Bishop Gooch suppressed the right of way through the nave and north transept of Norwich cathedral, while ten years later a slype was opened at the west end of Worcester cathedral to avoid the carrying of burdens through the north entrance and across the nave to the cloisters.[304]

Sometimes churches were used for what today would be regarded as bizarre activities. In 1571, for example, they were centres for the inspection of hats. This was the result of a measure to ensure the employment of the poor by compelling all citizens above the age of six to wear caps of wool on pain of being fined ten groats. So all 'bailiffs, constables, churchwardens, etc. every Sunday and festival day, are to make diligent view and search, in all churches, chapels, and all other places' to detect offenders.[305] In 1596 the London churches were the scene of another activity:

> On the morning of Easter Sunday, 1596, during the reign of Queen Elizabeth, the lord mayor and aldermen of London received the royal command to raise a thousand men with the utmost expedition, wherefore they repaired with their deputies, constables, and other officers, to the churches, and having caused their doors to be shut, took the people from divine service during their worship, till the number was completed, and having armed them, the men, so raised and equipped, were marched the same night to Dover, in order to their embarkation for France.[306]

Churches could be used as workshops, from weaving silk to painting scenery for plays. So the crypt of St Faith's under St Paul's was occupied in 1561 by French and Flemish refugees who used one aisle for worship and another for their looms.[307] At Chelmsford in 1562 a man named Lawrence was paid fourpence for 'watching in the church when the Temple was adrying'.[308]

These examples, however, belong mainly to the late sixteenth century and represent a survival of medieval uses, but as the years passed they became less and less common, as the preceding survey has demonstrated. Nevertheless, one activity had a future—the holding of concerts. As far back as 1552–3 minstrels were playing and singing in the church at Barnstaple,[309] but it was not until the eighteenth century that music displays began to come into vogue.

Dean Swift at Dublin agreed, not ungrudgingly, to 'lend his cathedral to players and scrapers' to act what he called 'their opera'.[310] On Saturday, 27th May 1749, the Prince and Princess of Wales attended a concert of Handel's music in the chapel of the Foundling Hospital, London, the performance being for the benefit of the foundation.[311] On 12th March 1825 in the Roman Catholic chapel in Sutton Street, London, Soho, there was 'a selection of music, chiefly from Haydn's masses, powerfully performed, by a very numerous choir, accompanied by a full band'.[312] Perhaps not everyday life but at least one aspect of its cultural side was finding a place in church buildings. Yet even this did not appeal to many nineteenth-century churchmen. M. A. C. Walcott, writing in 1872, had this observation to make:

The divorce of a modest instrumental accompaniment from the actual services, and the conversion of a Cathedral into a music hall with its attendant indecencies, began in a slothful and indifferent age.[313]

When such was the prevailing attitude one would look in vain for examples of many secular activities surviving the greater supervision exercised by the ecclesiastical authorities, the attacks of the Puritans and the now universal conviction that a church was and is only a place of worship.

# 7

# The Problem of Church-Building

THE STUDY of the relationship of the sacred and the secular is usually approached in one of two main ways. A writer may examine the subject phenomenologically, i.e. he may survey the attitudes and practices discernible in the world's faiths, seeking to discover the essence of the religious understanding of the subject by concentrating upon the characteristic structures of religious phenomena. The alternative is to begin by stating a position; if the writer be a Christian, this is likely to be an account of the biblical understanding of the relationship, which is then explored and expanded. Both these approaches are clearly of value and both will be adopted later in this chapter, but neither will provide our starting point. Instead, in keeping with the previous survey, we shall begin by examining the problem of church building. This will necessarily involve making certain affirmations about the uses to which such buildings may be put and this in turn will raise the question of attitudes to churches and so of the relationship of the sacred and the secular. Our analysis will then rest upon the examination of a concrete problem and our understanding of that problem will provide the guideline for further exploration. In this way it may perhaps be possible to avoid the dangers either of theorizing in a way which is irrelevant to the real world or of accepting an outlook simply because it is common to the majority of the world's religions.

The building of a church, as anyone who has engaged in the exercise knows, involves a whole range of subjects: financial, legal, technical, functional, theological and sociological. Some of these fall within the specialized province of the architect and others are the concern primarily of the client, although all need to be reviewed in dialogue between those having the essential expert knowledge. The architect, for example, has to decide how to make provision for the various services required within the budget available or if indeed all the services can be catered for within the price limit, but he will also seek the assistance of the quantity surveyor in making up his mind. It is the architect's responsibility to take decisions, with such professional assistance as he may need, that will affect the acoustics; the choice of materials lies within his purview, etc., etc. In the design process, however, the client is not a mute partner; he has to speak on matters of finance and of function, being assisted by questions that will elicit the necessary information, some of which he might otherwise pass over as self-evident—although not so to the architect—and aspects of which he might himself not have thought about at all. This process is rendered more complex by the inter-relationship of all the questions, e.g. of function and finance.

As our previous survey has shown, there is a general consensus among Christians of all denominations that a church is essentially a place set apart for worship; its function is therefore to be defined in terms of the liturgy that will be performed within it. Such definition, however, immediately turns the financial question into a moral one. It is no longer a matter of simply deciding that $x$ pounds or dollars are available and that this sum is not to be exceeded. The further question cannot be avoided: is it right to spend a large sum of money on a liturgical hall that will only be in use for a few hours each week? It is certainly unsound economics to freeze capital in plant that stands idle for a major part of the time. But what is more pertinent is the consideration of the rightness of such an action when there are so many human problems that require money for their solution—problems of housing, of malnutrition, of starvation, education, etc., on a global scale. Should a Christian community devote a large share of its financial resources to bricks and mortar or reinforced concrete? Should it not rather seek to serve the needs of mankind? Indeed, it is arguable that to build churches for cultic occasions only can be a self-regarding 'spiritual' luxury, when millions of men and women are suffering from lack of material assistance. Thus the primary question is not: how much can we afford, but, acknowledging that we are stewards of our financial

assets, how can we best exercise that stewardship for the furtherance
of God's purpose for the world? The subject of finance then raises
matters not only of ethics but of theology, and amongst the theological items are the nature of God and the function of the Christian
community in the world.

What kind of being is this God for whom churches are to be
erected? Is he one who delights in monuments to his honour rather
than in loving care for men? A church building may be the expression of devotion to a false, even tribal, God who is less humane than
many of his creatures. When the gods had to be propitiated to
ensure fine weather, a good harvest or victory in war, the building
of temples appeared to be eminently practical. They could be erected
before the events, thus placing the gods in debt and forcing a settlement, or after the events, in fulfilment of a vow, as payments for
services rendered. It was a way of safeguarding one's own interests by
eliciting a favourable response from the spiritual powers. But these
capricious, if not commercial, beings are scarcely to be compared
to the living God of the bible, who is above all self-offering, self-
sacrificing and self-giving. The concern of Jesus was always for men
and women and for their immediate problems. In his ministry the
works that are prominent are not those of 'sanctification and sacrifice but works of healing and proclamation, invitation and instruction, service and calling'.[1]

Moreover, the God of Abraham, Isaac and Jacob was not a residential being; in this respect he was the antithesis of the baals, each
with his own locality, over which he presided and outside of which
he had no authority, and his holy space where he could be encountered and honoured through the cult. The whole burden of Stephen's
speech in Acts is to this effect: 'the most High dwelleth not in houses
made with hands'.[2] Indeed 'our God is not a temple dweller. In the
strict sense of the term he is not even a church god. He advances
through time; ever again he lets the new conquer the old.'[3] He is a
God who gives himself without stint for the liberation of the world
in which he is continually active. The goal or goals of his action
must clearly determine the function of the Christian community in
the world, in so far as it claims and is intended to be an instrument
of God for the achievement of his purposes. Nor can Christian

buildings be dissociated from this; it would appear to be axiomatic that any buildings erected by Christians should themselves be conceived as means towards the achievement of the divine purposes. If they do not serve those ends, we may well doubt if they have any *raison d'être* at all. In other words, the question of church building is inseparable from the question of the Church and of its function in the modern world. The purpose of the *domus ecclesiae* is to be understood in relation to the purpose of the *ecclesia* itself. It is therefore no digression but of the very essence of our subject to examine the rôle of the Church, since only in this way can a functional analysis of a church building penetrate below the surface of crude utilitarianism.

The clue to the understanding of the divine purpose, according to Christian belief, is to be found in the ministry of Jesus, who both reveals that purpose and is the agent of its fulfilment. That purpose may be defined as the establishment of the Kingdom of God—'kingdom' being not so much a place over which God rules as God's reign itself, i.e. his sovereign power being manifestly effective in the world of human experience. According to Jewish expectation the *de jure* Kingship of God over the world was to be replaced at the *eschaton* or last day by his *de facto* rule;[4] according to the New Testament this hope is now in the process of realization because the rule has been inaugurated through Jesus of Nazareth. So Jesus was concerned with the present eschatologically conceived, i.e. understood in terms of the *eschaton* actually taking place—'the Kingdom of God is come upon you'.[5] It is true he could nevertheless teach his disciples to pray: 'Thy kingdom come', but this future consummation was already a present reality in his message and mission. According to him, the decisive moment of God's action had arrived; the exercise of the divine sovereign power was inaugurated. God is no longer the one about to come, rather the essential mystery of Jesus is to make the reality of God and of his rule present. But the tension in Jesus' teaching continues; the Kingdom is both 'already' and 'not yet'; it has broken in but it is not yet present in its fullness. The rôle of the Church is to fill the gap between the two; its members have both to proclaim the 'already' and be the instruments of the establishment of that which is 'not yet'. Church and Kingdom

are not identical—how can they be, since from one aspect the Kingdom is still a future reality?—but the former is or can be the
instrument of the latter.

The proclamation of the divine rule is also a proclamation of the
Lordship of Christ through whom that rule is exercised. This is to
proclaim the exaltation that has already taken place; it means
exposing the ever-present Christ and so it involves entering into
every situation to help men to see there, in terms of their everyday
life, the Christ who is already there and is their Lord. But this
Lordship is not like any other known to men, because its chief
characteristic is loving service. The sovereign rule of God is expressed and known not in domination, not in 'lording' it over others,
but in meeting human need. Jesus came not to be served, but to
serve,[6] to function as a waiter, subordinate, inconspicuous, available,
ready to help. Since the Christian life is the life of Christ lived in his
disciples, the form of the Church must be the form of the servant;
its rôle is to enter upon a life of service seeking to meet human need
wherever it may be found. It is by these acts that it witnesses to the
present reality of the Kingdom.[7]

The nature of the Kingdom is indicated by Paul when he says
that it is 'righteousness and *shalom* and joy in the Holy Spirit'.[8] Paul
wrote of course in Greek, but there is little question that he understood *eirene* as synonymous with the Hebrew *shalom*—hence the
substitution in this quotation. *Shalom* is a portmanteau word which
cannot therefore be rendered by a single English equivalent, such
as 'peace', which is the usual translation. Its fundamental meaning
is that of 'wholeness' or 'totality', and this includes the idea of
harmonious community, since man can only develop and mature in
conjunction with others. Consequently it denotes not a status but a
relationship; it is a matter of relation to one's total environment. It
is a social happening and can therefore never be enjoyed in isolation.
It includes unity, solidarity, the exercise of mutual responsibility, a
community of will. It embraces salvation, in the sense not of
deliverance from this world into another but of wholeness, well-
being and growth. So it involves neighbourliness, reconciliation,
responsible freedom and hope. God is himself the 'god of *shalom*'[9]
and Christ is 'our *shalom*' in that he unites men in himself with one

another.[10] So the establishment of the Kingdom, of which the inner reality is *shalom*, refers to unity and mature humanity. It refers to unity, because it is the divine purpose to bring all men into unity with himself and with one another. It concerns mature humanity, because it is the divine purpose to enable all men to be whole by overthrowing the forces of evil that separate men from their Creator and so stultify and dehumanize them that they cannot attain to the full stature of their creaturehood.

This divine purpose relates to the whole world; it is not confined to just one small sector of it. God is neither shut up in one part of life nor interested in only one part of life. Since he is the Creator, all creatures are his concern. In other words, God is world-centred, in the sense that his activity is cosmic and his purposes embrace the whole cosmos. This is repeatedly emphasized in the New Testament writings. We are informed that 'God was in Christ reconciling the *world* unto himself'[11] and that it is the divine intention 'to reconcile *all* things unto himself'.[12] God is the one who 'willeth *all* men to be saved',[13] and this word translated 'saved' really means 'made whole'. 'God so loved the *world* that he gave his only begotten Son'[14] and that Son is represented as saying: 'I came not to judge the world, but to save the world',[15] i.e. to restore it to wholeness, to enable it to experience *shalom*. The scope of the divine purpose cannot be less than all-embracing, otherwise God is not God; he becomes instead not the God of radical monotheism but a tribal deity.

This definition of the divine purpose and of its object—the world —should determine the rôle of the Church and its concern, and, indeed, what these are has already been partly expressed in the previous paragraph, but may be restated more fully for the sake of clarity. The rôle of the Church is to proclaim the Kingdom and therefore to actualize *shalom*, unity and humanization being comprehended in this. This proclamation is not simply a matter of words; it is to be achieved by service to the poor and outcasts of the twentieth century—to the alcoholics, homosexuals, delinquents, the aged and infirm, to the underprivileged. The actualization of *shalom* involves joining in the struggle for civil rights and in the fight against racial discrimination. This advance towards unity requires participation in industrial disputes and in the frustration and hatred caused by class divisions—all involve the struggle for mature humanity. Moreover, all envisage the world as the sphere of the Church's activity. 'The signs of God's *shalom* must, after all, be established in-the-situation. One cannot talk the *shalom* from the Church into the world; it wants to be *lived* in the world. That must take place on the spot, precisely because *shalom* involves a corrective intervention, a bringing about of wholeness.'[16] Nor is this simply a revival of the old social gospel. It is no more than what is found in the Sermon on the Mount. 'Let your light so shine before men that they may see your good works and glorify your Father which is in heaven.'[17]

It is good Reformed theology to see the glory of God, the *gloria Dei*, as the end of man and the purpose of the apostolate. That destiny and that purpose are fulfilled among people when they see the light shine. And it is stated here that they discover that light in good works. 'Good works' has often become a frightening term which causes us immediately (and quite unnecessarily) to become nervous. After all, what it simply means is that people get an insight into our lives and discover there that this life is directed and oriented by that which is good, that it reaches out for *shalom*. We are not so much talking about a whole series of isolated activities, but rather about the expression of a pattern of life that speaks also when one says or does nothing. If you want this pattern of life summarized in a few words, then look at the Servant of the Lord. His life can be described in five words: election, witness, self-identification, suffering, service.[18]

In the light of this discussion of the function of the Church in terms of the divine purpose for the world, we can now consider afresh the problem of church building from which we began. Our starting point was the financial aspect, which we have now seen to be inseparable from moral and theological questions. If the choice is between erecting a church and meeting human need, the Christian community has no grounds for hesitation. Its rôle of the servant is to participate in God's action in the world; if its task is in the office, the factory, the workshop, the hospital, the prison, etc., then this is a matter of dispersion and not of gathering within isolated and special ecclesiastical structures. It is a question of so deploying the available financial resources that they are at the disposal of God's mundane activity and are not locked up in buildings that are only used for cultic assemblies for a limited number of hours per week. This means that those responsible for church-building programmes should examine each project with the utmost care to see if it does assist and not hinder participation in God's action in the world. There is little doubt that such an investigation, honestly and rigorously carried through, with all the help, e.g. of sociologists, that can be obtained, would result in the cancellation of a number of projects and with the diversion of the money and labour required from them to the real needs of society. This, however, is not all that can be said.

Christians, it has been argued, are called to serve, and the service of others not infrequently involves the provision of buildings. A Church for others will plan its buildings in terms of the human needs of the neighbourhood, irrespective of whether or not those in need choose to call themselves Christians, since the object of the Church's service is not itself but the world. What is required therefore is not just centres for services but service-centres. Since the form of the Church is that of the servant, the form of a church must be for serving. The need is for multipurpose buildings, the functions of which are not defined primarily by the restricted liturgical requirements of a Christian group, but by the rôle of that group in the world today.

At the present time there is great stress on the need for liturgical architecture, i.e. liturgical factors are regarded as the essential determinants of the church-building programme. It would be stupid to attempt to go back on this—certainly buildings used for worship should be planned to provide for that activity. But the argument so far means that this is an inadequate concept for the churches of the future—they *must* be liturgically planned but, at the same time, they must also be planned to house those secular activities that are inseparable from the Church's service of the community in terms of need, work, leisure and everyday living. To quote J. C. Hoekendijk again:

> In church building a shift ought to take place from *sacral architecture* to the designing of a *fellowship house*. Not only does the church legitimize herself through her serving character, but she will want to be identified

as a servant community as well. One has to be able to see it. Her liturgy consists first of all in *diakonia*, service. The claim is frequently made that it must be evident from the architectural structure that a congregation gathers there whose members 'concentrate on the redemptive mysteries'. This would then mean that a sacral space must be designed, one that is separate and different from the world. This seems to me unacceptable. The redemptive mystery is not only Word and Sacrament; it is not only what takes place within the walls when the congregation gathers there. The mystery is that Christ wants to be present. According to his promise, he is not only where 'two or three are gathered in his name' (Matt. 18.20) but as well in the least of his brethren, the hungry and the thirsty, the strangers and the naked, the sick and the imprisoned (Matt. 25.31ff.). In the New Testament the wall between liturgy and *diakonia* has become transparent, and both have been placed in the context of pro-existence. One must be able to notice this from our houses.[19]

In this type of fellowship house or church, sacred and secular would be united, i.e. their relationship would be not one of division nor of identification nor of absorption of the one by the other but of unity. So the problem of church building, examined in the light of finance and of the Church's rôle in the world, points to the oneness of the sacred and secular as two aspects of an integrated whole. Our examination of a concrete problem thus leads to a more or less precise definition of the relationship of the sacred and the secular.

We have now to consider whether such an understanding of the relationship is in accord with the general phenomena observed by the students of comparative religion and whether it is contradicted or endorsed by the New Testament witness.

The categories of the sacred and the secular are not those with which the student of comparative religion is accustomed to work; instead he examines the division between the sacred and the profane, although he is ready to acknowledge that the profane and the secular are identical.[20] Further, in so far as in Christian thought the secular and the profane have been frequently equated, as evidenced by the repeated efforts to prohibit secular activities in churches on the grounds that this is a profanation, an understanding of that division is relevant to our study.

There is a general consensus of opinion that, in the words of Roger Caillois, 'the only thing that can be validly affirmed in general of the sacred is to be found in the actual definition of the term: it is that which is opposed to the profane'.[21] So to speak of the sacred and the profane is to refer to two antithetical entities. This opposition can be expressed in a variety of ways. The one is that which is potent, full of power, while the other is powerless; the one is the real and the other unreal. They cannot therefore approach one another without losing their proper nature. Their separation is essential for their integrity, otherwise either the sacred will consume the profane or the profane will contaminate and enfeeble the sacred. The sacred is therefore dangerous. It both attracts and repels man; it attracts him because it is the source of power and it repels him because to encounter it is to be in peril.[22]

The sacred is the 'wholly other'; it is a reality of an entirely different order from 'natural realities'. In general, therefore, the sacred and the profane must be kept apart because any contact between them would be fatal to both. Their contacts can only be intermittent and must be strictly regulated by rites which can have either a positive or a negative character. Included in the former are rites of consecration whereby someone or something is introduced into the realm of the holy. The negative ones take the form of prohibitions, raising barriers between the two and so isolating them and preventing a catastrophe. These rites allow a certain coming and going between the two spheres, since they provide the conditions within which intercourse is possible. But any attempt, outside the prescribed limits, to unite sacred and profane brings confusion and disaster.

Underlying all this is the concept of two worlds: a sacred world and a secular world—a divine world and the world of men. The sacred, then, represents the irruption into the world of men of the power of the divine world. It must therefore be carefully handled; it must be hedged in to preserve its nature and to prevent the world of men from being destroyed. When man encounters the holy he receives 'a revelation of a reality *other* than that in which he participates through his ordinary daily life'.[23] To allow this encounter, man must separate himself from the world of the profane in order to penetrate into the world of the sacred because 'the human must be abandoned before approaching the divine'.[24] There are, then, two realms of being and 'these two worlds, that of the sacred and that of the profane, can only be strictly defined in terms of each other. They exclude each other and they are opposed to each other.'[25]

Intimately associated with this concept of two worlds is the idea of the created order which has to be preserved from dissolution. Unless the limits of the two are recognized and kept intact chaos may supervene. To contaminate the holy or to allow the holy to penetrate the profane is to destroy this equilibrium. Consequently, separation between the two is essential if life is to go on. The source of this life is indeed the sacred and for that very reason it must be shielded from impurity.

This opposition finds its visible expression in holy places. The sacred space is first of all a means of ensuring the isolation and so preservation of both the sacred and the profane. The wall which keeps the one in also serves to keep the other out; it is the demarcation line between the two worlds. But within the sacred precincts, the profane world is transcended and hence the existence of the holy place makes it possible for men to pass from one world to the other by entering the shrine. The door is therefore an object of great importance for it is the means of moving from profane to sacred space and so from the world of men to the divine world.

This outlook means that space is discontinuous; man experiences interruptions, breaks in it. Nevertheless, despite this apartness of the sacred area, 'its holiness gives it a prominence as against the surrounding eternity of space. Hence also the relationship between the sacred place and the whole Universe: the shrine is the centre of power, a world in itself.'[26] It can therefore be conceived as a reflection of the divine world, and since by imitating the divine man remains in the sacred and so in reality, temples are to be constructed according to a heavenly plan.

To speak of the unity of sacred and secular in this context is meaningless; they can no more be brought into union than oil and water. It is only through the complete separation of the sacred from the secular that man, by observing the necessary safeguards, can approach the divine without risk. Having taken the necessary precautions, he may pass from one realm into another by entering the shrine which is a door of access to the divine. There, in the sacred enclosure, contact with the divine is possible, since 'the temple constitutes an opening in the upward direction and ensures communication with the world of the gods'.[27] Alternatively one may say that as a temple is a house of God, one has to enter that house in order to meet the owner-occupier. So Jacob, after his dream at Haran, says: 'How dreadful is this place! This is none other but the house of God, and this is the gate of heaven.'[28] This passage from Genesis is the foundation charter of the sanctuary at Bethel and it shows how holy places were at first constituted by theophanies. Where no such irruption of the sacred had taken place, a sign could be sufficient or one could be sought.[29] Ultimately, building was undertaken to fix the limits of both the sacred and the secular.

It will be immediately apparent to the reader of the previous chapters that in general the Christian understanding of the sacred and the secular in terms of church building fits into this pattern observed and described by the students of the phenomenology of religion. There is no need to reproduce all the evidence here, but some of the main items have to be recalled and some fresh ones added in order to make the argument fully comprehensible. In Christian thought and practice from the fourth century to the Reformation, and in certain Churches since, there is a clear separation of and opposition between the sacred and the secular. The sacred is the 'wholly other', the *mysterium tremendum*, the numinous, which by its very nature is dangerous to man—witness the countless stories in the lives of saints and elsewhere of paralysis, blindness and other calamities befalling individuals who approach the holy without first having completely separated themselves from the impurities of their secular life. Coupled with this understanding of the sacred is the basic concept of the two worlds, the idea of a juxtaposition and conflict of two spheres, the one divine, holy, supernatural and Christian, and the other worldly, profane, natural and unChristian. According to Dietrich Bonhoeffer:

This view becomes dominant for the first time in the Middle Ages, and for the second time in the pseudo-Protestant thought of the period after the Reformation. . . . In the scholastic scheme of things the realm of the natural is made subordinate to the realm of grace; in the pseudo-Lutheran scheme the autonomy of the orders of this world is proclaimed in opposition to the law of Christ, and in the scheme of the Enthusiasts the congregation of the Elect takes up the struggle with a hostile world for the establishment of God's kingdom on earth.[30]

But as far back as the fourth century this opposition was already apparent in the understanding of the church building. Then, as we have seen, churches came to be regarded as belonging to the same class of buildings as temples, the only distinction being the object of worship—the true God versus false idols. Hence the practice of incubation could be transferred from pagan to Christian shrines[31] and the latter were similarly recognized as affording sanctuary, it being believed that the fugitives became invested with some of the sacredness of the place and so could not be touched as long as they remained within it.[32] At the same time, the Jerusalem Temple came to be regarded as the prototype of Christian church buildings which acquired the same sanctity.[33]

In the Middle Ages this last identification reigned supreme, the division into sanctuary, nave and atrium being regarded as a direct copying of the holy of holies, the holy place and the forecourt.[34] Year after year the ecclesiastical authorities sought to prevent these buildings from profanation, attacking plays, games, meetings, church ales, etc., as desecrations of the holy places, which were regarded as being defiled by this intrusion of secular activities.

At the Reformation, the Roman Catholic branch of Christendom perpetuated the same outlook, emphasizing, in Jewish fashion, degrees of holiness and the correspondence of the Jerusalem Temple and the Christian church.[35] With the Renaissance the opportunity came to build churches in exact imitation of the classical pagan temples—a quite logical proceeding once it is held that they all belong to the same genre of edifices. While Baroque churches owed much to the contemporary theatrical architecture, they too were envisaged as palaces of the King of heaven.[36] Anglicans shared an identical outlook; if some were at first prepared to speak of a relative or derived holiness, the majority soon came to regard churches as sacred shrines set apart exclusively for worship.[37] Episcopal and archidiaconal injunctions, backed by state support, were gradually successful in expelling, as profanations of God's house, all secular activities, and with the Gothic Revival the view that it would be impious to think or act in any other way became riveted upon the mind of the Church of England.[38]

To the present day the same attitude persists. For the Roman Catholic position we may quote from the *Guiding Principles for the Design of Churches*, issued by the German Liturgical Commission in 1947. This states that a church is 'in a unique way "the tabernacle of God among men" (Rev. 21.3), the place in which God allows his people to be certain of finding him; it is "the Father's house" (cf. Luke 15.17); it is God's royal palace. . . . The interior of the ideal church should forcefully proclaim the greatness of God as something beyond all earthly standards. In this way it will lift the worshipper out of the atmosphere of his ordinary existence.'[39] A decade later the Diocesan Church Building Directives for Superior, Wisconsin, repeat the same themes, declaring a church to be a sacred building and emphasizing this by quoting from the mass of dedication: 'O how awesome is this place; this is the house of God and the gateway to heaven; it shall be called the majestic court of God'[40]— so Jacob's outlook is taken as representative of that which the twentieth-century Christian should adopt.[41]*

The official Anglican attitude is expressed in the draft canons published in 1947. Canon 108, section 1, reads as follows:

> The Churchwardens and their Assistants shall not suffer any Church or Chapel to be profaned by any meeting therein for temporal objects inconsistent with the sanctity of the place.

Canon 109 states:

> Forasmuch as Cathedral and other Churches and Chapels have been separated from all profane and common use and dedicated for the solemn worship of Almighty God, no Cathedral, Collegiate, or Parochial Church or Chapel shall be used for any play, concert, or exhibition of a cinematograph film without the permission of the Bishop of the Diocese, or in places exempt from his jurisdiction, the permission of such persons as exercise ordinary jurisdiction in the same. Such permission shall not be given until the Bishop or other persons exercising ordinary jurisdiction have first examined, or caused to be examined by some competent persons appointed by them for this purpose, the words, music, and pictures of the said play, concert, or film proposed to be exhibited, and have satisfied themselves that they are such as befit the House of God, are consonant with sound doctrine, and tend to the edifying of the people.[42]

This canon allows a certain measure of discretion to be exercised by the ecclesiastical authorities, but its whole tone stems from an implicit acceptance of the concept of the two worlds and it clearly states that a church is the house of God and that it is a place invested with sanctity.

This continuity of outlook has not escaped the notice of the phenomenologists. Mircea Eliade describes a church in a modern city in this way:

> For a believer, the church shares in a different space from the street in which it stands. The door that opens on the interior of the church actually signifies a solution of continuity. The threshold that separates the two spaces also indicates the distance between the two modes of being, the profane and the religious. The threshold is the limit, the boundary, the frontier that distinguishes and opposes two worlds—and at the same time the paradoxical place where those worlds communicate, where passage from the profane to the sacred world becomes possible.[43]

To the same effect Roger Caillois says:

> He who wishes to offer sacrifice, to penetrate into the temple, to communicate with his god, must, at the outset, break with his everyday habits. . . . The restrictions which make a man fit to meet the divine and which render him pure, exist with the same value for the Australian neophyte who prepares himself for the tests of initiation, for the magistrate of the ancient world who went to sacrifice in the name of the city, and for the modern Christian who kneels before the Holy Table.[44]

This correspondence between the Christian outlook and practice and those that emerge from an analysis of comparative religion goes even further. It has been stated above that a shrine is conceived to be a world in itself; such an understanding has been applied both to the Jerusalem Temple and to Christian churches. Josephus interpreted the plan of the temple as 'an imitation of the system of the world'.[45] He contended that 'when Moses distinguished the tabernacle into three parts, and allowed two of them to the priests, as places accessible and common, he denoted the land and the sea, these being of general access to all; but he set apart the third division for God, because heaven is inaccessible to men'.[46] So the temple was an *imago mundi*, and at the same time was the centre of the world.

This cosmological structure of the sacred edifice still persists in Christian thought and is most noticeable in a Byzantine church:

The four parts of the interior of the church symbolize the four cardinal directions. The interior of the church is the universe. The altar is paradise, which lay in the east. The imperial door to the altar was also called the door of paradise. During Easter Week, the great door to the altar remains open during the entire service; the meaning of this custom is clearly expressed in the Easter Canon: 'Christ rose from the grave and opened the doors of paradise unto us.' The west, on the contrary, is the realm of darkness, of grief, of death, the realm of the eternal mansions of the dead, who await the resurrection of the flesh and the last judgment. The middle of the building is the earth. According to the view of Kosmas Indikopleustes, the earth is rectangular and is bounded by four walls, which are surmounted by a dome.[47]*

The identical outlook is found in the West in the Middle Ages, when cathedrals were regarded as models of the cosmos.[48]

Not only is the holy place a world in itself, it is also an imitation of a divine plan. Here again the Jerusalem Temple and the church are regarded as being in correspondence. Various passages in the Old Testament indicate that the Temple was constructed after a divine model. Yahweh's instructions to Moses are to this effect: 'Let them make me a sanctuary; that I may dwell among them. According to all that I shew thee, the pattern of the tabernacle, and the pattern of the furniture thereof, even so shall ye make it. . . . and see that thou make them after their pattern, which hath been shewed thee in the mount.'[49] Similarly when David gave the plans for the Temple to Solomon, he informed him that 'all this have I been made to understand in writing from the hand of the Lord, even all the works of this pattern'.[50] In the Wisdom of Solomon, the king is represented as saying that what he has built is 'a copy of the holy tabernacle which thou preparedst aforehand from the beginning'.[51] The author of the Epistle to the Hebrews reproduces the same idea when he describes the Temple and its furniture as 'a copy and shadow of the heavenly things' and as 'the copies of the things in the heavens'.[52] The Temple was the centre of the city of Jerusalem and this too was based upon a transcendent model; it was that 'which was prepared beforehand here from the time when I took counsel to make paradise'.[53] In Christian thought a church is an imitation of the Temple of Solomon, but since that was believed to have been constructed according to a celestial plan, the church is also conceived to be an image of the heavenly Jerusalem;[54] it is a reflection of heaven upon earth and therefore a means of passage into the divine world.[55] According to the German Liturgical Commission, 'it is the place in which the ultimate union of God with his people is anticipated, and which has therefore been justifiably described as the heavenly Jerusalem descended to earth (cf. Rev. 21.2)'.[56]

Entrance into this divine realm must be carefully regulated. This was achieved in the churches of the fourth century by means of the *cantharus* or *phiale*, which was a fountain in the forecourt. An inscription on a column from Bieda (Blera) in the province of Viterbo reveals their purpose. *Christianae lava manus et ora ut remittant (tibi peccata)*.[57] Eusebius witnesses to the same concept when he records how Paulinus of Tyre had built an atrium before his basilica and 'there he places symbols of sacred purification, by erecting fountains right opposite the temple whose copious streams of flowing water supply cleansing to those who are advancing within the sacred precincts'.[58] The same idea explains the holy water stoups which are still used by Roman Catholics when they enter churches today, and the location of the font, close to the main door, derives from the same concept. So a passage is effected without risk from one world to another by observing the necessary ritual precautions. The transition from the secular world into the sacred enclosure requires and is provided with a means of purification.

Finally, in this list of point by point correspondence, we come to the constitution of holy places by theophanies. Just as Solomon knew where to build the Temple in Jerusalem because of a divine manifestation at the threshing floor of Araunah,[59] so, too, Constantine adorned the sites of Christ's ministry and death in Palestine, and he constructed a church at Mamre where the three men, interpreted as Jesus and two angels, appeared to Abraham.[60] The same practice has continued. The shrine at Monte Sant' Angelo, *c.* 1076, was built because it was believed that the archangel Michael had visited the place. Similarly the sixteenth-century church of Our Lady of Guadeloupe, near Mexico City, marks the spot where the Virgin presented herself to a peasant. Where such theophanies have not been experienced and places made sacred thereby, the orientation of the church supplies the lack. The position of the sacred place is determined by building the shrine facing in a certain direction. In this way, while man, in the absence of a theophany, cannot make a shrine nor select its position, he can discover it and be sure of the presence of the divine.[61] So the German document says:

The focal point of the eastward attitude is God and his only-begotten Son, who are thought of as being, like the sun, enthroned in and coming from the east. This coming of God, this theophany, takes place, however, on the altar and it is the altar that both priest and congregation must face.[62]

It is remarkable that the actual word 'theophany' is here used.

This interlocked scheme of belief and practice does of course rule out any idea of a multi-purpose church in which sacred and secular are united. But disagreements with it have been previously noted, especially in connection with the Lutherans, the Reformed and the English Puritans.[63] So it is necessary to re-examine the question of the relationship of the sacred and the secular, not in the light of Church history from the fourth century onwards, but in connection with the New Testament teaching and with some general considerations about the validity of the thesis of the two worlds.

The New Testament position has already been outlined in the first chapter when we sought to discover the reasons why the early Christians had no temples and indeed gloried in the fact that they were without them, our point of departure being the triumphant boast of Minucius Felix; 'We have no temples and no altars.'[64] The outlook of the New Testament writers generally may be summarized in the form of three propositions. First, the dichotomy between the sacred and the profane had been brought to an end through Christ. Whereas in the Old Testament the common or profane is that which does not pertain to God and is to be avoided as an impediment or hindrance to man's approach to him, in the New Testament the situation is entirely different. 'What God hath cleansed make not thou common', Peter is informed.[65] This act of cleansing has been effected once and for all through Jesus who 'made purification (*lit.* cleansing) of sins'.[66] Henceforward 'nothing is unclean (*lit.* common) of itself',[67] and so the sacred and the divine are no longer divided.

Secondly, there is according to the New Testament position no exclusive place of encounter with God; anywhere can be the place of his presence. He may be met by the member of a caravan on the road to Damascus or by an itinerant preacher in the desert between Jerusalem and Gaza.[68] The result of such encounters was not the erection of shrines but the acceptance of the service of God in the world. Thirdly, in so far as there is a temple any longer, it is not one constructed of stone; it is a community, living in and not apart from the world, of which the 'living stones' are men and women.

Nor is there in the New Testament any concept of the two worlds. The New Testament, comments Bonhoeffer, 'is concerned solely with the manner in which the reality of Christ assumes reality in the present world, which it has already encompassed, seized and possessed. There are not two spheres, standing side by side, competing with each other and attacking each other's frontiers. If that were so, the frontier dispute would always be the decisive problem of history. But the whole reality of the world is already drawn into Christ and bound together in him, and the movement of history consists solely in divergence and convergence in relation to this centre.'[69]* This in itself could be taken as sufficient refutation of the thesis that sacred and secular are mutually exclusive and that therefore any attempt to unite them in a multipurpose church is out of the question, but we must pursue the matter further.

It is possible to approach this subject from another angle; we may accept the hypothesis of two worlds and test its validity by examining its corollaries. Since there are two worlds, then

(1) God is to be conceived as the resident of the supernatural realm; he is the 'wholly other'; he is remote, transcendent, high and lifted up. Consequently there is a great gulf between him and men; indeed God and men are separate because each belongs to a totally distinct realm of being.

(2) The sacred and the secular must be kept entirely separate, for the former is that which is apart from common usage. This isolation is essential to protect the world of the sacred from contamination. Consequently there can be no direct relationship of the sacred and

the secular; the former can only influence the latter from outside, from a safe distance as it were, and the latter can only come into contact with the former by ceasing to be itself, by observing ritual precautions whereby it is sacralized and turned, if only for a time, into the sacred.

(3) God operates chiefly within his own realm of the sacred. Since he should observe its bounds, the secular is outside his direct purview; it only comes within it if the borders of his realm are extended to include, and by so doing to transform, the secular.

These ideas, which are essential concomitants of the idea of the sacred space defined above, have to be carefully examined.

(1) To speak of God as the 'wholly other' is to adopt the terminology of Rudolf Otto's work *The Idea of the Holy*, the German original of which was published in 1917 and the first English edition in 1923. In this truly classic study, Otto set out to examine those elements in religious experience that lie outside and beyond the scope of reason. He defined these elements as 'creature-feeling' or self-abasement into nothingness before an overpowering, absolute might; as awe before a *mysterium tremendum*, and as fear before a *mysterium fascinans*. He characterized these experiences as numinous (from the Latin *numen*, god) and declared that the numinous presents itself as the 'wholly other' (*ganz andere*); it is entirely unlike anything human; it is totally different from any natural reality. So brilliant was Otto's analysis of the psychological aspects of the experiences he passed under review that scarcely anyone who has thought or written about the holy since his work was issued has been able to avoid using his vocabulary. Criticism has been levelled at his exclusive concentration upon the non-rational and his picture has been supplemented by directing attention to the equally important rational elements, amongst which is numbered the moral, but his basic thesis has been generally accepted.[70]

At the same time scholars have not been unaware that modern man seldom appears to have these experiences and that an encounter with the numinous is something which many today fail to have. Hence arise lamentations that twentieth-century urbanized man has lost an important dimension in life and has become more or less incapable of appreciating the divine. This is a remarkable position to have reached. It means in effect that those who believe in God can say that God has ceased to be able to communicate himself to many of his creatures. If such indeed be the case, it is too simple to condemn his creatures as myopic, carnal, engrossed in and with the material and culpably turning their backs on the divine. God himself must bear the blame for being too feeble to reveal himself to mankind. But before accepting this extreme position, one can at least pose a series of questions: is Otto's definition of the holy really correct? Does the holy reveal itself only in the form of the experiences that he describes? Is it impossible for the holy to be encountered in ways which do not inspire awe and fear? There are certain considerations which suggest that the answer to all these questions could be in the negative.

In the first place, we must distinguish between the experience and the object of the experience. Phenomenologists of religion are today more cautious in this respect than was Rudolf Otto. Van der Leeuw, for example, in the very first paragraph of his *Religion in Essence and Manifestation*, is emphatic that while for religion God is the active agent in relation to man, for the sciences concerned with religion it is the activity of man in relation to God that must be considered; 'of the acts of God himself,' he comments, 'they can give no account whatever'. Otto, however, begins with man's experience and then deduces from this certain predicates which he ascribes to the object which may be supposed to have produced those experiences. He may or may not be right; but the correctness of his procedure and the truth of his definition are not self-evident. Otto failed to take account of the fact that the experiences he analysed could be produced by natural phenomena alone. The savage who beholds the heavens brilliant with lightning and is deafened by the crash of thunder may feel self-abasement before absolute power; he may experience awe and fear before a *mysterium tremendum*; he may believe that this phenomenon is the 'wholly other' and is in fact a demonstration of the divine wrath. He, and Otto with him, may interpret this as an experience of the numinous, but modern scientific man is scarcely likely either to share the experience or to accept the explanation. In other words the experience of the 'wholly other' may be no more than the experience of an overpowering natural reality. If this is so, then the realm of the 'wholly other' will progressively diminish as the borders of scientific knowledge are advanced and the sacred will be no more than a stop-gap for the incompleteness of that knowledge. The question at issue of course is not the reality of religious experience as such, nor the existence of God, but why feelings which can be induced by natural phenomena should be regarded as distinctive of religious experience. Otto's analysis does not determine whether or not the 'wholly otherness' of God is no more than a description of what is not yet intelligible in scientific terms.

But *is* God the 'wholly other' according to the New Testament? Apart from quoting a few isolated verses, the exegesis and relevance of which may be questioned, Otto rested his case upon four main points. First, he argued that the good news of the Kingdom was the proclamation of the 'wholly other'. 'The kingdom is just greatness and marvel absolute, the "wholly other" "heavenly" thing, set in contrast to the world of here and now, "the mysterious" in its dual character as awe-compelling yet all-attracting, glimmering in an atmosphere of genuine "religious awe".' Further, as its Lord, God is 'far more "holy", "numinous", mysterious, *qadosh*, *hagios*, *sacer* and *sanctus* than his kingdom'.[71] Secondly, Otto contended that the agony in the garden was the record of 'the awe of the creature before the *mysterium tremendum*, before the shuddering secret of the numinous'.[72] Turning next to the Pauline writings, he asserted that the apostle's concept of the wrath of God is 'permeated by the "awefulness" of the numinous'. The God here depicted 'pours out the blazing vials of his wrath over the whole world'.[73] Finally, he adduced the Pauline doctrine of predestination and maintained that the religious concept in this 'is nothing but that "creature-consciousness", that self-abasement and the annulment of personal strength and claims and achievements in the presence of the transcendent, as such'.[74]

A critical examination of these statements will reveal their tendentious nature. As regards the Kingdom of God there are three observations to be made.

(*a*) Whereas according to the Synoptic Gospels the Kingdom of God is undoubtedly the result of the divine initiative, this does not mean that it is separate from human actions since the agent of the

Kingdom is the man Jesus of Nazareth. To say that the Kingdom is a 'wholly other' reality is to question the humanity of Christ.

(*b*) The Kingdom, as we have defined it above, is the sovereign power of God being manifestly effective in the world of human experience, but we can only say, with Otto, that it is *therefore* a revelation of the 'wholly other' if we have previously accepted this as a definition of the holy. If the holy is the numinous, then the Kingdom is a 'wholly other' reality because it is an effective manifestation of the holy God, but whether or not the holy is the numinous is precisely the point at issue. Otto reads this into and not out of the New Testament material and the same applies to his characterization of God as the Lord of the Kingdom.

(*c*) In the Synoptic Gospels the Kingdom is something that men are to enter into; they are to accept it with joy; even children may inherit it. There is no suggestion that either adults or children are to abase themselves before it in dread and awe.

Otto's exegesis of the agony in the garden is equally an example of his finding what he wants to find. It is true that according to the Marcan account Jesus 'began to be greatly amazed, and sore troubled',[75] and that the Greek words used in this passage suggest shuddering awe, but this refers to an intense degree of horror and suffering at the prospect of the torture and death that lie before him.[76] In this connection it is helpful to appreciate the difference between the death of Socrates and the death of Jesus:

Socrates died without any fear. His belief in the immortality of the soul made death nothing but a door through which the magnificent soul could leave the prison of our body. But Jesus did not know about the immortality of his soul. He knew that death is the last enemy of man and also the great enemy of God. He is the annihilator, the one who throws us into nothingness, into the pit of ultimate loneliness. Therefore the Gospels, in the unbearable story of the Garden, tell us that Jesus was in anguish of spirit, his sweat falling to the ground like drops of blood, his heart breaking with grief. Jesus knew, as we do, that death is the end.[77]

So the incident depicts a natural human experience in the face of man's inhumanity to man and of the prospect of death; there is no need whatsoever to interpret it as an experience of the *mysterium tremendum*. Moreover, there is one feature of the account that suggests the exact opposite of Otto's exegesis. Jesus is represented as addressing God not in the normal fashion of the Aramaic-speaking Jew as *ahbi* but as *abba*, which is the more familiar term used of one's earthly progenitor. Such amazing familiarity is the very antithesis of 'awe . . . before the shuddering secret of the *numen*'.

Otto's third point about the wrath of God is less easy to criticize because of divergence of opinion about the meaning of this concept. Otto clearly regarded 'wrath' as a feeling (*affectus*) on the part of God, since he referred to him as 'jealous, passionate . . . and angry'.[78] This is indeed the general LXX understanding, but in the writings of Paul there is a complete change. There wrath is an activity (*effectus*); it refers to God's providential ordering of history, to the action of a personal God who hates sin; it describes an inevitable process of cause and effect in a moral universe.[79] As an *effectus*, it is ultimately under the control of an *affectus*, but this *affectus* is the divine love.[80] Once this has been said, Otto's position becomes entirely problematic.

Equally suspect is Otto's account of Paul's supposed doctrine of predestination. This is based upon Romans 9, but what Otto has failed to appreciate, and he has had many predecessors, is that this chapter is concerned not with predestination but with election. Paul's argument is that God is free; he chooses whom he will to act as agents of his purpose and his choice is not determined by the merit of those whom he elects. If they will not execute his will, he is said to 'harden' them, but this 'hardening', according to Old Testament usage, is not an act of divine power which forces men against their will to do what is required; it is rather an acceptance by God and a condemnation of their refusal to be obedient.[81] Hence Otto misinterpreted Paul and this allowed him once again to read in his own misunderstanding of the numinous. If election be the theme of Romans 9 and not predestination, the foundation of Otto's argument disappears.

Otto was perfectly well aware that the New Testament did not provide abundant evidence for his thesis. He attempted to explain this by using the argument from silence. He acknowledged that in the teaching of Jesus there is little about the numinous, but contended that this was simply because it was 'a self-evident fact to every Jew'.[82] Such an argument fails to allow for the possibility that neither Jesus nor his followers spoke of the numinous because they had a different experience and understanding of the holy. In other words, by stressing the continuity of the Old and New Testaments —a continuity which in many particulars it would be idle to pass over—Otto failed to face the question: are there not ideas in the Old Testament that require not merely correction but rejection in the light of the New? Paul had indeed stated that 'whatsoever things were written aforetime were written for our learning',[83] but he also observed a distinction between what was to be imitated and what was not: 'these things happened unto them by way of example; and they were written for our admonition'.[84] It is possible, and it certainly has to be investigated, that the Old Testament concept of the holy, in which Otto legitimately discovered the numinous, was written 'for our admonition'. It is possible that the understanding of the holy, common to Jesus and his followers, was not identical with that of the Jews, whose experience was patterned upon and interpreted exclusively in the light of the Old Testament record.

Jesus' familiarity with God has already been noted in speaking of the agony in the garden and his use of the term *abba*. This intimate mode of address even survived translation into Greek and was used by the Gentile Christians.[85] Their prayer was an encounter of personalities, a communing with a personal God. In this activity they enjoyed great freedom, for they now found it possible to approach God as Father; they were no longer slaves but adopted sons. God was not a remote being, but one who was remarkably accessible. Reverence and respect were obviously called for, but this was entirely different from fear and trembling and self-abasement before the 'wholly other'. Here, in part lay the scandal of the Christian message. Whereas it had been generally thought, especially by the Jews, that 'the holy object is that which is screened from profane gaze, or to be manifested only on solemn occasions',[86] Christians now asserted that the God revealed in Jesus had exposed himself to every aspect of human life. Indeed,

For a truly personal communion with man, God had to be God for man in a human way. Since his desire was to manifest a tri-personal life and to reveal to man his share in that life, only a person, only God living a human life, could adequately reveal this. Revelation from the beginning was concerned not so much with problems, facts, or events, but an inner personal life; finally, it was in the flesh of a human nature that the unsuspected and unsurpassable revealing took place.[87]

So he who is holy by nature has refused to remain at a distance from secular life. The apparent gulf between the sacred and the secular has been bridged. Since the initiative in this bridging process has been taken by God, there must be something in his nature that makes this possible; there must be an affinity between Creator and creature which, if one may so express it, allows God to enter into union with humanity without acting contrary to his own nature. If he were the 'wholly other', it is difficult to see how this could be achieved.

That there is an affinity between God and man according to Jesus may be seen from the statement: 'Ye, therefore, shall be perfect, as your heavenly Father is perfect.'[88] The term rendered 'perfect' should not be given a moralizing content: *teleios* means whole or complete. The 'wholeness' of God is the model of the 'wholeness' or full maturity and unity of man. Such a concept is only intelligible if there is a likeness between Creator and creature, a likeness which is expressed in the Old Testament in the words that man was created in God's image. If man were to become like the 'wholly other', he would cease to be man; he can only become 'perfect', like the heavenly Father, if he attains 'unto a full grown (*teleios*) man, unto the measure of the stature of the fulness of Christ'[89] who is himself the divine image in all its human completeness.[90]

So the first corollary of the idea of the two worlds, viz. that God is the 'wholly other' and, being remote, is separated from man by a great gulf, does not accord with the New Testament teaching on the subject. We must now go on to consider the second corollary.

(2) If the sacred has to be kept apart from the secular to preserve it in its integrity, then God was not in Christ reconciling the world unto himself; yet the New Testament affirms the opposite, viz. that God has not kept himself apart but has entered human life without any fear of compromising his holiness. The history of Jesus is an episode in *secular* history; he lived and died under a Roman official who was governor of Palestine from A.D. 26–36. So far from pre-

serving himself from contamination, he consorted with prostitutes and sinners, yet at the same time he could be recognized as 'the Holy One of God'[91] and his followers could speak of him as both 'the Holy and Righteous One' and the 'Holy Servant'.[92] The holy is now encountered in and through the secular, but the secular is not thereby changed into the sacred. The humanity of Christ is not sacralized; instead it becomes the locus of the unity of sacred and secular. Henceforth the holy does not influence the common life of mankind externally from a separate base as it were; the two are integrated so that the wholeness of life may be enjoyed in its full power. So God in human form is revealed as neither remote and terrifying nor absolute, metaphysical and infinite, but as the man for others. This is the manifestation of a direct relationship between the sacred and the secular, of their perfect unity, and this unity is achieved by a sublime lack of concern on the part of the holy about any supposed risk of contamination, by an assumption of the human condition in all its secularity. Yet this is not simply a display. Revelation is not a mere gesture which effects nothing beyond the declaration of what was already true before it happened. Revelation is God in action, and through his action in Christ he establishes the conditions within which the unity of the sacred and secular is possible. Henceforth in and through Christ sacred and secular can be one. So the divine love effectively bridges the gulf. Christianity is, therefore, to use the distinction made by van der Leeuw, not a religion of remoteness but of love.[93] God is not a distant being unconcerned with everyday secular life, but a loving Father who has the whole cosmos in his purview. In saying this, we are already moving towards a criticism of the third corollary.

(3) Briefly summarized, the third corollary to the concept of the two worlds is that God is primarily related to the world of the sacred and only indirectly to the world of the secular. The divine being is thus envisaged as an object of devotion to be worshipped and encountered within the religious enclave alone. Life is thus split up into two areas, one over which God is sovereign and one from which his presence and activity are largely banished. Hence, to quote a pungent remark by the Bishop of Woolwich, 'the space to watch, as it were, if one really wants to see what God is up to, is the Church

papers'.[94] It is to Dietrich Bonhoeffer that the credit for emphasizing the falseness of this outlook belongs. He argues that the
acceptance of the idea of two distinct realms leads to the division
of reality into two parts:

> . . . the cause of Christ becomes a partial and provincial matter within
> the limits of reality. It is assumed that there are realities which lie outside
> the reality that is in Christ. It follows that these realities are accessible by
> some way of their own, and otherwise than through Christ. However
> great the importance that is attached to the reality in Christ, it still always
> remains a partial reality amid other realities. The division of the total
> reality into a sacred and a profane sphere, a Christian and a secular sphere,
> creates the possibility of existence in a single one of these spheres, a
> spiritual existence which has no part in secular existence, and a secular
> existence which can claim autonomy for itself and can exercise this right
> of autonomy in its dealings with the spiritual sphere. . . . So long as
> Christ and the world are conceived as two opposing and mutually repellent
> spheres, man will be left in the following dilemma: he abandons reality as
> a whole, and places himself in one or other of the two spheres. He seeks
> Christ without the world, or he seeks the world without Christ. In either
> case he is deceiving himself. Or else he tries to stand in both spaces at
> once and thereby becomes the man of eternal conflict, the kind of man
> who emerged in the period after the Reformation and who has repeatedly
> set himself up as representing the only form of Christian existence which
> is in accord with reality.
> It may be difficult to break the spell of this thinking in terms of two
> spheres, but it is nevertheless quite certain that it is in profound contra-
> diction to the thought of the Bible and to the thought of the Reformation,
> and that consequently it aims wide of reality.[95]

We must also recognize that to think in terms of the two spheres
is to think statically and ontologically. The sacred belongs to one
clearly defined realm and the secular to another. The holy is experienced at specific places by means of a theophany which thereby
marks out an area and changes its nature; profane space is now
sacralized and becomes sacred. But 'when God the Father "shows"
himself in a radical and complete manner by becoming incarnate in
Jesus Christ, then all history becomes a theophany'.[96] This manifestation of the sacred in secular history means that the Christian's
vocation lies within his concrete, historical life, the life that was
chosen and lived by Christ. Any attempt to withdraw into a sacred
world is thus a contraction out of history; it is a denial that God has

acted and continues to act in history and that history is a means of the divine self-revelation and of communion with him.

To reject the concept of the two realms is not to accept monism; it is, however, to affirm that the sacred, which is that which pertains to God, is freely available to man in and through his secular existence. Bonhoeffer again gives a brilliant account of this unity:

There are not two realities, but only one reality, and that is the reality of God, which has become manifest in Christ in the reality of the world. Sharing in Christ we stand at once in both the reality of God and the reality of the world. The reality of Christ comprises the reality of the world within itself. The world has no reality of its own, independently of the revelation of God in Christ. One is denying the revelation of God in Jesus Christ if one tries to be 'Christian' without seeing and recognizing the world in Christ. There are, therefore, not two spheres, but only the one sphere of the realization of Christ, in which the reality of God and the reality of the world are united. . . .

Thought which is conducted in terms of two spheres regards such pairs of concepts as secular and Christian, natural and supernatural, profane and sacred, and rational and revelational, as though they were ultimately static antitheses, serving to designate certain mutually exclusive entities. It fails to recognize the original unity of these opposites in the reality of Christ, and in the place of this true unity it sets the forced unity of some sacred or profane system in which these contradictory concepts are combined. In such a system the static antagonism persists. But these things assume quite a different form with the recognition of the divine and cosmic reality in Christ. The world, the natural, the profane and reason are now all taken up into God from the outset. They do not exist 'in themselves' and 'on their own account'. They have their reality nowhere save in the reality of God, in Christ. It is now essential to the real concept of the secular that it shall always be seen in the movement of being accepted and becoming accepted by God in Christ. Just as in Christ the reality of God entered into the reality of the world, so, too, is that which is Christian to be found only in that which is of the world, the 'supernatural' only in the natural, the holy only in the profane, and the revelational only in the rational. The unity of the reality of God and of the world, which has been accomplished in Christ, is repeated, or, more exactly, is realized, ever afresh in the life of men. And yet what is Christian is not identical with what is of the world. The natural is not identical with the supernatural or the revelational with the rational. But between the two there is in each case a unity which derives solely from the reality of Christ, that is to say solely from faith in this ultimate reality.[97]

The unity of which Bonhoeffer speaks has to be lived; this is far more important than theoretical discussions about it. Yet this can be rendered difficult, if not impossible, if its nature is misconceived. It is in fact as important to know what the unity is not, as it is to define it positively. For illumination upon this we may turn to the Christological debate of the first half of the fifth century. By the year 400 Christians accepted three propositions about Christ: he is completely divine; he is completely human; he is one person. The Christological problem is to determine how anyone can be both divine and human and *at the same time* one person. The debate was in fact about the very subject we have been considering, viz. the unity of the sacred and secular. It is true that it was conducted in metaphysical terms that are now considered by many to be outdated, but the attempt to define Christ's person was not simply a struggle for truth in its metaphysical aspect; it was a struggle for a particular understanding of the whole of life. The Chalcedonian Definition did not solve the problem of the unity of Christ's person, although it did enunciate clearly the factors that must not be bypassed. We are therefore not appealing to it as an authoritative and final statement of absolute truth, but we are going to use it as a model from which there is something to be learned.

The prelude to the meeting of the Council of Chalcedon consisted of two controversies associated with the names of Nestorius and Eutyches respectively. Nestorianism, which may or may not have been identical with the teaching of Nestorius, was the belief that in Christ Godhead and manhood exist side by side in a kind of partnership. This is what is known in Aristotelian terms as a union of composition, or juxtaposition. 'A faggot held together by bands and pieces of wood held together by glue' are examples of such a union.[98] To the orthodox opponents of Nestorius this was no real unity; instead it was simply an association of two essentially separate beings which could be dissolved at any time if there arose a divergence between them. This corresponds to the view that the sacred and the secular may perhaps be occasionally associated but can never be truly united. The Nestorian 'Two Sons' is the equivalent of the two independent realms of the sacred and the secular. In rejecting such a concept Christians of the fifth century were affirming in their own terms that 'there is no real possibility of being a Christian outside the reality of the world and that there is no real worldly existence outside the reality of Jesus Christ. . . . The Christian is no longer the man of eternal conflict, but, just as the reality in Christ is one, so he, too, since he shares in this reality in Christ, is himself an undivided whole.'[99]

Reaction to Nestorianism went to the opposite extreme in the teaching of Eutyches. He asserted that in Christ the humanity was absorbed by the divinity. This was the Aristotelian union of predominance according to which the weaker of two uniting elements disappears in the one of greater power or action. So the humanity of Christ was changed into the divinity as a drop of honey vanishes and is transformed when it is mixed with the sea.[100] This was equally unacceptable to the orthodox party, who immediately recognized that there is no unity when the result is that one of the elements ceases to exist. The Eutychian 'one nature' teaching is the equivalent of the idea of sacralization, i.e. the absorption of the secular by the sacred so that it ceases to be secular. In rejecting such a view Christians of the fifth century were affirming in their own terms that one must not separate and alienate oneself from the world in order to live a 'righteous' life in an insulated compartment, within which the world, it is hoped, will be progressively included. The sacred is neither to subdue nor to dominate the secular, for it is a liberating force. Indeed, 'the whole issue of the interaction of the sacred and the secular, in so far as it is rightly effected, is the enabling of the latter to come into its own and to reveal its true nature and full potentialities'.[101]

The Chalcedonian Definition, opposing these two heresies, asserted that the Godhead and the manhood are in Christ 'without confusion, without change, without division, without separation'. The same adverbs are to be applied to the sacred and the secular; they are not to be confused by being merged with one another in an undifferentiated unity; by taking the common stuff of humanity, God in Christ reveals its capacity for embodying and manifesting the sacred. Further, the one is not to be absorbed by the other (Eutychianism); nor are they to be set in opposition to each other (Nestorianism). The Definition, further, asserted the unity of Christ's person but emphasized that he is 'acknowledged in two natures', i.e. while he is one person, rational analysis enables one to recognize that he is both God and man. Thus the sacred and the secular are both elements in a unified life; they are twin aspects of the whole of life seen and experienced as a totality. Bonhoeffer's illustration of this is vivid enough to be worth repeating. He points out how in polyphonic music there is a unity of *cantus firmus* and counterpoint. The two are not identical and can indeed be distinguished as we listen, but both are essential to this particular form of music. They are ' "undivided and yet distinct", in the words of the Chalcedonian Definition, like Christ in his divine and human natures'—so are the sacred and the secular—but both are united, and 'only a polyphony of this kind can give life a wholeness'.[102] So God is to be sought not on the borders of life, nor along the supposed boundary line between the sacred and the secular, but in the midst of life in and through the secular. Life in the secular world is the place of encounter with God; he is not to be found beyond or apart from it.

Fortunately, the situation in Western Europe today is such that the Church, often in spite of itself, is gradually being recalled to this vision of unity which is writ large in the New Testament and was a source of inspiration to the first Christians. Indeed 'from the moment that the Church finds itself faced by a world without religious structurization, by a world which encloses itself in its own autonomy, it is precisely then that it discovers the negative and absurd character of the separation between the religious and the profane'.[103] The two principal factors that impede this discovery are, on the one hand, an introversion which prevents Christians from seeing the contemporary world as it really is and, on the other hand, a theology which embodies the false concept of the two worlds. To break out of the first and to rethink the latter are enormous tasks, but since the unity is to be lived rather than treated as the object of theory a beginning may be made by building multipurpose churches in which sacred and secular are united—the theory can wait upon the reality of the experience and the theological reformulation can spring out of this encounter of gospel and world.

Against such a programme are to be set two factors, one arising from fear and the other from conservative prejudice. The first of these is the argument that unless the sacred and the secular are sharply distinguished the reality of the former will soon be forgotten. Without a fence around it, the sacred may be contaminated, as it were, and finally lost. The present situation, however, suggests precisely the opposite. The sacred and the secular have for centuries been sharply distinguished and the result is a complete inversion of the primitive understanding of the two. That understanding, as previously defined, is that the sacred is the real and the secular the unreal; today, for many people, it is the sacred that is the unreal and the secular the real. It is arguable that this is a direct result of the persisting separation and that the way to enable the reality of the sacred to be rediscovered is to promote circumstances in which it may be encountered in and through the secular. If the previous argument is correct, viz. that the sacred and the secular are integral elements in a unified life, then where there is no such unity the sacred soon comes to be regarded as irrelevant and the secular becomes subject to secularism. The secular then tends to elevate itself into an absolute; it vies, not with the Church, which should never seek to dominate, but with Christ who is its Lord. It invests itself with a sacral character which is spurious and is likely to lead it to prostitute men and make them less than human, for since man is created in the divine image the denial of God is the denial of man. The isolation of the sacred also denies its true character, for, according to the New Testament, it is of the nature of the sacred to communicate itself, to incarnate itself. To seek deliberately to perpetuate this separation is thus to acquiesce in circumstances which progressively denaturalize both sacred and secular.

It is arguable that this concern to protect the holy stems from an arrogation of authority which human beings simply do not possess. Can anyone seriously maintain that *we* are to defend God? That *we* are to build walls to safeguard him from the toil and stress of daily life? If God was in Christ, then this shows his willingness to empty himself, his readiness to enter into secular life. If God were so little worried about his apartness, who are we to worry in his stead? The reality of the sacred is the reality of God; presumably, if the phrase may be excused, he can look after himself. Perhaps our walls of defence are prison walls shutting God in rather than the secular out;

or alternatively, since God will not be so confined, creating unnecessary hindrances to his free activity. If we constitute ourselves
guardians of the holy, then we have a heavy responsibility to ensure
that it is preserved; but have we any authority so to constitute ourselves? The fear that to affirm the unity of sacred and secular will
issue in a devaluation of the former may be no more than a disguised
concern for the preservation of one's own status as a dispenser of
the holy. There seems little evidence, however, that God has surrendered his sovereign freedom to any human agency. Christ may
work through the Church, but he is its head.

Widespread prejudice among the laity against the use of churches
for secular activities is a comparatively recent growth—it is nevertheless an undeniable fact. This may be illustrated from one of the
findings of a sociological survey conducted in 1965 for the Institute
for the Study of Worship and Religious Architecture in the University of Birmingham. The Institute had been asked to plan and build
a new Baptist centre in the Balsall Heath district of the city. In order
to determine what kind of centre to build, it wanted to know the
attitudes of people to the idea of a multipurpose church and what
type of activity would be regarded as legitimate in the worship area.
The questionnaire used for the survey therefore contained the item:
'What would you think of having these sorts of meetings in a church
building as well as the usual services (i.e. not in adjoining rooms or
buildings)?' A list of possible activities was then appended and the
overall results were as follows:

| *Items* | *Number of Responses* |
|---|---|
| 1. Parish Meetings | 89 |
| 2. Lectures | 83 |
| 3. Plays | 79 |
| 4. Children's Activities | 72 |
| 5. Concerts | 69 |
| 6. Socials | 63 |
| 7. Parish meals | 57 |
| 8. Film Shows | 53 |
| 9. Wedding breakfasts | 49 |
| 10. Whist Drives | 45 |
| 11. Dances | 43 |
| 12. Ballet | 36 |

In this ranking only five items were responded to in a positive manner,[104]* i.e. only five of the activities were endorsed by more than 50 per cent of the one hundred and thirty-five people interviewed. So this particular sample expressed the view that most of the activities listed should not take place in the body of the church itself. Moreover, if the sample is further broken down into responses by churchgoers and non-churchgoers, then one finds that the former positively endorsed only two, i.e. parish meetings and lectures, while non-churchgoers were prepared to add to these the next three items, viz. plays, children's activities and concerts. In either case there is no great enthusiasm for using the church for a variety of activities—the holy place is to be kept apart and the sacred and the secular are not to be united. Even those who do not come regularly inside it regard it in the same light and therefore dismiss a number of activities as unsuitable to a sacred shrine. This represents not only a dichotomy of the sacred and secular but also a lesion of thought.

This lesion of thought may be illustrated also from the experience of the Institute in connection with another building project, viz. the planning of a new church at Hodge Hill, Birmingham. At an early stage of the discussions of the building committee the question of a multipurpose church was raised. The idea was clearly new to many of the members of the committee, but they were very willing to consider it. After some debate, the point was reached where it was agreed that plays could be legitimately staged in a church. The question then arose: What kind of plays? A division of opinion immediately became apparent. Some were in favour of classical plays only; others refused to draw any line. The lesion of thought revealed by the first group was this: its members did not realize that the choice of a play is to be determined by an estimation of the plays themselves and not by the place in which they are presented. The operative factor is not where a play is staged but what its standards are. If a play is not fit to be acted in a church because, for example, it is merely pornography, one may question if it should be acted or seen anywhere. Once admit plays into church, then none can be ruled out except those in which one should not participate in any building. But at Hodge Hill some of the members of the building committee were unwittingly dividing plays into sacred and profane, and their willingness to accept only certain ones corresponded to their understanding of a church as a holy space set apart from the secular. Their readiness to allow plays in church suggested that they acknowledged the unity of sacred and secular, but their discrimination between plays indicated that this was not really so; the sacred/secular dichotomy persisted in their minds. The church was to them still a holy place into which one might allow religious drama and classical plays become venerable with age, i.e. only drama more or less sacralized was permissible. Because this dichotomy persisted in their thought, they were providing evidence of a failure to live an integrated life and were prepared to see it compartmentalized—in this instance two types of plays corresponded to a secular compartment and a holy compartment.

How are this fear and this prejudice to be overcome? There are various factors that may contribute to this end—patient teaching, an appeal to past practice and a demonstration of the essential unity of life by employing existing churches for secular activities and by planning new ones for multipurpose use.

The content of the Church's teaching must be the unity of the sacred and the secular in and through Christ. Since this relates to the Christological problem, which has to be examined afresh and made intelligible in every age, this is not a matter of peripheral concern; it should be at the very centre of the Church's teaching ministry. Only as this is illuminated can people be expected to understand what the Church's message is about. The message is good news not about the *possibility* of unity but of the actualization of unity between God and man in Christ and of man and man in him here and now in the world. Man's divided existence—which is a way of describing what the New Testament writers call sin—is being overcome; in the fullness of his secularity he can attain maturity and experience *shalom*, even if that *shalom* is not complete because the present era belongs to the 'already' but 'not yet'.

Past practice has been documented in the previous chapters. For something like 1,800 years churches were used for almost every conceivable secular activity. Such practices, as we have noted, were under constant fire from the ecclesiastical authorities; bishop after bishop condemned, on an inadequate theological basis, what they considered to be acts of desecration, but their efforts had little immediate effect. It is only within the last two centuries that the battle has been largely won, with the consequence that to many a church appears to be totally irrelevant to their secular and daily life. The Christian appeal to tradition is often heard; here then is a lay tradition that is overwhelmingly in favour of the secular use of church buildings, and we must also take notice of the fact that in at least one country this tradition has never been broken.

Many of the buildings of the Reformed Churches in the Swiss Cantons are still in regular use for secular activities. They are the scenes of village assemblies, when all the voting members of the community discuss matters of local concern. They are used for elections, for concerts and for plays and films, the last two being of all kinds and not restricted to the 'religious'. Extra-mural university classes take place in them, as well as brass band rehearsals and, if there is no alternative accommodation, schools also are found within them.

Amongst the Pentecostalists, too, we find the same readiness to use churches for non-liturgical gatherings; in so far as these are in any way limited, this arises from the restricted range of the activities in which a Pentacostalist may legitimately engage and not from any concept of sacred space. Eating, for example, is quite common; individuals bring their provisions with them and share them for a lunch or supper in the church. In African Pentecostalist churches children are allowed to play games, and in Latin America dancing is not uncommon, although this latter example is usually given a liturgical setting.

Into many churches in England, too, a certain number of non-liturgical activities are now finding their way; concerts and religious plays are quite common, and with these may be included by way of illustration the liturgical pageant held in 1966 in Newport parish church, consisting of mime, readings and music. Choir and organ festivals may take the form of a competition with the presentation of prizes to the winners, e.g. the festival held in St Michael, Crickle-wood, London, in 1966. Even eating, although with a restricted menu, is finding its place. On Maundy Thursday, 1967, in St Francis, Westborough, Guildford, Methodists and Anglicans shared in a fellowship meal of bread and wine, sitting at trestle tables arranged in a semi-circle in the nave. Vestry and annual church meetings are once again penetrating the sacred precincts, as at Hope, near Sheffield, where in 1966 the vicar and wardens sat on the stone platform in front of the rood screen and the parishioners occupied their pews. The consecration festivities of the Roman Catholic cathedral in Liverpool included a danced mass, consisting of simple modern dances presenting the mass visually in choreographic images and set to Cavalli's *Missa Concertata* and to the unconventional electronics of Pierre Henry's *Mass of Christ the King*. It is, however, Coventry cathedral which provides the leading modern example in England of an attempt to use the liturgical area for secular activities. It has become customary to have five or six dramatic productions in the nave each year; films are shown and both the Royal Ballet and the Women's League of Health and Beauty have danced there; even a jazz concert has been staged and televised. This cathedral was not, however, designed primarily with secular activities in mind, and in other consecrated buildings, where there is less space, some re-ordering has to be effected. Woolwich parish church is one of the few instances where rigorous re-planning has been carried through. The inner core of this Georgian church now consists of a chapel to seat three hundred and fifty worshippers. The remaining space accommodates eight offices devoted to social service work, a lounge and a restaurant in the screened-off galleries, together with the parish office, the rector's office and the usual vestries.

It is important for clarity of thought to recognize that this Woolwich example is not a multipurpose church building in the sense in which that term is used throughout this book. The church at Woolwich accommodates divers functions but it does not do so within a single volume. What has happened is that the sacred area—the 'church'—has simply been reduced in size and then screened off; the space thus liberated, outside the smaller liturgical room, has then been put to secular use, but sacred and secular are as distinct as ever they were. There remains an inner shrine, a holy of holies, set apart for religious activities. If this plan were adopted for the churches of the future, then they would consist of a central chapel surrounded by a cluster of subsidiary rooms; the unity achieved between sacred and secular would be one merely of juxtaposition which, as argued above, corresponds to a Nestorian Christology; this is not a true union according to the classical Christological analogy. Perhaps it is better to have a Nestorian Christology than none at all—opinions may differ about this—but it is not a satisfactory solution. It masks the shocking nature of Christianity, i.e. the refusal of God in Christ to be hidden from 'profane' gaze. How then are we to visualize new churches for multipurpose use?

In seeking an answer to this question, it is not necessary to resort to theory; two examples may be cited, each of which has been deliberately conceived and planned as a multipurpose building. The design of SS. Philip and James, Hodge Hill, Birmingham, is an attempt to provide a fully integrated complex meeting the needs of the local community; it is to be a building serving all and not just accredited church members (Fig. 12). The worship area is the centre of the complex with the parsonage on one side and the youth centre on the other. This area is the major volume for worship, drama and whatever other uses the parish thinks desirable—social activities, games, etc. It has a fixed and defined space for sanctuary and choir and for the font, but no attempt has been made to shield 'sacred' objects during secular use. A stage along one side can serve as a children's playroom and to provide extra seating for a particularly large congregation, as does the lounge, which is raised above the level of the 'church floor'. The youth centre itself has a further hall and this for two reasons: first, the programme of activities envisaged is such that more than one large space will be needed *at the same time*, and, second, the playing of energetic games, e.g. with balls, would be inconvenient in a room with fixed and unprotected altar, etc. The architect has summarized his outlook in the following statement:

The design for SS. Philip and James at Hodge Hill did not materialize in a blinding revelation. It evolved, following an understanding of a complex group of changing functions, as a series of inter-relating spaces, covering and, it is hoped, enhancing the activities within. It is not intended to be an 'ideal' solution to a finite philosophy of church building. It is, however, an attempt to create a building for a real situation within inherent limitations. Its shortcomings are probably apparent: its ultimate success or failure has to be assessed.[105]

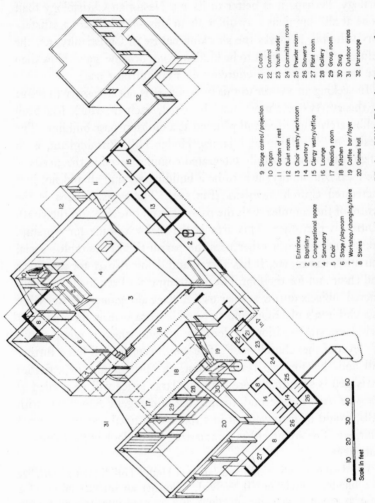

1 Entrance
2 Baptistry
3 Congregational space
4 Sanctuary
5 Choir
6 Stage/playroom
7 Workshop/changing/store
8 Stores
9 Stage control/projection
10 Organ
11 Garden of rest
12 Quiet room
13 Choir vestry/workroom
14 Lavatory
15 Clergy vestry/office
16 Lounge
17 Reading room
18 Kitchen
19 Coffee bar/foyer
20 Games hall
21 Coats
22 Control
23 Youth leader
24 Committee room
25 Powder room
26 Showers
27 Plant room
28 Gallery
29 Group room
30 Snug
31 Outdoor areas
32 Parsonage

Scale in feet
0 10 20 30 40 50

*Fig. 12* The Multipurpose Church: SS. Philip and James, Hodge Hill, Birmingham, 1967

The Hodge Hill church is Anglican, while the Highgate Centre has been commissioned by the Baptists, but the approach in each case has been identical. Those responsible for preparing the brief for the latter were quite clear that there was no need for a separate church and hall and that the worship area could be used for non-liturgical and secular activities. In the final design there is a central room containing the table, font and pulpit and seating some eighty people (Plate 16, facing page 195). This room can be extended in three directions and can eventually seat up to four hundred worshippers. The extensions form other accommodation such as a lounge for informal meetings and for an old people's day club, and a games hall. Each can be used independently or in conjunction with its immediate neighbours.[106]

In these two buildings there has been a deliberate break-away from immediate past practice, according to which a church is employed solely for worship. But this break-away has not resulted in a more refined form of the dual-purpose building, i.e. that type of hall with a sanctuary at one end which can be safely screened off when so-called non-religious activities are taking place under the same roof.[107]* Such a plan was the product in the main of economic circumstances after the last war and this, in its turn, failed to grapple with the problem of the unity of sacred and secular. In effect these buildings have been used on week days for the secular, with the holy in the sanctuary screened off; on Sundays the partition was opened and those who attended then engaged in 'sacred' activities. This was therefore an architectural expression of the dichotomy to which we have been objecting. In the two Birmingham churches the unity is visibly declared—hence the fixed altar-table, etc. These two plans thus enable the unity to be demonstrated and to be lived. How far they will be successful only time and experience will show, but at least they have a basis in a theological outlook which is nearer to that of the New Testament than those attitudes which have been adopted at certain times by some Christians in the centuries before our own.

This break with conventional church structures is all the more necessary when the situation is that of a new town. In the past secular planners have experienced two main difficulties in their relations with the Churches. On the one hand, the research and hard thinking that have contributed to the final plan have not been matched by a corresponding forethought on the part of the ecclesiastical authorities, who have not attempted to work in close conjunction with the consultants or the development corporation. On the other hand, the Churches have conveyed the impression that they were not really interested in supporting and fostering the life of the new communities, but only in creating a religious enclave within them. If, however, the Church accepts its rôle as the servant, then it will seek to build community life as a whole. It will recognize the interdependence of all social agencies, including itself with its pastoral concern. It will accept as a basic fact the inter-relationship of the work of doctor, psychiatric social worker, probation officer and priest or minister. The meaning and possibilities of this inter-relationship can be worked out in pastoral centres, which is another form that the multipurpose church can take. When neighbourhoods are designed as one community and are to act as one community, the Church must be able to serve within that one community. A traditional church plant, with liturgical room, etc. does not fit into this pattern; instead, the accommodation planned by Christians should be integrated with the provisions that are made for all kinds of social work. In other words, the community centre which houses the local caring agencies should also include the Church's pastoral centre. This should not be a holy shrine on a miniature scale nor a domestic chapel, but one that is suitable for pastoral counselling, for welfare for the aged, etc., as well as for the celebration of the eucharist for small groups. In this way the unity of the sacred and the secular can be vividly expressed and the Church's outgoing in concern can be embodied in a building that does not stand apart and is not set apart from life in the world.[108]

The concept of the multipurpose church has recently been brought to the attention of the public at large by the re-ordering at Woolwich previously described. In this form it has been subjected to some criticism and indeed a criticism of its theological basis has already been offered above. The Woolwich multipurpose *building* with its inner shrine is not the multipurpose *church* we have been advocating. Nevertheless, since some of the criticisms could be brought against our concept, they must be faced. There would appear to be three main objections. First, it is said that this is no more than an attempt to find a place for the Church in secularized society. Second, the rôle envisaged is described as one that really belongs to social agencies and not to the Christian community as such. Third, it is pointed out that secular activities do not need to be housed in hallowed buildings and indeed in so being they are merely given a false, churchly, character.[109]

On the face of it, there would appear to be nothing wrong in the Church attempting to understand and fulfil its rôle in secularized society. If it has no rôle, then it becomes irrelevant and can only concern itself with a 'religious' world set apart from the world of everyday living. The Church then gives up any idea of the unity of the sacred and the secular and passes its life entirely in the former sphere. In other words, the attempt is not to be condemned simply as an attempt; the essential question is rather whether the rôle is correctly conceived. Now we have previously discussed the rôle of the Church in the twentieth century; it is to help men to live the life of Christ in the world, i.e. to know and to live the unity of the sacred and the secular. Moreover, the life of Christ is a life of service and this service may in certain areas, though not necessarily in all, involve the provision of accommodation for secular activities. It is no valid objection to say that these activities are within the purview of social agencies, for to think in this way is to misunderstand the pioneer character of the Christian community in service. We may illustrate this pioneer nature of the Church from past history. In the centuries gone by the Church has led the way in providing both schools and hospitals. These forms of service were unquestionably right and proper in their day and age. To have argued that the State or other agencies should do this and not the Church would have meant that nothing was done. Once, however, the State has realized its responsibility and is fulfilling it, there seems little need for the Church to continue these forms of service. At the present day there are many social agencies that recognize the need to do some of the things that are proposed for a multipurpose church; but they cannot do them for lack of accommodation, finance, etc. The Church must then undertake these particular forms of service; in time these too may be assumed by secular agencies, and the Church, having fulfilled its pioneer task, will be grateful. Part of the Church's rôle is then to identify human need and meet it *now*. Its place in society will differ from district to district, from country to country and from age to age. How to live the life of Christ in the world is to be determined by the contemporary world and not by the world of yesterday or tomorrow. Even in the ideal society, when human need no longer exists—should that ever be established—the Church will still have to perform the rôle of assisting men to live the unity of sacred and secular. The multipurpose church, as defined in this study, is a possible means of doing this now.

If a church is conceived simply as a hallowed building, along traditional lines, this could lead to a 'churchifying' of secular activities. But this is not the concept of a church with which we have been working; the sacralization of the secular is not our intent. The secular is only 'churchified' if its unity with the sacred is denied and the attempt is made by the latter to dominate it. But, of course, this is not unity; it is the Eutychian approach which we have rejected. Nor will that unity be achieved by physical planning alone; it involves a revolution in thought and practice. When the ordained leader of a Christian group is clericalized, i.e. when he sees his function as solely within the sphere of the holy, anything that takes place in a building under his general control will be 'churchified'. The question of the relationship of sacred and secular is therefore not just one of church buildings; it affects the whole life and thought of the Christian community, but to consider all the ramification of this would be to go outside the limited, and therefore more manageable, scope of this study.

# 8

# The Consecration of Churches

In all the ages of the world thy servants have separated certain places from all profane and common uses, and hallowed them to thy divine worship and service. . . . We are now assembled here to put thy name upon this place, and the memorial of it, to make it thy house, to devote and dedicate it for ever to thee, utterly separating it from all former uses common and profane, and wholly and only to consecrate it to the invocation of thy glorious name.[1]

THESE SENTENCES, taken from the form of consecration devised by Lancelot Andrewes in 1620, are typical of the ideas expressed in countless other rites. Whether we turn to the medieval period or to more modern times, the same views are formulated. By consecration a church is set apart for holy use for ever and is not to be employed for secular activities. This understanding of consecration is not only common to the various services, it is also, in England, embodied in the law, according to which consecration 'has the effect of setting aside land or buildings *in sacros usus* for ever'.[2] This means that both liturgically and legally the multipurpose church is suspect. It is therefore necessary, in this final chapter, to examine the question of the consecration of churches to determine whether or not it constitutes a valid bar to the type of buildings advocated in this study. This examination has to be primarily theological, since the legal position should be regulated, and if necessary altered, so that it facilitates and does not constitute a hindrance to the performance by Christians of what they may legitimately believe to be right.

While the legal question can be largely left on one side, there is one aspect of the present position which has to be noted. In law, consecration differs from dedication. Dedication is understood to be no more than a pious act, a blessing of a building which may be only a temporary structure; whereas consecration is held to be an irrevocable act, so that the building can never be secularized.[3] This legal distinction has no basis in Christian usage nor in theological understanding. In the patristic period the terms were interchangeable. *Egkainismos* can be translated as either consecration or dedication. *Hagiazo* means to sanctify, hallow or consecrate, while *aphiero* can be rendered to treat as holy, to consecrate or dedicate. The last two words were used indifferently of churches and of the eucharistic species, of vestments and of vessels.[4] In Latin *dedico* and *consecro* are synonymous. So we find an inscription of 715 which refers to the chapel by the gate of Deerhurst priory and states that *Dodo consecrari fecit*, while of Clee Church, Lincolnshire, it is said in 1192 that *dedicata est*.[5] Hence in a theological analysis we do not need to observe any distinction between consecration and dedication; they each refer to the same thing.

In approaching the theological question, we may begin with the liturgical forms, since these embody a certain understanding of consecration.

As the first Christians had no holy shrines, the need for consecration did not arise. It was only in the fourth century, with the peace of the Church, that the practice of dedicating buildings began; even so, all that was required was the celebration of the eucharist. Eusebius's description of what took place at Tyre, which he gives as an example of 'festivals of dedication in the cities and consecrations of the newly-built houses of prayer',[6] shows that there were a number of addresses and that the service culminated in the performance of 'the sacred rites and stately ordinances', i.e. of the eucharist. From the moment that the eucharist was offered, within the context of a special festival service, the church was regarded as consecrated; consecration was thus effected by use. As late as Gregory the Great this was still the prevailing concept.[7]

From the end of the fourth century, however, there was added to the eucharist another element that was later to achieve considerable prominence; this was the deposition of the relics of martyrs within or beneath the altar. One of the earliest instances of this is described by Ambrose in a letter of 386 to his sister Marcellina, in which he tells her of the discovery of the remains of the saints Gervase and Protase and how these were borne to the new basilica and buried beneath the altar.[8]

At the beginning of the seventh century Gregory the Great prescribed the use of water when dedicating former pagan temples as churches; this aspersion was really a form of exorcism concerned to chase away the demons from their previous habitat, and this too was to become a feature of the developed medieval rite.[9] In its Roman form this rite consisted of the following elements:

I   The carrying of the relics in procession.
II  The entrance of the bishop and his party into the new building to prepare the mortar for sealing the altar stones and to wash the altar with exorcised water.
III The departure of the bishop's party, followed by the aspersion of the people.
IV  The entrance of all; the anointing of the four interior angles of the cavity; the deposition of the relics; the sealing of the stone and its anointing at the centre and four corners.
V   The blessing of the house, its vessels and of a lighted taper from which all the church lights are kindled.
VI  The mass.[10]

This consecration service is clearly modelled upon funerary rites; the church has become the mausoleum of a saint, with the altar as his tomb, and his burial, represented by the deposition of the relics, is the most prominent feature, the concluding mass serving as a requiem.

An entirely different rationale of consecration is represented by the Gallican form. Its general outline was as follows:

I   The bishop, having knocked on the door with his crozier, enters and leads the introductory prayers.
II  The bishop traces the letters of the alphabet with his crozier on the floor in two diagonal lines crossing in the centre of the church. This ceremony, of Celtic origin, would seem to correspond to the ancient Roman method of taking possession of a piece of land and marking out its boundaries. The Roman surveyor traced two transverse lines and connected them to form the perimeter; similarly the bishop marks the area which is to be Christ's by tracing the sign of the cross and the complete alphabet was an expansion of the alpha and omega.

III The bishop prepares lustral water, with exorcism, blessing and the
addition of salt and wine.
IV The altar is sprinkled.
V The church is sprinkled, a triple circuit being made inside and out,
the water being scattered on the walls.
VI A consecration prayer is uttered, eucharistic in character.
VII The altar is anointed.
VIII The church is anointed, the walls being touched with oil.
IX The objects used in worship are blessed.
X The relics are brought and placed in the cavity.
XI Lamps are lit.
XII The mass begins.[11]

This service is clearly modelled upon the rites of Christian initiation. The church is exorcised and then baptized with water and confirmed with oil—indeed *Ordo* 42 actually employs the terms *baptizat*
and *confirmat* in reference to the altar,[12] which is next dressed in
white, as were the catechumens. The lighting of the lamps is the
equivalent of the giving of tapers to the newly baptized, and the
mass corresponds to the baptismal eucharist in which the neophytes
joined as the climax of their entry into the Christian community.

The later medieval rite and, following it, the modern Roman form,
represents a fusion of these two services, but with the Gallican usage
predominating. So:

I The bishop is met by the clergy and in procession goes to fetch the
relics.
II The procession makes a threefold circuit of the exterior, while the
bishop sprinkles the walls.
III The procession enters, after the bishop has knocked on the door, and
the alphabet ceremony follows.
IV There are next the lustrations and anointings.
V The relics are placed in the altar which is censed and anointed.
VI The mass begins.[13]

Before proceeding to an account of the post-Reformation Protestant rites, a preliminary consideration of the rationale of the medieval
form will help to expose the basic theological ideas. Consecration is
an act whereby a certain volume of space is liberated from demon
infestation. So the blessing of the lustral water, according to the
Gelasian Sacramentary, includes the petition that it will acquire the

virtue to chase away all devils, illnesses and evil powers.[14] Consecration is further an act whereby that which was formerly profane is made holy. So the Gelasian has a prayer that God will 'pour out your grace upon this house of prayer',[15] and the *oratio super aquam et vinum* requests: 'Send down the Spirit upon this wine mixed with water that, armed with a celestial defence, it may serve for the consecration of this church.'[16] Hence the building ceases to be what it was before; there is a kind of transubstantiation of space whereby it becomes holy—holiness being understood as a quality of being. The new character is permanent, and hence the petition that 'the consecration of this place may remain for ever'.[17]

Consecration is effected by the combination of two main actions. The building becomes holy by being associated with the holy bodies of the saints. It also becomes holy by being baptized and confirmed; it is therefore treated exactly like a human being, and the effects predicted of Christian initiation, viz. liberation from evil, the transference of the believer from the secular world to the world of the Church and the imprinting with an indelible character are also attributed to the building. The fourth-century idea of consecration through use persists, in that the eucharist is invariably celebrated, but this has been displaced from its original prominence by the deposition, anointings, etc.

In general it may be said that the post-Reformation Protestant rites tend to think of the effects of consecration along similar lines, but consider it to be accomplished by use. Much of the Roman ceremonial has been stripped away: there is no deposition of relics, and anointing and lustrations are usually absent. Andrewes' form of 1620 begins with a perambulation with appropriate petitions at each stopping place—baptistery, pulpit, lectern, altar, etc.. Morning Prayer and the eucharist follow with special prayers added. In 1662 and 1663 the Anglican convocations discussed the provision of an official form, and one was eventually approved in 1712 and revised in 1714 but was never promulgated with authority. In 1887 and 1898 Bishop Wordsworth produced further revised forms and these have become the basis of many modern diocesan uses. Representative of these is that drawn up by the former Bishop of Sheffield, L. S. Hunter, and published in 1965. The structure is as follows:

    I   Circuit of the church.

   II  The bishop knocks on the door and receives the petition for the consecration and the keys.

 III  A prayer of dedication is followed by parts of the litany.

 IV  A lesson.

   V  The consecration prayer in eucharistic form.

 VI  Sermon.

VII  Blessing.[18]

Provinces of the Anglican communion, outside England, have been more forward in producing authorized forms. The Irish Order (1666) may have been that compiled by Bishop Cosin in 1662. It provides special lessons at various parts of the church, a dedication of the altar, a solemn presentation of ornaments, Morning Prayer with proper psalms and lessons and prayers for the donors, and the eucharist with its own collect, epistle and gospel and post-communion prayers. The American order, first introduced into the *Prayer Book* in 1799, was based upon the English of 1712. After the bishop has been received at the door, he goes in procession to the altar during the singing of Psalm 24. He then receives the instruments of donation and endowment, offers a prayer and next, facing the congregation, prays with reference to baptism, confirmation, the eucharist, reading, preaching and matrimony. A collect, epistle and gospel are provided for the eucharist. The Canadian form is very similar, while the African and Scottish allow for a circumambulation.

There is little to be gained by describing other services in detail; one non-Anglican example will suffice to demonstrate the general similarity of structure. The order published by the United Evangelical Church in Germany in 1952 consists of four parts:

   I  The bishop, clergy, elders, confirmation candidates, builders, etc., all gather in the building that has been in use for worship prior to the erection of the new church. A short service takes place, including an address and prayers.

  II  A procession goes to the new building to the singing of hymns and the blowing of trumpets. One of the confirmation candidates carries the key, while the clergy bear bible, vessels, etc. A hymn is sung before the door, while the key is passed from the master-builder to him who has commissioned the church, to the bishop and finally to the parish priest who opens the door.

III After an introit psalm, there is prayer and a short address, followed by a reading. Next there is the Lord's Prayer and the consecration formula. The vessels, books, etc., are placed in position with a prayer said over each, beginning with the altar furnishings, crucifix, vessels, etc., next to the font, then the lectern and bible, the organ and finally the bells.

IV The main Sunday service follows with, frequently, the communion.

More important than the precise order adopted by any one Church is the rationale. There is little or nothing in these Protestant rites corresponding to the medieval idea of liberating a certain volume from demon possession. There is, on the other hand, general agreement that consecration is an act whereby what was formerly profane is made holy, the building ceasing to be what it was before. Andrewes included a prayer to this effect:

Blessed Spirit, without whom nothing is holy, nor person, nor place can be sanctified aright; send down upon this place thy sanctifying power and grace; hallow it, and make it to thee a holy habitation for ever.[19]*

One section of Bishop Hunter's service is indeed entitled: 'The Separation of the Church from All Unhallowed Uses'. It has become, in the words of the *Book of Common Prayer* of the Protestant Episcopal Church in the United States, 'separated from unhallowed, worldly and common uses'. Indeed the building has now become a dwelling place of God. So the *Book of Common Order* of the Church of Scotland (1940) has this petition:

Dwell in this house, built to the honour of Thy most glorious name, that it may be, to all who seek Thee within its courts, a temple of the living God, a sanctuary of the Most High.

The new character acquired by the building is permanent, and the Scottish form, just quoted, is typical, when it prays that 'this place may be separated to Thy glory and hallowed for ever'. The consecration is regarded as effected by the Word of God, prayer and use. As regards the last item, many of the seventeenth-century Anglican services actually provided for the performance of baptisms, confirmation and the eucharist.[20] The *Ordinal and Service Book* of the Church of Scotland (1954) makes this attitude quite plain when it states:

If Holy Communion be not celebrated at the Service of Dedication, a celebration shall follow on the first Sunday thereafter, completing the dedication by putting the building to its full use.

What are we to make of all this? In the first place, it is difficult not to dismiss out of hand the belief that consecration liberates a particular space from demon possession. But because this ties in closely with the idea of consecration for ever and because it is still an element in the Roman rite,[21] though discarded in the Protestant forms, some attention must be paid to it. Experimental demonology means little or nothing to modern western man. It is of course writ large in the New Testament, where the belief is prominent that nervous disorders and even sickness in general are the product of devilish activity. 'The demonological theory about such evils was no mere speculation, it provided recipes for dealing with them. The essential point of diagnosis was not (let us say) to isolate the bacillus, but to name the demon; for if you named him you could exorcise him.'[22] One cannot deny that this was the child of scientific ignorance, and, to quote Austin Farrer, 'since we have long abandoned the practical part of the doctrine, it seems odd that we should trouble our heads over the theoretical'.[23] In reference to consecration it is obviously a speculative and apparently unfounded theory— not even the New Testament provides a basis for regarding all secular space on earth as inhabited by demons; they are associated essentially with human beings. Can anyone indeed point to a virgin patch of ground on which a church is to be built and seriously declare that it is demon infested? A new town is emerging from the drawing board; some plots are assigned for houses or flats, some for schools and shops, and some for churches. It would be nonsense to exorcise the whole area. Is it any less nonsensical to exorcise the church site?

This belief as to one of the effects of consecration is closely connected with the idea that it is an act the consequences of which are permanent. To hold that consecration may come to an end is, against this background of thought, to allow the possibility of what has been God's territory being surrendered and so returned to the devil. Since Christians in the past have held this to be unthinkable, they have also insisted on the permanence of consecration. This is quite logical, but remove the premiss and the deduction has no basis. Indeed, those who believe in the present Lordship of Christ and therefore do not accept that the world is largely under the sway of Satan, assuming he exists, cannot endorse a theology of consecration which is founded upon such a view. Moreover, past practice and rational consideration tell against the idea of permanence. One need not go further back than the eighteenth century to discover that Anglicans, at least, in those days, were 'not sentimental about old churches, and saw no point in spending money on the repair of a church that was inconveniently placed and seriously dilapidated. The purpose of a church was to accommodate the parishioners; and why should money be spent on a church to which they did not want to go? If there were sufficient room in a more convenient church, the obvious thing to do was to pull down the unwanted building, and to use the material for repairing the church that was more accessible and less ruinous.'[24] To cite just one example: in 1753 Hallington church was demolished and the materials salvaged and the money realized for the site were used for the repair of the church at Raithby. No idea of a permanent effect of consecration was allowed to stand in the way of the sensible redeployment of resources. The same conclusion follows from another line of argument.

In the medieval rite the alphabet ceremony, as we have seen, was understood to be the means whereby a certain area of land and the building upon it were conveyed to God. The same idea, that through consecration a church becomes the property of the deity, is expressed in modern rites. But, as the *Report of the Committee on Deconsecration* in 1961 cogently reasons:

though something is given to God, it is, of necessity, held by human agents as stewards or trustees for God. A gift cannot be taken back by the donor; but the beneficiary may dispose of the gift; and, where the gift is held by trustees as stewards, the trustees may dispose of it on the beneficiary's behalf provided they devote the proceeds to the benefit of the beneficiary. In secular affairs this is happening daily. Trustees who are possessed of land or shares on behalf of a beneficiary are expected to realize them from time to time when that can be done profitably; but, of course, the proceeds must be used only to the advantage of the beneficiary. It seems to us that the same principle should apply to land or buildings given to God by an act of consecration. The gift should not be revocable, but the human agents who hold the property as stewards in trust for God should have power to dispose of it when God's purposes are better served thereby, such proceeds as there may be from the disposition being held in trust for a godly purpose. The most obvious example of what we have in mind would be provided by the sale of a redundant church, the proceeds being devoted to the erection of a new church elsewhere where one is wanted.[25]

So consecration should not be deemed to have the effect of setting aside land or buildings in *sacros usus* for ever. The Committee goes on to support its thesis with four other considerations. It points out, first, that in the Early Church there seems to have been no scruple about leaving a house and allowing the room used for worship to revert to non-sacred use; second, that in England there have been numerous examples of consecration being nullified by parliamentary action; third, that by canon 1187 of the Roman *Codex Juris Canonici* authority is bestowed upon the ordinary to convert a church to profane, though not to sordid, uses when it can in no way be used for worship and there is no means of restoring it:

Fourthly, it seems to us to be simple common sense that God's property should be used in the way which best advances God's purposes, even though this should involve the disposal of the property. Human foresight cannot anticipate every contingency for ever. When a church is first built and consecrated it may seem probable that it will be used as a church for all time. Experience shows how often this probability is illusory. When this proves to be the case, the fact were better effectively acknowledged. The principle to which we firmly adhere is that the initial gift to God by consecration must be irrevocable in the sense that thereafter God alone is the beneficiary of the gift; but as stewards or trustees it is for us to see that the greatest benefit accrues, whether by continuing the gift in its original use or by disposing of it for the benefit of some godly purpose.[26]

To endorse the view that consecration, from one aspect, is the giving of something to God, or, more strictly, the giving back to God of something which he first gave us, does not mean that we are also accepting the idea that a church is thereby made a habitation of the deity. According to Matthew, Christ said: 'Where two or three are gathered together in my name, there am I in the midst of them.'[27] Anywhere, as we have previously contended, can be the place of encounter with the God who, through his Holy Spirit, dwells in his community. Consecrated architectural space is not necessary for this.

Indeed, 'the New Testament puts us on our guard against a pagan concept and even against the pre-exilic Jewish concept of a habitation of God in the temple. The Lord cannot be circumscribed in a dwelling-place made by the hands of men.'[28]

We have, however, still to examine the one feature common to all consecration rites, viz. the idea that through them space is hallowed, sanctified, or made holy and so set apart from secular use. In order to test the validity of this thesis we have to pass the theology of consecration briefly under review. This involves considering eucharistic consecration, for unless there is some affinity between the consecration of bread and wine and the consecration of bricks and mortar, the use of the identical term is inexcusable and can only lead to confusion. But the very fact that the same word is employed suggests that to understand the one may help to interpret the other.

Modern scholarship enables us to assert with confidence that consecration in the earliest days of the Church was understood to be identical with the Jewish giving of thanks. In the Jewish *Berakah* God himself is blessed; there is no blessing of inanimate objects. The 'blessing' of wine, for example, is really the blessing of God over the wine. When Jesus at the Last Supper is reported to have 'blessed' the bread, we know from Jewish sources that this would have taken the form: 'Blessed art thou, O Lord our God, King of the universe, who bringest forth bread from the earth.' The wording of his thanksgiving over the wine would have been in a similar vein: 'Blessed art thou, O Lord our God, King of the universe, who createst the fruit of the vine.' So God was blessed for some particular act—in this instance the creation and bringing to fruition of the corn and grapes—and this 'consecrated' the food. 'The blessing was in fact a thankful remembrance before God of a gracious act of his divine omnipotence and for that reason it conferred sanctity.'[29] The result was not a change of nature in the objects, but the explicit acknowledgement of their relationship to God. This same functional and non-ontological outlook underlies Jesus' words at the Last Supper.

In the Upper Room, according to Paul and the Synoptists, Jesus said of the bread: 'This is my body', and of the wine: 'This is my blood.' What did this mean? An essential clue to the interpretation of these sayings is the fact that Jesus was a Hebrew; his ideas have then to be understood within the context of Hebrew modes of thought. It is indeed necessary to recognize that there is a vital difference between the Greek and Hebrew ways of looking at things.

The Greek considers a thing in itself; he analyses it, dissects it, defines it in terms of what it is. He is concerned with its empirical nature, with its objective reality. He looks at it in its pure state, geometrical and physical, what it is as it is seen, as it is weighed. He defines its material composition according to his powers of observation. He apprehends its substance according to its empirical data. He sees it as an independent entity set in the exterior world, which is an objective closed system, capable of mathematical measurement. This attitude leads to the study of the natural sciences and of physics; it leads, too, to a natural anthropology since man is understood to 'apprehend himself by objectifying himself from his own observation like the phenomena of nature'.[30] The Greek language is consequently logical; it expresses the object, the reality objectively given. From this point of view to speak of bread as a body and wine as blood is nonsense, since it involves calling certain things what they are not.

When we turn to consider the Hebrew attitude we find ourselves in an entirely different climate of thought which provides the clue to Jesus' meaning. The Hebrew knows of no natural sciences; he never objectifies the world as a natural order whose laws are to be discerned,[31] instead the world is a place beyond man's control, though not beyond God's. Again there is no natural anthropology: man is not considered in himself, but always in his situation before God. Man only *is*, according to Hebrew thought, in his existence before God. Moreover, to know God is not, as it is for the Greeks, to contemplate his metaphysical nature but to know his will, and to know his will is to acknowledge him. God cannot, as for the Greek, be apprehended simply by reason, but by his self-revelation to the receiving subject. Truth therefore is not 'propositional knowledge, but that which is valid and demands recognition, that which can be trusted'.[32] The Hebrew attitude to things is consequently in contrast to the Greek. The Hebrew considers a thing, not as it is in itself, but as it is in relation to himself, and the Hebrew language expresses

not the object but the subject, his domination over things. He is
therefore not primarily concerned with things as they are but with
what he makes of them. He associates them with their end which is
defined by his existence before God and their place in the divine
purpose. Thus where the Greek language is logical, the Hebrew is
eschatological. So far from passively observing objective reality, the
Hebrew actively endeavours to master it in view of its final purpose
or destiny. He seeks 'beyond the natural things what they have to
say, their meaning, the will which is expressed by them'.[33] When,
therefore, Jesus speaks of bread as his body, this is not to be understood from the Greek point of view. Logically the bread is bread and
the wine is wine, but Jesus associates them with an end that trans-
cends their empirical reality. It is not a question of what the elements are as such but what they become in relation to their final
reference and that reference is the realization of his presence among
his followers.

Enfolded and, as it were, immersed in the will of Jesus Christ, this
bread remains bread; that is quite certain. Physico-chemical analysis will
continue to find in it the same elements. There is no *transmutation* of matter in it. Christianity has always reacted against an interpretation of the
words of Jesus which ends by saying that the bread is materially the
body.[34]

The bread remains bread therefore, and the wine remains wine,
but both are now given another dimension; they function as instruments of Christ's presence. When the communicants receive the
elements, their relationship to them has become different, since
through this reception the divine intention is realized, i.e. the species
are the means of personal communion. The 'secular' nature of the
bread and wine persists, but in and through them the sacred is also
present in indissoluble unity. Hence consecration, which includes
*berakah* as well as giving, eating and drinking, is an action whereby
the objects, without ceasing to be what they were, acquire a new and
additional end to that of physical nourishment, which they do not
lose, and their reality is to be understood not in terms of meta-
physics but of function. This does not mean that that which was
profane has been made sacred; man originally accepted the whole
world as sacred, and consecration was not the creation of the holy

but the preservation of that which had been sacred from the beginning.[35] But it is possible to speak of the consecrated bread and wine as holy objects, understanding holiness not in the sense of a quality of being but as God-relatedness, duly acknowledged in word and action. Yet in order that this relatedness may exist, the objects must preserve their physical and secular reality; they are not withdrawn from a human and profane world into a divine and sacred realm, but in and through them the unity of the sacred and the secular is manifested and becomes a reality in the life of the communicants as they enter into union with the God-man.

This functional understanding of eucharistic consecration may also fittingly be applied to the consecration of churches. It is necessary however to recognize that in so doing the various ways in which, according to the several rites, consecration is effected are rendered both meaningless and unnecessary. Indeed they can scarcely be said to stand from the point of view of simple rational analysis. No one is likely to argue that the presence of relics is a *sine qua non* of Christian worship. Not only was the eucharist celebrated for decades before any existed, but to this day it can be and is performed in houses, in hospital wards, on battle fields, etc., apart from any of the remains of the saints. Further, to treat a building as a human being, and so to baptize and confirm it, cannot be regarded as anything other than a pious fiction. Nor is the idea that consecration is effected by use any more tenable. If that were true, then the regular celebration of the eucharist in places other than churches, to which we have just referred, would consecrate those too.

Basically, consecration is thanksgiving. The rendering of thanks to God upon the opening of a new church is natural and right; this is its consecration. The result, however, is not that the nature of the space is changed; rather the result is that its God-relatedness is acknowledged. Understood in functional terms then consecration is an act whereby a church does not cease to be what it is, i.e. secular space in which secular activities may be held, but it does acquire a new and additional end. It becomes the place of assembly of God's people where they can with convenience offer their corporate worship to their Lord. The space is then holy, but this holiness is not a quality of being, but an explicitly acknowledged relationship to

God. So by consecration a building is dedicated as an instrument of the mission of God; its nature is not altered, but its function is declared.

The parallelism between eucharistic consecration and the consecration of churches should now be clear. The former does not change the nature of the species; it increases their function. The function of bread and wine is that of physical nourishment; the function of consecrated bread and wine includes physical nourishment but it also allows union with God through Christ. The function of a building is to serve human need, in terms of leisure, shelter, etc.; the function of a consecrated building includes the serving of human need but it also provides for the worship of God. So the consecration of a building does not transform the nature of the space enclosed; it increases its function. It is now capable of serving both sacred and secular ends. To believe that the consecration of a building sets it apart from secular uses would be to restrict its function; there is no such restriction in and through eucharistic consecration and there is no sound theological reason for supposing that the consecration of a building necessarily involves a restriction either.

To treat a church as a holy place, set apart from the secular, is tantamount to treating the eucharistic species as the body and blood of Christ apart from the reality of the bread and the wine. The eucharistic analogy, as previously the Christological analogy with which it is closely associated, thus confirms the thesis of the unity of sacred and secular and of the validity of multipurpose churches.

How then is a consecrated building to be defined? Negatively, it is not to be defined as a habitation of God nor as a shrine of the divine presence; it is not the modern counterpart of the Jerusalem Temple. Nor is it a holy place, in the sense that it has a character of 'wholly otherness' set apart from the world. There is then no depersonalization of the holy. In so far as the term 'holy' can be used of it at all, this must be understood functionally to mean 'God-relatedness'. A consecrated building is therefore one in which the secular is God-related explicitly and the unity of life thereby shown forth. In emphasizing this functional aspect we are not proposing

any startling innovation. In the past a church has always been understood functionally, but this function has been restricted to worship
conceived solely as a cultic activity. Our argument leads to the
affirmation that either it is wrong to limit the meaning of worship
in this way or that it is necessary to acknowledge that the function
of a church building is more complex than has previously been
conceived. Its function is to serve the mission of God; it is to be an
instrument of his outgoing in concern to the world; it must therefore minister to human need and at the same time its explicit God-
relatedness declares the unity of all life in Christ.

# NOTES

# CHAPTER 1

[1] *Octavius*, 32.  [2] James 1.10.
[3] I Cor. 1.26.
[4] E. Lohmeyer, *Lord of the Temple*, E. T. Oliver & Boyd, Edinburgh, 1961 and John Knox Press, Richmond, Va., 1962 *passim*.
[5] Mark 12.33.  [6] Matt. 6.6.
[7] Lohmeyer, 72.  [8] Matt. 18.20.
[9] Mark 11.15–18.  [10] Lohmeyer, 39.
[11] Mark 14.58.  [12] Mark 15.38.
[13] John 4.21, 23.  [14] Gal. 5.12, RV margin.
[15] Berach, 32*b*.  [16] II Cor. 6.16.
[17] D. G. Delling, *Worship in the New Testament*, E. T. Darton, Longman & Todd, London, 1962, 9, and Westminster Press, Pa.
[18] F. W. Young in *Worship in Scripture and Tradition*, ed. M. H. Shepherd, O.U.P., N.Y., 1963, 88.
[19] St. *Daniel* I.17.6, 7.  [20] *Strom.*, VII.5.
[21] Luke 24.35.  [22] I Peter 2.5.
[23] Lohmeyer, 104.  [24] Acts 2.46.
[25] I Cor. 16.19.  [26] Col. 4.15.
[27] Philemon 2.  [28] 1.13; 9.37.
[29] Acts 20.9.  [30] *Acta Justini et Sociorum*, 2.
[31] 131 ff.  [32] 20.
[33] This was not immediately universal; as late as 304 a congregation of 49 was meeting at Abitina in the house of Octavius Felix (*Acta SS. Saturnini*, etc., 2). The ownership of community houses would in any case be vested probably in an individual since the Church had no legal standing.
[34] Gregory of Tours, *Hist. Franc.*, 1.29.
[35] *de Idol.*, 7.  [36] *adv. Val.*, 3.
[37] M. Rostovtzeff, *Dura-Europos and Its Art*, O.U.P., 1938.
[38] Acts 8.36.  [39] Acts 16.13ff.
[40] *Apol.*, I.61.  [41] *de Bapt.*, 4.
[42] 26.  [43] 49.
[44] *Clem. Hom.*, 14.1.  [45] *Clem. Recog.*, 4.32.
[46] For the history of the provision for baptism see J. G. Davies, *The Architectural Setting of Baptism*, Barrie & Rockliff, 1962.
[47] *C.S.E.L.*, XXVI, 186.  [48] See pp. 22–28.
[49] J. G. Davies, *The Origin and Development of Early Christian Church Architecture*, SCM Press, 1952, 20, and Philosophical Library, N.Y.

268 · *Notes*

⁵⁰ The word *titulus* refers to the marble slab bearing the owner's name and establishing his title to the property.

⁵¹ R. Krautheimer, *Early Christian and Byzantine Architecture*, Penguin Books, 1965, 8.

⁵² R. Krautheimer, *Corpus Basilicarum Christianarum Romae*, I, Pontificio Istituto de Archeologia Cristiana, 1939, 267–303.

⁵³ E. Junyent, *Il titolo di San Clemente in Roma*, 1932.

⁵⁴ P. B. Whitehead, 'The Church of St Anastasia', *A.J.A.*, XXXI, 1927, 405–20.

⁵⁵ R. Vielliard, *Les origines du titre de Saint-Martin-aux-Monts à Rome*, Les Belles Lettres, 1931.

⁵⁶ Frag. 76 quoted by Krautheimer, *Early Christian and Byzantine Architecture*, 15.

⁵⁷ Krautheimer, *Corpus*, 144–64.

⁵⁸ Krautheimer, *Early Christian and Byzantine Architecture*, loc. cit.

⁵⁹ *adv. Gent.*, 6.3.

⁶⁰ R. H. Connolly, *Didascalia Apostolorum*, O.U.P., 1929, 119f.

⁶¹ *Ibid.*, 127.

⁶² In 313; Lactantius, *de Mort. Per.*, 48.

⁶³ In 324, after the final overthrow of Licinius; Eusebius, *de Vita Const.*, 2.46.

⁶⁴ *Ibid.*, *H.E.*, x.2.1.          ⁶⁵ *Ibid.*, *de Vita Const.*, 3.34.

⁶⁶ Krautheimer, *Early Christian and Byzantine Architecture*, 21.

⁶⁷ *Ibid.*, 23.

⁶⁸ Eusebius, *H.E.*, x.4. The date is uncertain.

⁶⁹ Krautheimer, *loc. cit.*

⁷⁰ Davies, *The Origin and Development of Early Christian Church Architecture*, 99ff.

⁷¹ Davies, *The Architectural Setting of Baptism*, 2–39.

⁷² Davies, *Origin and Development*, 51.

⁷³ The evidence is assembled and interpreted by R. Krautheimer, 'Mensa-Coemeterium-Martyrium', *Cahiers archéologiques*, XI, 1960, 15–40.

⁷⁴ Some other examples of covered cemeteries are known in North Africa, e.g. at Tabarka and Bishop Alexander's chapel at Tipasa.

⁷⁵ *Cod. Theod.*, 2.8.1.

⁷⁶ Paulinus, *Ep.*, 32.12; *Carmen*, 28.187. The practice, at the eucharist, of kissing the altar was borrowed from paganism and is another indication of the way church and temple were identified (J. A. Jungmann, *The Mass of the Roman Rite*, E.T. Burns & Oates, London, 1959, 210, and Benniger Bros., N.Y.).

⁷⁷ *Div. Inst.*, 5.2.          ⁷⁸ e.g. *de Vera Relig.*, 55.

⁷⁹ Gregory of Nyssa, *Or. Catech.*, 18.   ⁸⁰ Prudentius, *Peristeph.*, 2.527f.

⁸¹ Cf. Eusebius, *H.E.*, x.2.1          ⁸² *Ibid.*, *de Vita Const.*, 3.30.

⁸³ *Ibid.*, 3.53.          ⁸⁴ *Ibid.*, 4.56.

⁸⁵ *c. Auxent.*, 12.

⁸⁶ *P.G.*, 52.429. For other quotations see Y. M.-J. Congar, 'L'eglise, ce n'est pas les murs', *Maison-Dieu*, 70, 1962, 105–14.

⁸⁷ *P.G.*, 46.1011.          ⁸⁸ *Ep.*, 58.3.

⁸⁹ *Ep.*, 46.11.          ⁹⁰ *Ep.*, 130.14.

⁹¹ *Ep.*, 60.12.          ⁹² *Ep.*, 46.5.

[93] *H.E.*, x.4.3.

[94] *Ibid.*, x.4.45.

[95] *Ibid.*, x.4.42.

[96] *Mystag.*, 1.11.

[97] *de Myst.*, 5.

[98] *de Sacramen.*, 4.1f.

[99] 2.57. The orientation of the Constantinian buildings, with their sanctuary at the west end and their entrance at the east, may be another example of Old Testament influence, since the Temple was oriented with its entrance to the east and the holy of holies at the west.

[100] *Quaest. in Hept.*, II.177.

[101] *de Adorat. in Sp. et verit.*, 9.

[102] *Ep.*, 46.8.

[103] Cassian, *Inst.*, 1.10.

[104] Ex. 3.5; Josh. 5.15.

[105] Eusebius, *de Vita Const.*, 3.56.

[106] There was Old Testament precedent in the case of Samuel who received a divine visitation while asleep in the temple at Shiloh (I Sam. 3).

[107] M. Hamilton, *Incubation*, Simpkin, 1906, 119–25.

[108] *Ibid.*, 126.

[109] The Greek text is printed by L. Deubner, *de Incubatione*, 1900, 120–34.

[110] *H.E.*, ii, 3.

[111] Hamilton, 149–56.

[112] Gregory of Tours, *de Virt. Mart.*, 2.4.

[113] Hamilton, 163f.

[114] ii, 6.

[115] iii, 12.

[116] iv, 31.

[117] iv, 3.

[118] Canons, 90, 92.

[119] Hamilton, 165.

[120] W. Jaeger, *Demosthenes*, C.U.P., 1938, 197.

[121] e.g. Ex. 21.12ff.

[122] Basil of Caesarea, for example, had previously protected a widow who had fled to the altar in fear of the governor of Pontus (Gregory Nazianzus. *Or.*, 43.56).

[123] *Cod. Theod.*, 9.45.1. Augustine once refused to give up a debtor named Fastius and had to pay what was owing; he organized a collection in church and argued that he could not deliver Fastius up to be tortured by his creditors (*Ep.* 215).

[124] *Cod. Theod.*, 9.45.2.

[125] *Ibid.*, 9.45.5.

[126] Evagrius, *H.E.*, ii, 8.

[127] *Cod. Theod.*, 9.45.5. The *Sirmondian Constitutions*, 13, contain a law of 419 to the same effect.

[128] *H.E.*, vi, 2.

[129] Canon 97.

[130] I Cor. 11.17–32.

[131] Jude 12.

[132] e.g. Hippolytus, *Trad. Ap.*, 25.

[133] *Ibid.*, *loc. cit.*

[134] Canon 11.

[135] Canon 28.

[136] Paulinus, *Ep.*, 13.11ff.

[137] F. van der Meer, *Augustine the Bishop*, E.T. Sheed & Ward, 1961, 499.

[138] *C.I.L.*, VIII, 20277, translation in *ibid.*, 501.

[139] *Ibid.*, 507.

[140] R. Krautheimer, 'Mensa-Coemeterium-Martyrium', *Cahiers archéologiques*, XI, 1960, 36.

[141] *Ibid.*, *loc. cit.*

[142] 8.42.

[143] *Quaest. in Hept.*, I, 172.

[144] *de Civ. Dei.*, 8.27.

[145] *Ep.*, 29.10.

[146] Paulinus, *Carmen*, 27.559, 576.

[147] Krautheimer, *art. cit.*

[148] *Or. ad Sanct. coetum*, 12.

[149] *de Helia et ieiunio*, 17.

[150] 6.2.

[151] *Lib.* I. *Tract.*, 15.6.

[152] *Ep.*, 22.3, 4, 6.

[153] Cf. 273.8; 310.2.                   [154] Matt. 7.6.

[155] E. K. Chambers, *The Mediaeval Stage*, I, O.U.P., 1903, 161, n. 3.

[156] Sozomen, *H.E.*, vii, 19; Socrates, *H.E.*, v, 22.

[157] *H.E.*, iii, 11.                     [158] *Lib.*, I. *Ep.*, 14.

[159] *Lib.* II, *Ep.*, 76.

[160] L. A. Bocquillot, *Traité historique de la liturgie sacrée ou de la messe*, 1701, 417.

[161] Canon 99.        [162] T. Smith and L. Brentano, *English Gilds*, 1870, lxxxii.

[163] A. Aube, *Polyeucte dans l'histoire*, 1882, 79.       [164] van der Meer, 514.

[165] *Sermo*, 311, 5.                     [166] *Hom.*, 14.

[167] *H.E.*, i, 14.

[168] Texts of this and other statements are given in full with references by F. Cabrol and H. Leclerq, *Dictionnaire d'archéologie chrétienne et de liturgie*, IV, I, Le Jouzy, Paris, 1920, 252f.

[169] Mansi, VII, 949.                     [170] Canon 76.

[171] *Regulae Fusius Tractatae*, 40.      [172] Eusebius, *de Vita Const.*, 3, 7.

[173] *H.E.*, ii, 13.                      [174] Mansi, IV, 1332C.

[175] *Ibid.*, V., 241A.                   [176] *H.E.*, ii, 3, 18.

[177] Sozomen, *H.E.*, iv, 22.            [178] Mansi, III, 851.

[179] Hefel, V, 309.                       [180] *Ibid.*, 362.

[181] *Ep.*, 55. 8.                        [182] *Ep.*, 67.4.

[183] *Apol. c. Arianos*, 6.              [184] Sozomen, *H.E.*, vi, 24.

[185] Evagrius, *H.E.*, ii, 5.            [186] *Ibid.*, ii, 8.

[187] *C.S.E.L.*, XXXV, I, 2f.            [188] Eusebius, *H.E.*, v, 16.3

[189] Theodoret, *H.E.*, iv, 19.11.       [190] Sozomen, *H.E.*, vi, 21.

[191] *c. Fortunat.*, I, superscription.  [192] *de Acta c. Felic.*, 2.21.

[193] van der Meer, 90.                    [194] *Ibid.*, 100.

[195] I Cor. 6.6.                          [196] *Cod. Theod.*, I, 27.1.

[197] Gregory of Tours, *Hist. of Franc.*, 5, 12(18).

[198] The baptistery at Canterbury, built in 741, was to serve also as a law court and a mausoleum (C. E. Woodruff and W. Danks, *Memorials of the Cathedral and Priory of Christ in Canterbury*, Goulden, 1915, 11).

[199] *Cambridge Ancient History*, X, C.U.P., 1934, 430.

[200] *Cod. Theod.*, 4.7.1.               [201] *Sermo*, 21.6.

[202] Gregory of Tours, *Hist. Franc.*, 10.9.       [203] *Ibid.*, 6.32 (45).

[204] H. Lansdell, *The Sacred Tenth*, S.P.C.K., 1906, 256ff.

[205] Gregory of Tours, 4.32 (46).

[206] *Ibid.*, in *Gloria Mart. Beat.*, 57; for other examples see 19 and 33, and *Hist. Franc.*, 8.16, 40.

[207] Sozomen, *H.E.*, vii, 5.            [208] Evagrius, *H.E.*, iii, 13.

[209] Gregory of Tours, *Hist. Franc.*, 3.12.       [210] *Ibid.*, 7.35.

[211] Cabrol and Leclerq, VI, I, 391.

[212] Quinisext canon 88. Animals were also brought into church to be healed.

[213] iv, 10.                              [214] *Ep.*, 33.

[215] *Vit. Pont.*, 47.                    [216] *Ep.*, 32.16.

[217] VIII, 10.1.

## CHAPTER 2

[1] *de Rebus Eccl.*, I, 1.                [2] *Gemma animae sive de Divin. offic.*, I., 123f.

[3] *de Consecrat.*, II, in E. Panofsky, *Abbot Suger on the Abbey Church of St Denis*, O.U.P., 1947, 91.

[4] *Rationale divin. offic.*, I, 1.5.                [5] *Ibid.*, I, 1.39.

[6] *Ibid.*, I, 1.42.

[7] *Nova Legenda Anglie*, ed. O. Horstman, II, O.U.P., 1901, 624.

[8] I Kings 5.16.                [9] *English Hist. Review*, LI, 1936, 357.

[10] Ex. 30.22–9.

[11] A.-G. Martimort, 'Le rituel de la consécration des églises', *Maison-Dieu*, 63, 1960, 89f.

[12] I Kings 8.63.

[13] Before this period a building was dedicated to God simply by celebrating the eucharist within it.

[14] M. Andrieu, *Les 'Ordines Romani' du haut moyen âge*, IV, Spicilegium sacrum Lovanieuse, Louvain, 1956, 340.

[15] *Ibid.*, 344.                [16] G. G. Coulton, *Ten Medieval Studies*, C.U.P., 1930, 54.
[17] Andrieu, 398.                [18] I.6.6., 9, 12.

[19] The Latin text is printed in L. Duchesne, *Christian Worship*, E.T., S.P.C.K. 1903, 487f.

[20] *Mitrale seu de offic. eccles. summa*, I, 1.

[21] R. A. R. Hartridge, *A History of Vicarages in the Middle Ages*, C.U.P., 1930, 137.

[22] *Ibid., loc. cit.*

[23] G. H. Cook, *The English Medieval Parish Church*, Phoenix House, London, 3rd ed. 1961, 23, and Hillary House, N.Y.

[24] Hartridge, 14.                [25] *Ibid.*, 138.

[26] G. G. Coulton, *Five Centuries of Religion*, I, C.U.P., 1923, 240.

[27] M. Hamilton, *Incubation*, Simpkin, 1906, 167f.

[28] Cabrol and Leclerq, *Dictionnaire*, VII, 1, 514.

[29] J. B. Macklinay, *Saint Edmund, King and Martyr*, 1893, 297f.

[30] *Ibid.*, 286–9.

[31] C. Pendrill, *Old Parish Life in London*, O.U.P., 1937, 136.

[32] J. C. Cox, *The Sanctuaries and Sanctuary Seekers of Medieval England*, Allen & Unwin, 1911, 299.

[33] *Ibid.*, 107.                [34] *de Admin.*, XXI, in Panofsky, 57.
[35] Cox, 208.                [36] *Ibid.*, 303.

[37] H. T. Riley, *Memorials of London and London Life in the XIIIth, XIVth and XVth Centuries*, 1868, 633.

[38] Previously watches had been kept upon the initiative of the local justices, e.g. in 1276–7 there is a record of a watch upon St Mary, Staining Lane (*ibid.*, 17). But Edwards' injunction was not always obeyed: in 1298 the London Aldermen decreed that no watch should take place upon fugitives 'so long as they remain within the same churches' (*ibid.*, 36)—this seems a singularly ineffective statement, since without a watch there could be no means of ensuring that they did so remain.

[39] *Liber Albus. The White Book of the City of London, compiled by J. Carpenter and R. Whitington* (1419), trans. by H. T. Riley, 1861, 244.

[40] Cox, 30.  [41] *Ibid.*, 289.
[42] *Ibid.*, 304f.  [43] *Liber Albus.*, 82
[44] Cox, 293f.  [45] *Ibid.*, 239.
[46] *Ibid.*, 291f.  [47] *Ibid.*, 50, 127, 198.

[48] A complete account of the practice of sanctuary would also include references to eating and drinking and to the courts held in churches in connection with them; these two aspects are reviewed below in the appropriate subsections.

[49] S. Heath, *Pilgrim Life in the Middle Ages*, Allen & Unwin, 1911, 17.
[50] *Ibid.*, 201, 205.  [51] *Ibid.*, 46.
[52] J. Wickham Legg, *The Clerk's Book of 1549*, H.B.S., XXV, 1903, 66.
[53] T. D. Fosbroke, *Encyclopaedia of Antiquities*, I, new ed., 1843, 124.
[54] G. G. Coulton, *The Mediaeval Village*, C.U.P., 1925, 205.
[55] A. F. Leach, *Visitations and Memorials of Southwell Minster*, Camden Soc., N.S., XLVIII, 1891, 210.
[56] *Register W. Stapledon*, ed. F. C. Hingeston-Randolph, 1892, 111.
[57] J. C. Cox, *Churchwardens' Accounts*, Methuen, 1913, 19.
[58] *Ibid.*, 28.
[59] H. Littlehales, *The Medieval Records of a London City Church (St Mary-at-Hill), A.D. 1420–1559*, E.E.T.S., O.S., CXXVIII, 1905, 243, 340.
[60] Wickham Legg, 78.
[61] *Revelations of Divine Love*, ed. G. Warrack, Methuen, 11th ed., 1940, xvii.
[62] Heath, 84f.  [63] *Ibid.*, 87.
[64] F. J. Snell, *The Customs of Old England*, Methuen, 1919, 154.
[65] Cox, *Sanctuaries*, 317.  [66] *Ibid.*, 18.
[67] *Ibid.*, 256.  [68] *Ibid.*, 60.
[69] J. Brand, *Popular Antiquities of Great Britain*, ed. W. C. Hazlett, II, 1870, 229f.
[70] F. R. Salter, *Some Early Tracts on Poor Relief*, Methuen, 1926, 22.
[71] A. R. Powys, *The English Parish Church*, Longmans, Green & Co., 1930, 61f.
[72] E. L. Cutts, *Parish Priests and their People in the Middle Ages in England*, 1898, 459.
[73] Quoted by S. Denne, 'An Attempt to Illustrate the Figures Carved in Stone on the Porch of Chalk Church', *Archaeologia*, XII, 1809, 17n.
[74] L. A. Bocquillot, *Traité historique de la liturgie sacrée ou de la messe*, 1701, 425.
[75] Brand, II, 148.
[76] In the East this could have originated in the remains from the rite of the prothesis rather than in the *agape*.
[77] Wickham Legg, 58.  [78] Coulton, 28.
[79] In Bassingbourne Church, Cambridge, there were ten church ales in 1497–8; these raised a total of £14 7s 3½d towards the cost of a new tenor bell made in London (Cook, 28).
[80] So the eating and drinking in connection with *obits* really falls within this category.

[81] Denne, *art. cit.*, 13n. He provides numerous other examples.

[82] Pendrill, 62.

[83] J. Nichols, *Illustrations of the Manners and Expences of Antient Times in London*, 1797, 183.

[84] Cox, *Churchwardens' Accounts*, 287.

[85] D. Wilkins, *Concilia Magnae Britanniae*, II, 1737, 528.

[86] *Ibid.*, I, 530f., 574, 635–40, 672.      [87] Denne, *art. cit.*, 22.

[88] E. Peacock, 'Church Ales', *Archaeological Journal*, XL, 1883, 15.

[89] Cook, 28.      [90] Cox, 205.

[91] Quoted in J. Strutt, *Sports and Pastimes of the People of England* (1801), ed. J. C. Cox, Methuen, 1903, 290.

[92] Wilkins, I, 600, 624, 642.

[93] *Tract. de modo Gen. Concil. habendi*, II, 36.

[94] Cook, 29.

[95] Bishop Hobhouse, *Church-Wardens' Accounts*, Somerset Record Soc., IV, 1890, 84.      [96] Littlehales, 275.

[97] Nichols, 187.      [98] Cox, 128.

[99] *Ibid.*, 178.      [100] *Ibid.*, 255.

[101] *Ibid., loc. cit.*      [102] *Ibid.*, 260.

[103] Littlehales, 305.      [104] *Ibid.*, 100, 302, 305.

[105] E. K. Chambers, *The Medieval Stage*, II, O.U.P., 1903, 389.

[106] Cox, 70ff.      [107] *Ibid.*, 8.

[108] Nichols, 6.      [109] Cited by Cook, 31.

[110] H. F. Westlake, *The Parish Gilds of Medieval England*, S.P.C.K., 1919, 91.

[111] *Ibid.*, 79.

[112] K. Edwards, *The English Secular Cathedrals in the Middle Ages*, Manchester University Press, 1949, 62.

[113] *Archaeologia*, XVIII, 1817, 412.      [114] *Rationale Div. Off.*, 72, 120.

[115] VII, 42.      [116] Chambers, I, 276.      [117] Mansi, XXII, 842.

[118] J. Gougaud, 'La danse dans les églises', *Revue d'Histoire ecclésiastique*, XV, 1914, 232.

[119] *P.L.*, CCVII, 1169.      [120] Chambers, I, 321.

[121] *Ibid.*, I, 305.      [122] *Itinerarium Cambriae*, I, 2.

[123] *Collections des meilleurs dissertations, notices et traités particuliers relatifs à l'histoire de France*, ed. C. Leber, IX, 1838, 430. This dance continued until the middle of the seventeenth century.

[124] *Ibid., loc. cit.* This dance was eventually suppressed by Bishop Cyrus de Thyard (1594–1624).

[125] Chambers, I, 163.      [126] Gougaud, 237.      [127] Snell, 94.

[128] So A. Tenenti, *La vie et la mort à travers l'art du XV$^e$ siècle*, Colin, Paris, 1952, 28.

[129] Emile Mâle, *L'art religieux de la fin du moyen âge en France*, Colin, Paris, 2nd ed., 1922, 360ff.

[130] 231.      [131] *Ibid.*, 230.

[132] *Ibid.*, 12f., 234.      [133] *Summa major*, III, 2.4.13.

[134] Leber, IX, 438.      [135] Cox, 66.

[136] G. van der Leeuw, *Sacred and Profane Beauty*, E.T. Weidenfeld & Nicolson, London, 1963, 50, and Holt, Rinehart & Winston, N.Y.

[137] *Ibid.*, 37.

[138] White Kennett, *Parochial Antiquities*, II, 1818, 307. Bishops of both Nevers and Tréguier condemned the sale of goods in churches in the thirteenth century (O. Dobiache-Rojdestvensky, *La vie paroissiale en France au XIII^e siècle*, A. Picard, 1911, 141).

[139] *Ibid.*, 308f.

[140] J. B. Thiers, *Dissértations sur les porches des églises*, 1679, 61.

[141] G. G. Coulton, *Ten Medieval Studies*, 155.

[142] Quoted by J. C. Jeaffreson, *A Book about the Clergy*, 2nd ed., I, 1870, 149n.

[143] Cutts, 317.     [144] Jeaffreson, I, 346.

[145] *Hist. MSS. Com.*, V, 436.     [146] Powys, 66.

[147] *Letters and Papers of John Shillingford*, ed. S. A. Moore, Camden Soc., N.S., II, 1871, 93.

[148] W. Johnson, *Byways in British Archaeology*, C.U.P., 1912, 192.

[149] H. H. Milman, *Annals of St Paul's Cathedral*, 1868, 83.

[150] O. von Simpson, *The Gothic Cathedral*, Routledge & Kegan Paul, 1956, 167.

[151] Cook, 32.     [152] Milman, 42, 46.

[153] *Ibid.*, *loc. cit.*     [154] *Ibid.*, 46f., 61.

[155] *Ibid.*, 85, 88, 178, 289.

[156] J. Stow, *A Survey of London* (1603), ed. C. L. Kingsford, 2nd ed., I, O.U.P., 1908, 340.

[157] S. O. Addy, *Church and Manor*, Allen & Unwin, 1913, 226.

[158] Mrs J. R. Green, *Town Life in the Fifteenth Century*, I, 1894, 401.

[159] Addy, 227.     [160] Green, 156.

[161] Addy, 234.     [162] Cook, 34.

[163] Addy, 225.     [164] *Ibid.*, 248.

[165] Green, II, 227.     [166] Addy, 228f.

[167] Green, II, 358.     [168] Powys, 78.

[169] Addy, 234.     [170] *Notes and Queries*, 10th Series, XII, 1909, 148.

[171] Cox, 31.     [172] T. Smith and L. Brentano, *English Gilds*, 1870, 448.

[173] *Ibid.*, 189.     [174] F. Heer, *The Medieval World*, E.T. 1963 (Mentor ed.), 116.

[175] *Ibid.*, 131.     [176] *Ibid.*, 148.

[177] *Ibid.*, 269.     [178] Johnson, 137.

[179] Pendrill, 160.     [180] Hobhouse, 3.

[181] *Ibid.*, 11.     [182] *Ibid.*, 35.

[183] *Ibid.*, 37.     [184] *Ibid.*, 14–17.

[185] e.g. 1516–17, 1520–21, Littlehales, 294, 312.

[186] e.g. 1524–5, *ibid.*, 325.     [187] *Ibid.*, 319.

[188] Smith and Brentano, 174.     [189] Strutt, xxxii.

[190] *Hist. MSS. Com.*, V, 546.     [191] *Ibid.*, V, 494.

[192] Green, I, 410.     [193] *Ibid.*, I, 139, n.2.

[194] S. O. Addy, *The Evolution of the English House*, Allen & Unwin, 1898, 180.

[195] G. G. Coulton, *Social Life in Britain from the Conquest to the Reformation*, C.U.P., 1918, 55.

[196] Addy, *Church and Manor*, 210.     [197] I, 253f.     [198] Johnson, 138.

[199] B. L. Woodcock, *Medieval Ecclesiastical Courts in the Diocese of Canterbury*, O.U.P., 1952, 31–5.

[200] Cox, *Sanctuaries*, 243f.     [201] *Ibid.*, 258ff.

[202] Riley, *Memorials*, 618.    [203] Addy, 186.

[204] Heer, 50.

[205] De Moléon, *Voyages liturgiques de France*, 1718, 180, 188.

[206] L. Gougaud, *Dévotions et pratiques ascétiques du moyen âge*, Desclée, de Brouwer et Cie, 1925, 51.

[207] I, 68.    [208] Addy, 193.

[209] *Ibid.*, 186.    [210] *Ibid.*, 185.

[211] *Ibid.*, 195.

[212] M. E. C. Walcott, *Traditions and Customs of Cathedrals*, 1872, 95.

[213] Addy, 197.

[214] Gougaud, 52.    [215] Milman, 100f., 105.

[216] Addy, 240.    [217] Snell, 132f.

[218] Addy, 216f.    [219] *Ibid.*, 214.

[220] G. L. Gomme, *Primitive Folk-Moots*, 1880, 59.    [221] Addy, 184.

[222] Cox, *Churchwardens' Accounts*, 70.    [223] Gomme, 137.

[224] Addy, 204.    [225] *Ibid.*, 185.

[226] *Ibid.*, 202.    [227] *Hist. MSS. Com.*, III, 316.

[228] Coulton, *Ten Medieval Studies*, 197.    [229] Gomme, 137.

[230] Green, I, 401.

[231] J. Paterson, *Pietas Londiniensis*, 1714, 158. Any part of the church might be used, but sometimes special seating was provided, as in the ground floor of the late tenth-century west tower at Barnack, Northants. (*The Ecclesiastical Courts*, S.P.C.K., 1954, 2.)    [232] *Liber Albus*, 100.

[233] Riley, *Memorials*, 14.    [234] Addy, 186.

[235] *On the Laws of England*, trans. F. M. Nichols, I, 1865, 17.

[236] Cox, *Sanctuaries*, 113f.    [237] Riley, 6.

[238] *Ibid.*, 24.    [239] Cox, 225.

[240] *Ibid.*, 277. For further examples see *Liber Albus*, 85–8.

[241] Coulton, *Social Life*, 73.    [242] Addy, 204.

[243] *Ibid.*, 187f.    [244] *P.L.*, 106, 147ff.

[245] *Tract. de modo Gen. Concil. habendi*, II, 35.

[246] Addy, 203.    [247] Thiers, 60.

[248] F. A. Inderwick, *The King's Peace*, 1895, 13.

[249] *Shillingforth's Letters*, 48, 94.    [250] Stow, II, 316.

[251] W. Sparrow Simpson, *St Paul's Cathedral and Old City Life*, 1894, 81.

[252] Addy, 194f.    [253] *Ibid.*, 198.

[254] Walcott, 94f.    [255] Addy, 184.

[256] Riley, *Memorials*, 472f.    [257] Addy, 237f.

[258] Woodcock, 98.    [259] *Ibid.*, 186.

[260] G. G. Coulton, *The Medieval Village*, C.U.P., 1925, 294.

[261] Coulton, *Ten Medieval Studies*, 125.    [262] Addy, 194.

[263] *Ibid.*, 201. The church was a kind of lost-property office; cf. one of the thirteenth-century statutes of the diocese of Nîmes, which directs anyone who had found money in the street to ask the priest to publish the fact in church (Dobiache-Rojdestvensky, 100).    [264] Green, I, 155, n.1.

[265] Addy, 201.    [266] Milman, 177.

[267] W. Hone, *Every-Day Book*, I, 1841, 345.    [268] Addy, 91.

[269] Cutts, 307f.    [270] Riley, 168.

271 S. O. Addy, *The Evolution of the English House*, Allen & Unwin, 1898, 180.
272 Cox, 62.                         273 Smith and Brentano, 287f.
274 Westlake, 84.                    275 Addy, *Church and Manor*, 54.
276 Coulton, *Ten Medieval Studies*, 68. French churches were also used for storing grain in the thirteenth century (Dobiache-Rojdestvensky, 137).
277 Addy, 57.
278 C. A. T. Bannister, 'Visitation Returns of the Diocese of Hereford in 1397', *English Hist. Review*, XLV, 1930, 94.
279 W. Edwards, *A Medieval Scrap-Heap*, Rivingtons, 1930, 292.
280 Hartridge, 180.                  281 Coulton, *The Medieval Village*, 341.
282 J. R. H. Moorman, *Church Life in England in the Thirteenth Century*, C.U.P., 1945, 148.
283 Coulton, 340.                    284 Addy, 91.
285 Strutt, 21.                      286 Coulton, *Social Life*, 396.
287 Stow, I, 333ff.; Sparrow Simpson (236) gives 1375 as the date.
288 M. D. Anderson, *Looking for History in British Churches*, John Murray, 1951, 76. There is a patristic precedent for this but it is extremely doubtful if there was any continuity of use. The cubit that measured the increase of the Nile waters was kept in the temple of Serapis, and then by order of Constantine was removed to a church (Socrates, *H.E.*, i, 18).
289 Powys, 155.                      290 Sparrow Simpson, 242f.
291 Wickham Legg, 96f.               292 Johnson, 197ff.
293 Wickham Legg, 96f.
294 A. F. Leach, *The Schools of Medieval England*, Methuen, 2nd ed., 1916, 189.
295 *Ibid.*, 211.                    296 Stow, II, 38.
297 S. J. Curtis, *History of Education in Great Britain*, University Tutorial Press, 4th ed. 1961, 43.      298 Wickham Legg, 69, 77.
299 G. G. Coulton, *Art and the Reformation*, Blackwell, 1928, 81.
300 J. S. Purvis, *Educational Records*, St Anthony's Press, York, 1959, I, 11.
301 Powys, 141.                      302 Quoted by Stow, I, 71f.
303 *The Parochial Libraries of the Church of England*, Faith Press, 1959, 14.
304 J. C. Cox and A. Harvey, *English Church Furniture*, Methuen, 2nd ed., 1908, 331f.
305 Edwards, *English Secular Cathedrals*, 214.
306 Stow, II, 51.                    307 Milman, 186ff.
308 G. M. Trevelyan, *English Social History*, Longmans, Green & Co., 1944, 90.

# CHAPTER 3

[1] F. R. Salter, *Some Early Tracts on Poor Relief*, Methuen, 1926, 87.
[2] *Ibid.*, 89.   [3] See above, p. 53.
[4] E. K. Chambers, *The Medieval Stage*, O.U.P., I, 1903, 274–335.
[5] *Ibid.*, I, 325.
[6] K. Young, *The Drama of the Mediaeval Church*, O.U.P., I, 1933, 105, 551.
[7] Chambers, I, 287.
[8] Chambers provides a multitude of references (I, 274–335).
[9] Chambers again provides a thorough account (I, 363–71); see further, J. M. J. Fletcher, *The Boy-Bishop at Salisbury and Elsewhere*, Brown & Co., Salisbury, 1921.
[10] T. D. Fosbroke, *Encyclopaedia of Antiquities*, new ed., II, 1843, 824.
[11] *Collection des meilleurs dissértations, notices et traités particuliers relatifs à l'histoire de France*, ed. E. Leber, IX, 1838, 338f.
[12] Chambers, I, 186, n.5.
[13] *Rationale div. offic.*, 120.   [14] *Rationale div. offic.*, VI, 86.
[15] Leber, IX, 394ff.   [16] *Ibid.*, 399ff.
[17] D. Wilkins, *Concilia Magnae Britanniae*, III, 1737, 194.
[18] Chambers, I, 156.   [19] Leber, X, 1838, 128.
[20] Chambers, I, 91.   [21] Wilkins, I, 666.
[22] *Regist. R. Baldock*, ed. R. C. Fowler, Canterbury and York Society, 1911, 145f.
[23] Wilkins, II, 129.   [24] Chambers, I, 93.
[25] A. R. Powys, *The English Parish Church*, Longmans, Green & Co., 1930, 72.
[26] See above, p. 55.
[27] H. H. Milman, *Annals of St Paul's Cathedral*, 1868, 84.
[28] G. G. Coulton, *Art and the Reformation*, Blackwell, 1928, 73.
[29] F. J. Snell, *The Customs of Old England*, Methuen, 1919, 28f.
[30] G. G. Coulton, *Social Life in Britain from the Conquest to the Reformation*, C.U.P., 1918, 407.
[31] Chambers, I, 9.   [32] Young, I, 1f.
[33] The text of Book III, the vital section of the *Liber officialis*, is printed in *P.L.*, CV, 1101–64. For a detailed analysis of this see O. B. Hardison, Jr., *Christian Rite and Christian Drama in the Middle Ages*, Johns Hopkins Press, Baltimore, 1965, 48–77.
[34] *P.L.*, CLXXII, 570, quoted by Hardison, 39f.
[35] J. G. Davies, *Holy Week: A Short History*, Lutterworth Press, London, 1963, 30, 32, and John Knox Press, Richmond, Va.
[36] See the discussion by Hardison, 178–219.
[37] *Regularis Concordia*, ed. Dom T. Symons, Nelson, 1953, 49f.
[38] Hardison, 226.   [39] *Ibid.*, 253–84.
[40] G. H. Cook, *The English Mediaeval Parish Church*, Phoenix House, London, 3rd ed. 1961, and Hillary House, N.Y.
[41] Quoted by Chambers, II, 98, n.2.   [42] *Ibid.*, II, 98f.
[43] S. Denne, 'An Attempt to Illustrate the Figures Carved in Stone on the Porch of Chalk Church', *Archaeologia*, XII, 1809, 21 n.

[44] J. Nichols, *Illustrations of the Manners and Expences of Antient Times in England*, 1897, 130f.

[45] J. Payne Collier, 'The Performance of Drama by Parish Clerks and Players in Churches', *Shakespear Society Papers*, III, 1847, 40–7.

[46] Coulton, *Art and the Reformation*, 395.

[47] Chambers, II, 379.                    [48] Snell, 60, 66.

[49] J. C. Cox, *Churchwardens' Accounts*, Methuen, 1913, 276.

[50] Cook, 32.

[51] J. Payne Collier, 'Players and Dramatic Performances in the Reign of Edward IV', *Shakspear Society Papers*, II, 1843, 90.

[52] W. Kelly, *Notices Illustrative of the Drama*, 1865, 15 n.

[53] Cook, 32.                    [54] Kelly, 14.

[55] Chambers, II, 377.                    [56] Kelly, *loc. cit.*

[57] Chambers, II, 107.                    [58] *Ibid.*, II, 275.

[59] *Ibid.*, II, 342.                    [60] *Ibid.*, II, 367.

[61] C. Pendrill, *Old Parish Life in London*, O.U.P., 1937, 3.

[62] W. Hone, *Every-Day Book*, I, 1841, 435.

[63] Young, II, 400f., quoted by permission of the Oxford University Press.

[64] Chambers, II, 84.                    [65] Young, II, 420.                    [66] *Ibid.*, II, 414f.

[67] W. Johnson, *Byways in British Archaeology*, C.U.P., 1912, 102.

[68] C. Enlart, *Manuel d'archéologie française*, II, A. Picard, 1902, 474, 548–53. In 1203 the canons of Béziers sought authority to fortify their church of St Pierre-du-Bois for fear of the Albigenses (O. Dobiache-Rojdestvensky, *La vie paroissiale en France au XIII<sup>e</sup> siècle*, A. Picard, 1911, 139 n.4; see further: R. Métivier, *Les bastides et églises fortifiés du Gers*, 1903; R. Roger, 'Quelques églises fortifiés de l'Ariège', *Bulletin de la Société Ariégeoise des sciences, lettres et arts*, VIII, 1901).

[69] Johnson, 127–32, gives a great number of examples.

[70] M. D. Anderson, *Looking for History in British Churches*, John Murray, 1951, 141.

[71] H. T. Riley, *Memorials of London and London Life in the XIIIth, XIVth and XVth Centuries*, 1868, 417f.

[72] W. E. Tate, *The Parish Chest*, C.U.P., 1946, 36.

[73] Riley, 664f.

CHAPTER 4

[1] *Disput.*, II, iii, 4.  [2] *Comment. ad cap.* i, *Lib.* III, *Decret. tit.* i, n.7.
[3] *Anal. ad an.*, 57, n.104.  [4] *Rer. liturg.*, I, xx, 4.
[5] *Dissértation sur les porches des églises*, 1679, 75f.
[6] Trans. H. Danby, O.U.P., 1933, 605. Quoted by permission.
[7] 25f.  [8] 26.  [9] 27, n., 29, 34.
[10] F. Louvel, 'Le mystère de nos églises', *Maison-Dieu*, 63, 1960, 20.
[11] A.-G. Martimort, 'Le rituel de la consécration des églises', *ibid.*, 94.
[12] *Ecc. Pol.*, V, xi, 1.  [13] *Ibid.*, V, xvi, 1.
[14] G. W. O. Addleshaw and F. Etchells, *The Architectural Setting of Anglican Worship*, Faber & Faber, 1948, 109. An excellent account of the Laudian controversy is given in this work; I have added certain facts and references which it does not provide but I have also abbreviated the story.
[15] P. Heylyn, *Cyprianus Anglicus*, 1668, 69.
[16] *Works*, V, 1853, 381.  [17] *Ibid.*, 405.
[18] *Ibid.*, 342f.  [19] Heylyn, 285.  [20] *Works*, V, 439.
[21] *Ibid.*, 367. Hence the appointment of men to act as dog whippers, e.g. the entry in Pittington registers for 3rd May 1646: 'John Lazing was appointed to be bedel for driving dogs out of the church in times of public worship and other necessary duties' (E. Trotter, *Seventeenth Century Life in the Country Parish*, C.U.P., 1919, 7, n.6).  [22] *Works*, V, 362.
[23] Heylyn, 435.  [24] W. Prynne, *Canterburies Doome*, 1646, 113ff.
[25] *Works*, IV, 247f.
[26] *Anglicanism*, ed. P. E. More and F. L. Cross, S.P.C.K., 1935, 608.
[27] Heylyn, 289.  [28] 153.  [29] 3.
[30] 26f.  [31] 3.
[32] Published posthumously in 1650, 46.  [33] *Anglicanism*, 606.
[34] *Second Report of the Ritual Commission*, 1868, 579f.
[35] Prynne, 99.  [36] Ed. F. E. Brightman, Methuen, 1903, 272f.
[37] *The Beauty of Holiness of the Common Prayer as Set Forth in Four Sermons Preach'd at the Rolls Chapel in the Year 1716*, 8th ed., 1721, 143.
[38] M. H. Port, *Six Hundred New Churches*, S.P.C.K., 1961, 9.
[39] *Ibid.*, 31.  [40] *Ecclesiologist*, II, 1843, 131.
[41] *Ibid.*, N.S. II, 1846, 134.
[42] *A Few Words to Church Builders*, 2nd ed., 1842, 5.
[43] *Ecclesiologist*, III, 1844, 39.
[44] *A Few Words to Church Builders*, 21.
[45] *A Few Words to Churchwardens*, I, 12th ed., 1842, 4; II, 5th ed., 1842, 4.
[46] *Church Enlargement and Church Arrangement*, 1843, 10.
[47] *A Few Words to Churchwardens*, 12, 23.
[48] *Ecclesiologist*, N.S. II, 1846, 222.
[49] *A Few Words to Churchwardens*, 16.
[50] *Ecclesiologist*, N.S. II, 1846, 40.
[51] *Church Building: A Study of the Principles of Architecture in Relation to the Church*, 3rd ed. 1924, 89, quoted by J. F. White, *Protestant Worship and Church Architecture*, O.U.P., N.Y., 1964, 138.

[52] J. G. Davies, *The Architectural Setting of Baptism*, Barrie & Rockliff, 1962, 124.
[53] J. M. Neale and B. Webb, *The Symbolism of Churches and Church Ornaments*, 1893, xxiii.
[54] *Ibid.*, xxvi.          [55] *A Few Words to Churchwardens*, 15.
[56] *Ecclesiologist*, III, 1844, 59.          [57] 1846, 52–9.
[58] A. J. B. Beresford Hope, *Worship and Order*, 1883, 76.
[59] *A Book about the Clergy*, 2nd ed. I, 1870, 338.
[60] *An Admonition to Parliament* 1572, in W. H. Frere and C. E. Douglas, *Puritan Manifestoes*, S.P.C.K., 1907, 28.
[61] T. Cheshire, *A True Copy of That Sermon*, 1641, 12.
[62] Frere and Douglas, 46.          [63] *Ibid.*, 51.
[64] J. Whitgift, *Works*, III, 1853, Parker Society, 109.
[65] Davies, 96–100.
[66] R. A. Marchant, *The Puritans and the Church Courts in the Diocese of York, 1560–1642*, Longmans, Green & Co., 1960, 92–6.
[67] Quoted in *Hierurgia Anglicana*, III, revised ed. by V. Staley, De la More Press, 1904, 337.
[68] A. Tindal Hart, *The Man in the Pew, 1558–1660*, John Baker, 1966, 176.
[69] Davies, 99.
[70] M. E. C. Walcott, *Traditions and Customs of Cathedrals*, 1872, 31–46.
[71] M. D. Anderson, *Looking for History in British Churches*, John Murray, 1951, 249.
[72] C. H. Firth and R. S. Rait, *Acts and Ordinances of the Interregnum, 1642–1660*, I, H.M.S.O., 1911, 607.
[73] Quoted in R. Hooker, *Ecclesiastical Polity*, Everyman Ed., II, Dent, 1940, 52, n.4.
[74] *The Writings of Henry Barrow, 1587–1590*, ed. L. H. Carlson, Allen & Unwin, 1962, 466f.
[75] *Ibid.*, 469.          [76] *The Journal of George Fox*, 8th ed., 1891, I, 8.
[77] *Ibid.*, I, 91.          [78] *Ibid.*, I, 93.
[79] *Ibid.*, I, 99.          [80] *Ibid.*, I, 112.
[81] *Ibid.*, I, 115.          [82] *Ibid.*, II, 64f.
[83] *The Works of Martin Luther*, Philadelphia Ed., IV, United Lutheran Publication House, 1931, 48.
[84] *Reformation Writings of Martin Luther*, II, trans. B. Lee Wolf, Lutterworth Press, London, 1956, 117, and Philosophical Library, N.Y.
[85] *Ibid.*, 118–21.          [86] *Ibid.*, 121.
[87] Philadelphia Ed., V, 1932, 93.
[88] *An Exhortation to the Clergy Assembled at the Diet of Augsburg*, 1530, *ibid.*, IV., 376.
[89] *Inst.*, III, 20, 30.          [90] *Loc. cit.*
[91] *Ibid.*, IV, 1, 5.          [92] *Ibid.*, IV, 5, 18.
[93] Sermon C in Deut. 16.13–17, quoted by A. Biéler, *Architecture in Worship*, E. T. Oliver & Boyd, Edinburgh, 1965, 49, and Westminster Press, Pa.
[94] See below, p. 241.
[95] *Calvin: Theological Treatises*, trans. J. K. S. Reid, Library of Christian Classics, XXII, SCM Press, London, 1954, 61, and Westminster Press, Pa.

[96] *Ibid.*, 81.  [97] *Ibid.*, 62.  [98] *Ibid.*, 79.

[99] J. Summerson, *Heavenly Mansions*, Cresset Press, 1949, 29–50.

[100] L. B. Alberti, *Ten Books on Architecture*, edited by J. Leoni, Alec Tiranti Ltd, 1955, VII, I, 133.

[101] VII, 13, *ibid.*, 154.  [102] VII, 3, *ibid.*, 136.

[103] VII, 6, *ibid.*, 141.  [104] VII, 13, *ibid.*, 154f.

[105] VII, 4, *ibid.*, 138.  [106] *ed cit.*, 247, n.144.

[107] *Lib.* IV, *praefatio.* Trans. in B. F. Fletcher, *Andrea Palladio*, Bell, 1902, 81.

[108] IV, 2, trans. *ibid.*, 82. Very few classical temples were in fact centralized, but many of the circular and polygonal remains of Roman tombs and secular buildings were believed, at the time of the Renaissance, to have been temples in antiquity (R. Wittkower, *Architectural Principles in the Age of Humanism*, Alec Tiranti Ltd., 1949, 4f.).

[109] L. Bouyer, *Life and Liturgy*, Sheed & Ward, Stagbook, 1962, 4.

[110] M. Brion, *Ces palais où Dieu habite*, Fayard, 1960, 69.

[111] *Ibid.*, 71.  [112] Bouyer, 7.

[113] G. W. O. Addleshaw and F. Etchells, *The Architectural Setting of Anglican Worship*, Faber & Faber, 1948, 154.

[114] Quoted *ibid.*, 249.  [115] *Ibid.*, 58.

[116] *The Present State of Ecclesiastical Architecture in England*, 1843, 29.

[117] M. S. Briggs, *Puritan Architecture*, Lutterworth Press, 1946, 15–18. This gives an excellent account of the history of these buildings in England: for other countries see A. L. Drummond, *The Church Architecture of Protestantism*, T. & T. Clark, 1934.

[118] *Ibid.*, 24–7.

[119] *Works*, Philadelphia ed., IV, 178.

[120] Quoted by B. Biéler, *Architecture in Worship*, E. T. Oliver & Boyd, 1965, 57.

[121] J. G. Davies, *The Architectural Setting of Baptism*, Barrie & Rockliff, 1962, 104.

[122] Biéler, 59ff.  [123] *Ibid.*, 63.

[124] J. G. Davies, *The Origin and Development of Early Christian Church Architecture*, SCM Press, 1952, 37, and Philosophical Library, N.Y.

[125] Quoted by J. C. Cox and A. Harvey, *English Church Furniture*, Methuen, 1907, 283.

[126] *Ibid.*, 284.  [127] *Loc. cit.*

[128] B. F. L. Clarke, *The Building of the Eighteenth-Century Church*, S.P.C.K., 1963, 149.

[129] W. Hone, *Every-Day Book*, II, 1841, 664.

[130] C. J. Abbey and J. H. Overton, *The English Church in the Eigtheenth Century*, II, 1878, 423.

[131] II, 1843, 139, 168.

[132] Addleshaw and Etchells, *The Architectural Setting of Anglican Worship*, 86f.

[133] A. R. Powys, *The English Parish Church*, Longmans, Green & Co., 1930, 164.

## CHAPTER 5

[1] W. Longman, *A History of the Three Cathedrals dedicated to St Paul in London*, 1873, 55.

[2] See above, pp. 52, 56f., 64, 70f., 73, 84.

[3] F. Osborne, *Traditional Memoyres on the Raigne of King James the First, 1658*, in *Secret History of the Court of James the First*, I, 1811, 209ff.

[4] See the extract from Churchyard's *Challenge* of 1593, lines 180f., printed in *Harrison's Description of England A.D. 1577–87*, ed. F. J. Furnivall, New Shakespeare Society, Series VI, 8, 1881, 171.

[5] J. Timbs, *Curiosities of London*, 1885, 106.

[6] F. Bacon, 'Observations on a Libel', *Works*, 1862, VIII, 207.

[7] Longman, 55.

[8] J. Shirley, *The Witty Fair One*, 1628, Act II, scene 1.

[9] O. von Simpson, *The Gothic Cathedral*, Routledge & Kegan Paul, 1956, 167.

[10] *Paston Letters*, 1479, No. 828.

[11] Quoted in *The Gull's Hornbook*, reprinted with notes and illustrations by J.N., 1812, 123, n.30.

[12] W. Sparrow Simpson, *St Paul's Cathedral and Old City Life*, 1894, 81.

[13] *ed. cit.*, Series VI, I, 1877, 204.

[14] *The Diary of Henry Machyn*, ed. J. G. Nichols, Camden Society, XLII, 1848, 26f.

[15] *Origines Juridicales*, 1680, 142.

[16] J. Strype, *Annals of the Reformation*, I, 1, 1824, 390.

[17] *Ibid.*, I, 1, 392.          [18] *Satires*, II, V.

[19] Percy Society, V, 1841, no, 3, 11.          [20] *Ibid.*, 14.

[21] *Ibid.*, 11.

[22] *Pennyless Parliance of Threadbare Poets*, quoted by W. Jenkinson, *London Churches before the Great Fire*, S.P.C.K., 1917, 20f.

[23] Ed. J.N., 1812, 94f.          [24] *Ibid.*, 96f.

[25] *Ibid.*, 101f.

[26] The pillars also, according to an epigram of 1598, were plastered with notices (quoted by Jenkinson, 20).

[27] Text reprinted by Sparrow Simpson, 197.

[28] J. Weever, *Ancient Funerall Monuments*, 1631, 362.

[29] *ed. cit.*, 48.          [30] *English Reprints*, V, ed. E. Arber, 1869, 73.

[31] Weever, 372. For further references to Duke Humphrey, see Jenkinson, 21f.

[32] *Ibid.*, 373.

[33] Quoted by Longman, 54.

[34] *Works*, V, 1853, 489.

[35] H. H. Milman, *Annals of St Paul's Cathedral*, 1868, 353.

[36] *Notes on London Churches and Buildings, and on Public Events in England, A.D. 1631–58*, printed in *Harrison's Description, ed. cit.*, VI, 8, 1881, 203.

[37] J. P. Malcolm, *Anecdotes of the Manners and Customs of London*, II, 1811, 131.

[38] Sparrow Simpson, 278.

[39] Malcolm, 150.

[40] *Ibid.*, 158.

[41] Quoted by Horton Davies, *Worship and Theology in England. The Ecumenical Century, 1900–1965*, O.U.P., 1965, 52, n.6.

[42] C. J. Abbey and J. H. Overton, *The English Church in the Eighteenth Century*, II, 1878, 419.

[43] J. C. Jeaffreson, *A Book about the Clergy*, II, 2nd ed., 1870, 35f.

[44] *ed. cit.*, 16.

## CHAPTER 6

[1] W. Lambarde, *A Perambulation of Kent*, 1826, 434.

[2] *Voyage littéraire de deux religieux bénédictins*, I, 1717, 54.

[3] L. Deubner, *de Incubatione*, 1900, 62.

[4] M. Hamilton, *Incubation*, Simpkin, 1906, 219.

[5] *Ibid.*, 178.　　[6] *Ibid.*, 195.　　[7] *Ibid.*, 188, 208.　　[8] *Ibid.*, 221f.

[9] *Ibid.*, 184.　　[10] J. Strype, *Annals of the Reformation*, I, 2, 1824, 229.

[11] E. Trotter, *Seventeenth Century Life in the Country Parish*, C.U.P., 1919, 46.

[12] C. Pendrill, *Old Parish Life in London*, O.U.P., 1937, 214.

[13] J. Nichols, *Illustrations of the Manners and Expences of Antient Times in England*, 1797, 141f.

[14] J. C. Cox, *Churchwardens' Accounts*, Methuen, 1913, 86.

[15] S. P. Widnell, *A History of Grantchester*, 1875, 91.

[16] According to S. O. Addy, *Church and Manor*, Allen & Unwin, 1913, 44, the upper aisles of some Coptic churches, such as Abou Sargh in Old Cairo, were used as habitations.

[17] M. E. C. Walcott, *Traditions and Customs of Cathedrals*, 1872, 82.

[18] J. E. Vaux, *Church Folklore*, 1894, 7.

[19] W. Hone, *An Every Day Book*, II, 1841, 1255.

[20] Outside England we may note that in Serbia, forty years ago, the priest poured a glass of wine into the tomb; in Greece, on All Saints' Day, a dish of meat is placed on the grave; the Polish gypsies buy a ham and empty *raki* in the cemetery, which is the scene of an annual picnic in Naples (R. Krautheimer, 'Mensa-Coemeterium-Martyrium', *Cahiers archéologiques*, XI, 1960, 33).

[21] *Remaines of Gentilisme and Judaisme, 1686-7*, ed. J. Britten, 1881, 24.

[22] J. Timbs, *Curiosities of London*, 1885, 146.

[23] J. Brand, *Popular Antiquities of Great Britain*, ed. W. C. Hazlitt, II, 1870, 209.　　[24] Hone, II, 443-7.

[25] D. McClatchey, *Oxfordshire Clergy, 1777-1869*, O.U.P., 1960, 131f.

[26] Brand, II, 84.　　[27] Cox, 315.

[28] L. A. Bocquillot, *Traité historique de la liturgie sacrée ou de la messe*, 1701, 425.

[29] de Moléon, *Voyages liturgiques de France*, 1718, 420.

[30] J. C. Cox, *The Parish Registers of England*, Methuen, 1910, 47; cf. *The Diary of Henry Machyn*, ed. J. G. Nichols, Camden Society, XLII, 1848, 216.

[31] P. H. Ditchfield, *The Parish Clerk*, Methuen, 1907, 39.

[32] J. Wickham Legg, *The Clerks' Book of 1549*, H.B.S., XXV, 1903, 96f.

[33] A. Tindal Hart, *The Man in the Pew, 1558-1660*, John Baker, 1966, 70.

[34] Ditchfield, *loc. cit.*　　[35] 418.

[36] 407, 421.　　[37] *Ibid.*, 101, 119, 177, 210.

[38] F. Baker, *Methodism and the Love-Feast*, Epworth Press, 1957, 9. This is a comprehensive study of the subject with full documentation; I have therefore omitted further references from my text.

[39] W. H. Frere and W. M. Kennedy, *Visitation Articles and Injunctions of the Period of the Reformation*, III, Alcuin Club, XVI, 1910, 285. The year previously, in 1570, one William Kethe had preached a sermon at Blandford against church ales (W. Andrews, *Curiosities of the Church*, 1890, 40).

[40] *Phillip Stubbes's Anatomy of the Abuses of England*, ed. F. J. Furnivall, 1877–9, 150f.

[41] W. P. M. Kennedy, *Elizabethan Episcopal Administration*, III, Alcuin Club, XXVI, 1924, 143.

[42] *Ibid.*, 179.

[43] However, a canon was formulated in 1571 which said that *aeditui convivia, symposia, coenas, ac invitationes publicas-templis celebrari non patientur.*

[44] A. H. A. Hamilton, *Quarter Sessions from Queen Elizabeth to Queen Anne*, 1878, 28f.

[45] These are conveniently printed, together with similar documents, in the *Second Report of the Ritual Commission*, 1868. The page references for this and the following are: 442, 452, 455, 458, 461, 466, 473, 474, 480, 487, 491, 492, 497, 503, 508, 515, 531, 538, 550, 555, 558, 568, 598, 596.

[46] Printed in *Hierurgia Anglicana*, III, ed. V. Staley, 1904, De la More Press, 133–7.

[47] *Ritual Commission*, 613, 625.   [48] Andrews, 50.

[49] *Antiquary*, VII, 1883, 34.   [50] Andrews, *loc. cit.*

[51] A. R. Powys, *The English Parish Church*, Longmans, Green & Co., 1930, 63.

[52] Hone, I, 1414.

[53] G. H. Cook, *The English Medieval Parish Church*, Phoenix House, 3rd ed., 1961, 34.

[54] Cox, *Churchwardens' Accounts*, 9.   [55] Nichols, 14.

[56] W. Kelly, *Notices Illustrative of the Drama*, 1865, 13. Where the singing of the passion continued, refreshments were also provided, e.g. St Martin's, Leicester, for 1544–7 (*Ibid.*, 23).

[57] J. Stow, *A Survey of London* (1603), ed. C. L. Kingsford, II, O.U.P., 2nd ed., 1908, 36.

[58] Hone, I, 642.   [59] Aubrey, 40f.

[60] Vaux, 185f.   [61] *Ibid.*, 233.

[62] *Ecclesiologist*, II, 1843, 62.   [63] Cox, 94f.

[64] 240f.   [65] *Ibid.*, 251.

[66] *Four Supplications 1529–1553*, E.E.T.S., Extra Series, XIII, 1871, 41.

[67] Tindal Hart, 75.   [68] Nichols, 133.

[69] Frere and Kennedy, III, 271.   [70] Kennedy, II, 110, 166, 220, 228.

[71] *Ritual Commission*, 442, 446, 480, 503, 508, 531.

[72] *Ibid.*, 619, 656.   [73] Aubrey, 5.

[74] E. K. Chambers, *The Medieval Stage*, I, O.U.P., 1903, 198 n.1.

[75] *Collection des meilleurs dissértations, notices et traités particuliers relatifs à l'histoire de France*, ed. C. Leber, IX, 1838, 432.

[76] *Ibid.*, 438.   [77] Stubbes, 325.

[78] Leber, 426ff.   [79] L. Grove, *Dancing*, 1895, 226f.

[80] Chambers, I, 163.   [81] *Ibid.*, *loc. cit.*

[82] Grove, 317.   [83] *Notes and Queries*, 7th Series, IX, 1890, 381.

[84] Grove, 118.   [85] *Ibid.*, 309.

[86] *Ibid.*, 120.

[87] L. Gougaud, 'La danse dans les églises', *Revue d'histoire ecclésiastique*, XV, 1914, 237f.   [88] *Ibid.*, 243.

[89] Grove, 106f.   [90] Frere and Kennedy, II, 195.

[91] *Ibid.*, 245, 277, 294, 287.  [92] Kennedy, II, 78, 143.

[93] *Ritual Commission*, 442, 446.  [94] Pendrill, 263f.

[95] S. O. Addy, *Church and Manor*, Allen & Unwin, 1913, 295.

[96] Ditchfield, 225f.  [97] Stubbes, 339.

[98] J. B. Thiers, *Dissértation sur les porches des églises*, 1679, 105, 155.

[99] *Ibid.*, III, 128–36.  [100] Strype, I, 1, 472; I, 2, 115; IV, 552, 554.

[101] J. B. Thiers, *Dissértations ecclésiastiques sur les principaux autels des églises*, 1688, 59.  [102] Addy, 240.

[103] *Ibid.*, 259, 263.  [104] Nichols, 68f.

[105] C. J. Abbey and J. H. Overton, *The English Church in the Eighteenth Century*, II, 1878, 462.

[106] Tindal Hart, 62.  [107] 'Seven Sketches from one Parish', IV.

[108] *Notes and Queries*, 10th series, XII, 1909, 337.

[109] Addy, 230–6.  [110] Walcott, 88f.

[111] M. D. George, 'Elections and Electioneering, 1679–81', *E.H.R.*, XLV, 1930, 566.

[112] Vaux, 10f.  [113] Powys, 114.

[114] Addy, 190f.  [115] W. E. Tate, *The Parish Chest*, C.U.P., 1946, 242.

[116] Addy, 193.  [117] II, 1626.

[118] *The State of the Church in the Reigns of Elizabeth and James I*, Lincoln Record Society, XXIII, 1926, lxxv.

[119] Tindal Hart, 181.

[120] Bishop Hobhouse, *Church-Wardens' Accounts*, Somerset Record Society, IV, 1890, 222f.  [121] Strype, II, i, 421.

[122] S. and B. Webb, *English Local Government*, I, O.U.P., Home University Library, new ed., 1963, 105, n.1.

[123] Addy, 269.  [124] *Bibliotheca Topographica Britannica*, 1790, 62.

[125] Tate, 165.  [126] Addy, 193.

[127] W. Johnson, *Byways in British Archaeology*, C.U.P., 1912, 140.

[128] S. and B. Webb, 107.  [129] *Ibid.*, 96f.

[130] *Ibid.*, 99f.  [131] II, 1843, 170.

[132] W. Gresley, *Portrait of an English Churchman*, 6th ed. 1841, 250–65.

[133] Stow, I, 75f.

[134] T. F. Thistleton-Dyer, *Old English Social Life as told by the Parish Registers*, 1898, 37.

[135] Nichols, 148f.  [136] John Evelyn's *Diary* under 17 June 1655.

[137] *Ibid.*, under 29 March 1686.  [138] Thistleton-Dyer, 38.

[139] Trotter, 46, n.1.

[140] *Harrison's Description of England A.D. 1577–1587*, ed. F. J. Furnivall, New Shakespere Society, Series VI, 1, 1877, 75.

[141] H. H. Milman, *Annals of St Paul's Cathedral*, 1868, 222.

[142] *Ibid.*, 242, 252.  [143] Hone, II, 214.

[144] R. A. Marchant, *The Puritans and the Church Courts in the Diocese of York, 1560–1642*, Longmans, Green & Co., 1960, 135.

[145] Strype, II, 2, 62.  [146] *Ibid.*, III, 1, 131.

[147] E. R. Brinkworth, *The Archdeacon's Court*, Oxfordshire Record Society, XXIII, 1942, vii, x.

[148] Strype, IV, 75.

[149] H. T. Ellacombe, 'Malt Rate levied in the Parish of Woodbury, Co. Devon. From an Ms. in the possession of the late General Lee of Ebford Barton', *Archaeological Journal*, XL, 1883, 229–31.

[150] Tindal Hart, 62.

[151] 'Act Book of the Archdeacon of Taunton', Somerset Record Society, XLIII, 1928, 1–175.

[152] *Works*, V, 1853, 483, 487.    [153] *Gentleman's Magazine*, XXIX, 1759, 93.

[154] Thiers, *Dissértation sur les porches*, 61–4.    [155] Addy, 187, 258.

[156] *Ritual Commission*, 458.

[157] *Ibid.*, 461, 474, 492, 497, 508, 531, 538, 558, 589, 596.

[158] *Ibid.*, 625.

[159] *Miscellany Accounts of the Diocese of Carlisle*, ed. R. S. Ferguson, Cumberland, and Westmorland Antiquarian and Archaeological Society, 1877, 42.

[160] J. C. Cox, *Three Centuries of Derbyshire Annals*, I, 1890, 79f.

[161] Addy, 193.    [162] *Ibid.*, 129.

[163] *Ibid*, 195f.    [164] Strype, II, 2, 382.

[165] Addy, *loc. cit.*    [166] Trotter, 46, n.3.

[167] Powys, 78.    [168] Addy, 196.

[169] Powys, 75.    [170] Wickham Legg, xlv.

[171] Johnson, 140.    [172] Abbey and Overton, II, 463.

[173] Tate, 112f.    [174] *Ibid.*, 151.

[175] Hone, II, 1157.    [176] Wickham Legg, *loc. cit.*

[177] Ditchfield, 170.

[178] J. G. Lockhart, *Memoirs . . . of Sir Walter Scott*, I, 1837, 192.

[179] Ditchfield, 311.

[180] T. Smith and L. Brentano, *English Gilds*, 1870, 257.

[181] Strype, II, 2, 577.    [182] Johnson, 186.

[183] *Ibid.*, 497.    [184] Hone, II, 916.

[185] Cox, *Churchwardens' Accounts*, 319f.    [186] Nichols, 65.

[187] II, 172.

[188] F. H. Cripps-Day, 'Arms and Armour in Churches in England', *The Archaeological Journal*, XLI, 1935, 59–65.

[189] Strype, I, 2, 275.    [190] Nichols, 16, 19.

[191] J. C. Cox and A. Harvey, *English Church Furniture*, Methuen, 2nd ed., 1908, 330, 333.    [192] Cox, *Churchwardens' Accounts*, 248.

[193] Johnson, 167.    [194] Cox, 302.

[195] *Bishop Redman's Visitation, 1597*, ed. J. F. Williams, Norfolk Record Society, XVIII, 1946, 147.

[196] Tindal Hart, 103, 175.    [197] Stow, I, 275.

[198] A. P. Stanley, *Historical Memorials of Westminster Abbey*, 1876, 343–8.

[199] John Evelyn visited this on 12th November 1643.

[200] Act III, scene 2, line 84.

[201] A. F. Leach, *The Schools of Medieval England*, Methuen, 2nd ed., 1916, 39.

[202] W. K. Jordan, *The Charities of Rural England, 1490–1660*, Allen & Unwin, 1961, 54.

[203] Thistleton-Dyer, 36.    [204] Jordan, 321.

[205] Pendrill, 274.    [206] Jordan, 55.

[207] *Ibid.*, 331.    [208] *Ibid.*, 162.

[209] Pendrill, 122.

[210] J. S. Purvis, *Educational Records*, St Anthony's Press, York, 1959, 87.

[211] Aubrey, 40f.     [212] *Miscellany Accounts, passim.*

[213] *Ritual Commission*, 497, 508.     [214] Purvis, 6, 107.

[215] *Miscellany Accounts*, 4.     [216] *Ibid.*, 5, 22, 27, 52, 66, 75.

[217] *Ibid.*, 76.     [218] Addy, 269.

[219] Purvis, 69.     [220] *Ecclesiologist*, II, 1843, 171, 175.

[221] II, 1843, 62f., 172; III, 1844, 58; New Series, I, 1845, 46, 196; II, 1846, 269; IV, 1847, 37.

[222] S. O. Addy, *The Evolution of the English House*, Allen & Unwin, 1898, 186.

[223] *Kilvert's Diary, 1870–1879*, ed. W. Plomer, Jonathan Cape, 1944, 122.

[224] Hone, I, 446.

[225] *Accounts of the Churchwardens of St Michael, Cornhill, 1456–1608*, ed. W. H. Overall, 1871, 167.

[226] *The Parochial Libraries of the Church of England*, Faith Press, 1959, 16.

[227] Cox and Harvey, 333ff.     [228] *Miscellany Accounts*, 14, 16, 44.

[229] *Parochial Libraries*, 20.     [230] For the text see *ibid.*, 48ff.

[231] Walcott, 54.     [232] *Parochial Libraries*, 28.

[233] *The Diary of Henry Machyn*, ed. J. G. Nichols, Camden Society, XLII, 1848, 135.

[234] W. H. Frere and C. E. Douglas, *Puritan Manifestoes*, S.P.C.K., 1907, 28.

[235] Jordan, 39.     [236] J. Paterson, *Pietas Londiniensis*, 1714, 121f.

[237] Stow, II, 24.     [238] Frere and Kennedy, II, 126ff.

[239] *Ibid.*, 182.     [240] *Ibid.*, 240, 266.

[241] W. Kelly, *Notices Illustrative of the Drama*, 1865, 202.

[242] Frere and Kennedy, III, 3.     [243] Tindal Hart, 22.

[244] Trotter, 77.     [245] Nichols, 25, 14.

[246] Cox and Harvey, 312.     [247] Trotter, 46, n.2.

[248] Chambers, I, 366ff.     [249] Leber, IX, 397f.

[250] Wickham Legg, 82.     [251] Stubbes, 147.

[252] Chambers, I, 419.     [253] Frere and Kennedy, II, 88.

[254] *Ibid.*, III, 209.     [255] *Ibid.*, 271.

[256] *Ritual Commission*, 531.     [257] Brinkworth, 43.

[258] *Ibid.*, 27.     [259] *Diary*, 27.

[260] Kelly, 149.     [261] Tindal Hart, 175n.

[262] Leber, X, 1838, 89.     [263] Chambers, I, 368 n.1.

[264] *Ibid.*, 247.     [265] See above, p. 128.

[266] Quoted in Stubbes, 337.     [267] Hone, II, 1093f.

[268] Chambers, II, 102 n.     [269] Cox, *Churchwardens' Accounts*, 274.

[270] *Ibid.*, 269.     [271] *Ibid.*, 276.

[272] Chambers, II, 222.     [273] Cox, 277.

[274] Kelly, 15.     [275] Machyn, 138.

[276] Cox, 277.     [277] *Ibid.*, 278.

[278] R. Lennard, *Englishmen at Rest and Play*, O.U.P., 1931, 87.

[279] Cox, 279.

[280] A. Tindal Hart, *The Country Clergy in Elizabethan and Stuart Times*, Phoenix House, London, 1958, 37, and Transatlantic Arts, Flo., 1959.

[281] Cox, 278.     [282] Kelly, 68.

[283] Brinkworth, 124f.  [284] Cox, 280.

[285] Kennedy, I, lxxx. There is documentary evidence of the possession by churches of copies of plays and of costumes; this suggests that plays were performed in those churches or in those to which they were occasionally hired, but since no direct statement is made to that effect, the evidence has not been included.

[286] G. Burnet, *The History of the Reformation of the Church of England*, ed. N. Pocock, I, 1865, 503.

[287] Frere and Kennedy, II, 88.  [288] Chambers, II, *loc. cit.*

[289] Frere and Kennedy, II, 234, 291.

[290] Frere and Douglas, 29.  [291] Thistleton-Dyer, 205.

[292] Stubbes, 302.  [293] Frere and Kennedy, III, 271.

[294] *Ibid.*, III, 383; Kennedy, II, 59; III, 179, 220.

[295] Tindal Hart, 37.  [296] Kennedy, I, lxxx.

[297] Brinkworth, 124.  [298] Thistleton-Dyer, 204.

[299] Hone, II, 419f. Drama was used extensively by the Jesuits for the purpose of religious propaganda, in Europe, Latin America, China and Japan, but they usually presented their plays in theatres and I have been unable to find any evidence of their being staged in churches (R. Fülöp-Miller, *The Power and Secret of the Jesuits*, Putnam, 1930, 409–14).

[300] Addy, 92–5.

[301] *Visitation of the Diocese of Norwich*, *A.D. 1492–1532*, ed. A. Jessopp, Camden Society, New Series, XLIII, 1888, 295.

[302] Frere and Kennedy, III, 235.  [303] *Works*, V, 1853, 460, 462.

[304] Walcott, 79f.  [305] Strype, II, 1, 189.

[306] Hone, II, 449.  [307] Walcott, 97.

[308] Tindal Hart, *The Man in the Pew*, 75.

[309] Cox, 277.  [310] Abbey and Overton, II, 487.

[311] J. P. Malcolm, *Anecdotes of the Manners and Customs of London*, II, 1811, 10.

[312] Hone, I, 370.  [313] Walcott, 108.

## CHAPTER 7

[1] E. Lohmeyer, *Lord of the Temple*, E.T. Oliver & Boyd, 1961, 85.
[2] Acts 7.48.
[3] J. C. Hoekendijk, *The Church Inside Out*, E.T. SCM Press, London, 1967, 68, and Westminster Press, Pa., 1966.
[4] A. Richardson, *An Introduction to the Theology of the New Testament*, SCM Press, London, 1958, 85, and Harper & Row, N.Y., 1959.
[5] Luke 11.20.       [6] Mark 10.45.
[7] See J. G. Davies, *Worship and Mission*, SCM Press, London, 1966, 51, and Association Press, N.Y.; *Dialogue with the World*, SCM Press, 1967, 15.
[8] Rom. 14.17.       [9] Rom. 15.33.
[10] Eph. 2.14.       [11] II Cor. 5.19.
[12] Col. 1.20.       [13] I Tim. 2.4.
[14] John 3.16.       [15] John 12.47.
[16] Hoekendijk, 85.       [17] Matt. 5.16.
[18] Hoekendijk, 86.       [19] *Ibid.*, 80f.
[20] G. van der Leeuw, *Religion in Essence and Manifestation*, E.T. Allen & Unwin, 1938, 47.
[21] R. Caillois, *L'homme et le sacré*, Gallimard, 3rd ed., 1963, 11.
[22] van der Leeuw, 48.
[23] M. Eliade, *The Sacred and the Profane*, E.T. Harper and Row, N.Y., 1959, 24.
[24] Caillois, 44.       [25] *Ibid.*, 18.
[26] van der Leeuw, 39.       [27] Eliade, 26.
[28] Gen. 28.17.       [29] Eliade, 27.
[30] *Ethics*, SCM Press, London, 1955, and Macmillan Co., N.Y. (Fontana edition, 1964, 196).       [31] See above, p. 18.
[32] See above, p. 20.       [33] See above, p. 16.
[34] See above, p. 36.       [35] See above, p. 96f.
[36] See above, p. 127f.       [37] See above, pp. 99, 103.
[38] See above, p. 109.
[39] *Towards a Church Architecture*, ed. P. Hammond, Architectural Press, 1962, 248, 253.       [40] *Ibid.*, 255.
[41] Such an attitude, however, is not without criticism within Roman Catholicism itself; see especially F. Louvel, 'Le mystère des églises', *Maison-Dieu*, 63, 1960, 5–23; but these criticisms have themselves been the object of attack; cf. J. Hani, *Le Symbolisme du temple chrétien*, La Colombe, 1962.
[42] *The Canon Law of the Church of England*, S.P.C.K., 1947, 190f.
[43] Eliade, 25.       [44] Caillois, 44f.
[45] *Ant. Jud.*, III, 6.4.       [46] *Ibid.*, III, 7.7.
[47] Eliade, 61f., quoting H. Sedlmayr, *Die Entstehung der Kathedrale*, Atlantis Verlag, 1950, 119. As early as Maximus the Confessor (*c.* 580–662) this cosmological interpretation of a church was in evidence. So Maximus, speaking of St Sophia in Edessa, compared its roof to the heavens, its mosaic to the firmament and its arches to the four corners of the world (Hani, 34).
[48] O. von Simpson, *The Gothic Cathedral*, Routledge & Kegan Paul, 1956, 35.

[49] Exod. 25.8f., 40.    [50] I Chron. 28.19.
[51] Wisdom 9.8.    [52] Heb. 8.5; 9.23.
[53] Apocalypse of Baruch 4.3.    [54] von Simpson, 11.
[55] O. Frankl, *Gothic Architecture*, Penguin Books, 1962, 233–6.
[56] Hammond, 248.
[57] J. G. Davies, *The Origin and Development of Early Christian Church Architecture*, SCM Press, 1952, 98.
[58] *H.E.*, x, 4.    [59] II Sam. 24.15–25; I Chron. 21.22–22.6.
[60] See above, p. 15.    [61] van der Leeuw, 398.
[62] Hammond, 251.    [63] See above, pp. 112–23.
[64] See above, p. 1.    [65] Acts 10.15.
[66] Heb. 1.3.    [67] Rom. 14.14.
[68] Acts 9.1–9; 8.26–40.
[69] *Ethics*, 198. Nor does the popular distinction between this world and the world to come have any New Testament basis; on this see the lively article by J. A. T. Robinson, 'The Christian Society in this World: The Biblical Teaching' in his *On Being the Church in the World*, SCM Press, London, 1960, 9–22, and Westminster Press, Pa., 1962.
[70] Otto's thesis has of course not been immune from criticism, cf. the remark of John Oman that his 'fervour . . . often produces more heat than light' (*The Natural and the Supernatural* C.U.P., 1931, 474).
[71] Otto, 85f.    [72] *Ibid.*, 88.
[73] *Ibid.*, 89.    [74] *Ibid.*, 92.
[75] Mark 14.33.
[76] D. E. Nineham, *Saint Mark*, Penguin edition, 1963, 391, and Seabury Press, N.Y., 1968.
[77] Albert H. van den Heuvel, *These Rebellious Powers*, SCM Press, London, 1966, 52, and Friendship Press, N.Y.    [78] Otto, 89.
[79] C. H. Dodd, *The Epistle to the Romans*, Hodder & Stoughton, 1932, 23.
[80] D. E. H. Whiteley, *The Theology of St Paul*, Blackwell, London, 1964, 61–71, and Fortress Press, Pa., provides a very balanced survey of the subject.
[81] F. J. Leenhardt, *The Epistle to the Romans*, E.T. Lutterworth Press, 1961, 248–63.
[82] Otto, 86.    [83] Rom. 15.4.
[84] I Cor. 10.11.    [85] Rom. 8.15; Gal. 4.6.
[86] N. Smart, *The Teacher and Christian Belief*, James Clarke, 1966, 29.
[87] G. Moran, *Theology of Revelation*, Burns & Oates, 1967, 58f.
[88] Matt. 5.48.    [89] Eph. 4.13.
[90] e.g. II Cor. 4.4.    [91] Mark 1.24.
[92] Acts 3.14; 4.27.    [93] *Religion in Essence and Manifestation*, 598f.
[94] Robinson, 20.    [95] *Ethics*, 196f.
[96] M. Eliade, *Myths, Dreams and Mysteries*, E.T. Harvill Press, London, 1960, 153, and Harper & Row, N.Y.
[97] *Ethics*, 197ff.    [98] *Metaph.*, V, 6, 1015b, 36–1016a.
[99] Bonhoeffer, 200f.
[100] J. G. Davies, *The Early Christian Church*, Weidenfeld & Nicolson, London, 1965, 253f., and Holt, Rinehart & Winston, N.Y.
[101] P. A. Micklem, *The Secular and the Sacred*, Hodder & Stoughton, 1948, 52.

[102] *Letters and Papers from Prison*, SCM Press, London, and Macmillan Co., N.Y., Revised edition, 1967, 162.

[103] R. Mehl, *Traité de sociologie du protestantisme*, Delachaux et Niestlé, 1966, 72.

[104] C. R. Hinings, 'The Balsall Heath Survey—A Report', *Research Bulletin*, 1967 (Institute for the Study of Worship and Religious Architecture), 56–72. However, according to a similar survey conducted at Hodge Hill, the general sample positively endorsed 10 items and the Church sample all 12 (*ibid.*, 1968).

[105] 'The Hodge Hill Project—Second Report', *ibid.*, 23.

[106] D. Hinton and C. Brown, 'Highgate Baptist Church', *ibid.*, 30–4.

[107] The Free Church at Perivale, Middlesex, really belongs to this category. It has a sanctuary at one end and a stage at the other; the intervening space can either seat worshippers or spectators and the floor is marked out for badminton (M. S. Briggs, *Puritan Architecture*, Lutterworth Press, 1946, 81).

[108] P. Bridges, 'The Function of the Pastoral Centre', *Research Bulletin*, 1966 (Institute for the Study of Worship and Religious Architecture), 63–8.

[109] D. Jenkins, 'Swinging Church Strikes a False Note', *The Times*, 11 February 1967

## CHAPTER 8

[1] J. Wickham Legg, *English Orders for Consecrating Churches*, H.B.S., XLI, 1911, 55, 61.

[2] *Report of the Committee on Deconsecration to the Church Assembly*, Church Assembly Document, C.A. Misc., 3, 1961, 3, quoted by permission.

[3] I am referring to the law as it is at the time of writing. There are indications that changes may be made in the near future.

[4] See the entries in *A Patristic Lexicon*, ed. G. W. H. Lampe, O.U.P. 1961–2.

[5] R. W. Muncey, *A History of the Consecration of Churches and Churchyards*, Heffer, 1930, 90f.

[6] *H.E.*, x.3.2.    [7] *Dial.*, 3, 30.
[8] *Ep.*, 22.    [9] *Registr.*, 11, 56.

[10] For a text containing the majority of these elements see *Ordo*, 42, printed in M. Andrieu, *Les 'Ordines Romani' du haut moyen âge*, IV, 1956, 387–402.

[11] For text see *Ordo*, 41 in Andrieu, 339–47.    [12] Andrieu, 399, 402.

[13] Cf. A.-G. Martimort, 'Le rituel de la consécration des églises', *Maison Dieu*, 63, 1960, 86–95.

[14] H. A. Wilson, *The Gelasian Sacramentary*, 1894, 285.

[15] *Ibid.*, 133.    [16] *Loc. cit.*

[17] *Ordo*, 42, Andrieu, 400.

[18] *A Diocesan Service Book*, O.U.P., 1965, 7–14.

[19] Wickham Legg, 58. This prayer was repeated in the Bishop of St David's rite of 1634–5 and in the second form devised by Bishop John Cosin of Durham in 1665 (*ibid.*, 160, 229).    [20] *Ibid.*, xxxiii.

[21] For the revised modern Roman rite see A.-G. Martimort, 'Le nouveau rite de la dédicace des églises', *Maison-Dieu*, 70, 1962, 6–31.

[22] A. Farrer, *Love Almighty and Ills Unlimited*, Collins, 1962, 143.

[23] *Ibid.*, 143f.

[24] B. F. L. Clarke, *The Building of the Eighteenth-Century Church*, S.P.C.K., 1963, 146f.

[25] *Report on Deconsecration*, 3.

[26] *Ibid.*, 6.    [27] Matt. 18.20.

[28] A.-G. Martimort, 'Le rituel de la consécration des églises', *Maison-Dieu*, 63, 1960, 94.

[29] G. A. Michell, *Eucharistic Consecration in the Primitive Church*, S.P.C.K., 1948, 5.

[30] R. Bultmann, *Primitive Christianity in its Contemporary Setting*, E.T. Thames & Hudson, London, 1956, 128f., and Meridian Books, N.Y.

[31] *Ibid.*, 17.    [32] *Ibid.*, 24.

[33] O. Cullmann and F. J. Leenhardt, *Essays on the Lord's Supper*, E.T. Lutterworth Press, 1957, 46, and John Knox Press, Richmond, Va.

[34] *Loc. cit.*

[35] L. Bouyer, *Rite and Man*, E.T. Burns & Oates, London, 1963, 80f., and University of Notre Dame Press, Ind., 1962.

# INDEXES

# INDEX OF PLACES

# GENERAL INDEX